Inside Rwanda's
Gacaca Courts

"about substance not form"

Critical Human Rights

Steve J. Stern and Scott Straus
Series Editors

Books in the series Critical Human Rights emphasize research that opens new ways to think about and understand human rights. The series values in particular empirically grounded and intellectually open research that eschews simplified accounts of human rights events and processes.

Following genocide in Rwanda in 1994, the government decided to pursue a strategy of extensive domestic justice, in which it would prosecute hundreds of thousands of people accused of having participated in crimes related to the genocide. A centerpiece of that effort was *gacaca*, a traditional, open-air justice mechanism revamped in this case to handle genocide crimes. As a huge experiment in localized transitional justice that ultimately led to more than a million cases, *gacaca* has attracted a great deal of interest from scholars and policy-makers. Based on extraordinary field research and close observation of the *gacaca* proceedings, Bert Ingelaere's study distinguishes itself not only for the rich empirical work but also for its nuanced analysis. He attends both to the top-down force of the state and to the practical, decentralized ways in which Rwandans manage their everyday lives. The book is an excellent example of in-depth place-based research that focuses on human rights issues of transnational concern.

# Inside Rwanda's *Gacaca* Courts

Seeking Justice after Genocide

Bert Ingelaere

The University of Wisconsin Press

Publication of this book has been made possible, in part, through support from the Anonymous Fund of the College of Letters and Science at the University of Wisconsin–Madison.

The University of Wisconsin Press
1930 Monroe Street, 3rd Floor
Madison, Wisconsin 53711-2059
uwpress.wisc.edu

3 Henrietta Street, Covent Garden
London WC2E 8LU, United Kingdom
eurospanbookstore.com

Printed in the United States of America

This book may be available in a digital edition.

Library of Congress Cataloging-in-Publication Data

Names: Ingelaere, Bert, author.
Title: Inside Rwanda's gacaca courts : seeking justice after genocide / Bert Ingelaere.
Other titles: Critical human rights.
Description: Madison, Wisconsin : The University of Wisconsin Press, [2016] |
    Series: Critical human rights | Includes bibliographical references and index.
Identifiers: LCCN 2016012951 | ISBN 9780299309701 (cloth : alk. paper)
Subjects: LCSH: Gacaca justice system. | Transitional justice—Rwanda. |
    Criminal procedure—Rwanda. | Trials (Genocide)—Rwanda.
Classification: LCC KTD157.7 I54 2016 | DDC 345.67571/014—dc23
LC record available at https://lccn.loc.gov/2016012951

ISBN 9780299309749 (pbk. : alk. paper)

April is the cruelest month, breeding
Lilacs out of the dead land, mixing
Memory and desire, stirring
Dull roots with spring rain.

—T. S. Eliot, *The Waste Land*

Contents

Illustrations

Figures

Map

Tables

Supplementary Tables (in Appendix II)

 # Acknowledgments

This study grew out of an interaction between me and a computer screen. Luckily, the latter sentence qualifies only the last leg of the journey. Indeed, this book did not take shape in isolation but through interaction with and the support of a great number of individuals. It is only now, after many years of study, that I can finally thank these people on paper.

I could not have collected the data that drives this study without the assistance of a great many Rwandans. Over the years, I had the pleasure of working with more than twenty-five people who assisted me with various tasks in the research process (I do not provide full names given the nature of Rwanda's political climate): Vivine, Augustin, Alice, Jean-Baptiste, Yves, Stany, Anthère, Theodomir, Christine, Bonne Année, Frank, Jean-Paul, Victor, Jean, Bibiane, Judith, Jean-de-Dieu, Marguerite, Olivier, Bihoyiki, Ladislas, Florence, Sylvestre, and Jean-Bosco. Although I was technically their boss, I consider them colleagues. I thank them for their continued perseverance, motivation, and courage in undertaking fieldwork or capturing data in often difficult circumstances. A very special thanks to Sylvestre and Jean-Bosco, who were part of the research project from the beginning to the end. It is virtually impossible to put into words the effort, at times even sacrifice, they made to make sure we succeeded in every aspect of our work. Their contributions went well beyond what I had expected them to do. And their families became part of my family. *Murakozi cyane, cyane. Turi kumwe.*

Rwandans and non-Rwandans residing in the country enabled me to take necessary breaks from my research activities. If it were not for them, I would not have been able to continue for such a long time. The list of names is too long to recite. A special mention, however, for Amos: I vividly remember the moment he came to pick me up at the bus station when I arrived in Kigali from Uganda's capital, Kampala, in July 2004. At the time, I did not know it was the start of a long voyage in, through, and with Rwanda, often in his good company. And along the way I met Margaux. She made Rwanda home for me in a very special way. This book might not have seen print without her moral support, patience, and encouragement. Her lived experience accentuates the urgency of my quest for understanding but also the shortcomings of my insights.

This book grew out of a research trajectory that started in August 2005 when I arrived at the Institute of Development Policy and Management (IOB) at the University of Antwerp in Belgium. I sincerely thank Professor Filip Reyntjens for encouraging and supervising my research. While discussing the nature of fieldwork activities planned for an upcoming trip to Rwanda during a meeting in 2005, Professor Reyntjens suggested, "If you understand what sharing beers in the Rwandan countryside means for reconciliation, you will have been there too long." I was aware he made this suggestion not because such knowledge was not important but in the interest of time. In the end, and as I hope this book will show, I decided I wanted to explore in depth all the vicissitudes of justice and reconciliation in the Rwandan countryside. And so I had to return many times and for long periods. This is precisely the reason why I want to extend my sincere gratitude to Filip: it was his stimulating interest and never-ending support that allowed access to the necessary financial means that made my research possible and relevant. I also thank the staff at the IOB for creating a stimulating and supportive environment.

Over the years I have had the privilege to interact with many other researchers/scholars who gave valuable input by sharing their knowledge and insights, discussing particular topics of interest to me, commenting on work in progress, or giving practical advice. Here too, the list is too long to recite, but I must thank especially Lars Waldorf, Stef Vandeginste, and Luc Huyse. During fieldwork in Rwanda or somewhere else around the globe, Lars has always been an interesting and pleasant discussion partner, especially regarding our topic of mutual interest: the modernized *gacaca* courts. Stef has been a trusted *companion de route* throughout these years. He once characterized his take on transitional justice and political transition as a "helicopter" view, unlike my "frog" perspective, and our two points of view turned out to be complementary. The present study benefited from my participation in a research project on "traditional justice and reconciliation after violent conflict under the guidance of Luc Huyse. His pioneering work in the domain of transitional justice was and is an overall source of inspiration.

Filip, Stef, and Luc, as well as René Lemarchand, Susan Thomson, and Claudine Vidal, all gave crucial advice on converting my research on Rwanda's *gacaca* courts into an accessible book. I thank Scott Straus for his interest in my work and his suggestion that I submit my manuscript to the University of Wisconsin Press. Both he and the acquisitions editor Gwen Walker made critical comments that helped me develop the necessary focus. Their support, and that of the Critical Human Rights series coeditor, Steve J. Stern, was invaluable. Two anonymous reviewers gave instructive comments that helped me rework the manuscript. Craig Rollo undertook a careful proofreading of an early version. Kathleen Kearns's impeccable style editing not only polished my English but made my sentences sound much better. The usual disclaimer applies regarding shortcomings in the final version.

I also thank my funding sources: no results are possible without the necessary financial means, especially in a data-driven approach. The Research Foundation Flanders (FWO) and the University of Antwerp provided generous financial means for the research projects on which this book is built. Subsequently, the Flemish Interuniversity Council (VLIR-UOS) granted me a VLIR-VLADOC scholarship to continue the research activities. The FWO supported me further with a travel grant for additional fieldwork in Rwanda. The receipt of an Auschwitz Foundation Award in October 2014 motivated me to pursue publication of the book despite a Belgian academic climate that is often averse to book publications, and the financial support that came with the award allowed me to do so.

I based some sections of this book on work I have previously published. Chapter 2 is a modified version of "Learning to Be Kinyarwanda in Postgenocide Rwanda: Immersion, Iteration, and Reflexivity in Times of Transition," *Canadian Journal of Law and Society/Revue Canadienne droit et société* 30 (2): 277–92. Chapter 5 contains sections that were published in "What's on a Peasant's Mind? Experiencing RPF State Reach and Overreach in Post-Genocide Rwanda (2000–10)," *Journal of Eastern African Studies* 8 (2): 214–30. A version of chapter 7 was published in French as "Mille collines, mille *gacacas*: La vie en marge du processus *gacaca*," in *L'Afrique des Grands Lacs, Annuaire 2008–2009*, edited by F. Reyntjens and S. Marysse (Paris: L'Harmattan, 2009), 29–42. I have incorporated throughout the text insights and arguments published earlier in "The Gacaca Courts in Rwanda," in *Traditional Justice and Reconciliation after Violent Conflict: Learning from African Experiences*, edited by L. Huyse and M. Salter (Stockholm: International Idea, 2008); "'Does the Truth Pass Across the Fire without Burning?': Locating the Short Circuit in Rwanda's *Gacaca* Courts," *Journal of Modern African Studies* 47 (4): 507–28; "Do We Understand Life after Genocide? Center and Periphery in the Construction of Knowledge on Rwanda," *African Studies Review* 53 (1): 41–59; and "From Model to Practice: Researching and Representing Rwanda's 'Modernized' *Gacaca* Courts," *Critique of Anthropology* 32 (4): 388–414. I thank the reviewers of these articles and the editors of these journals for valuable suggestions during the article review and publication process.

I also thank my family and friends. I realize I have been a very absent friend, son, grandson, or brother during the years that I was doing fieldwork for this book. I learned, however, that things were always as before when I returned after another round of research that often took more than six months. Knowing this, it was always a pleasure to return to my first home, Belgium. Many of you made sure I did not forget this first home or that there are other things in life besides research, Rwanda, and *gacaca*. If I were to mention all of you and what you did, I would need to add at least a chapter to this already voluminous study. You know who you are and you know what you did. Thanks, guys and girls. The same is true for my father, mother, sister, and grandfather. To all of them, thanks *umuryango*.

And now I reserve a final word for the subjects of this study: Rwanda's peasants. I once said in jest that everyone does research on his or her level. Some speak with ministers or policymakers, I interact with peasants. In fact, I am proud and grateful to inhabit their world to a certain extent. And this was only possible because they let me do so.

Abbreviations

ASF	Avocats Sans Frontières (Lawyers Without Borders)
CIA	Central Intelligence Agency
DRC	Democratic Republic of the Congo
FAR	Forces Armées du Rwanda (Rwandan Armed Forces)
FARG	Fonds d'Assistance aux Rescapés du Génocide (National Fund for the Assistance of Genocide Survivors)
FGD	Focus Group Discussion
FIND	Fonds d'Indemnisation (National Compensation Fund)
HRW	Human Rights Watch
ICTR	International Criminal Tribunal for Rwanda
MINALOC	Ministry of Local Government
MRND	Mouvement National pour le Développement
NGO	nongovernmental organization
NURC	National Unity and Reconciliation Commission
PRI	Penal Reform International
RPA	Rwandan Patriotic Army

RPF	Rwandan Patriotic Front
SA	South Africa
SNJG	Service National des Juridictions Gacaca (National Service of the Gacaca Courts)
TIG	*travaux d'intérêt général* (community service)
TRC	Truth and Reconciliation Commission
UN	United Nations
UNHCHR	United Nations High Commissioner for Human Rights
US	United States

 Inside Rwanda's
Gacaca Courts

Introduction

This book opens the black box of Rwanda's grassroots transitional justice processes: the *gacaca* courts. Both the practice of and scholarship on transitional justice recently took a turn toward localized or grassroots mechanisms, processes, or approaches. Dealing with a violent past used to be primarily a matter of (inter)national tribunals or truth commissions. These institutions, however, were modeled on a Western idea of doing justice, which is dominantly retributive. Or they hinged on Western assumptions that establishing the truth would lead to spiritual or Christian redemption. In addition, they often operated mainly in capital cities, sometimes even abroad. For the ordinary population, of whom a significant part had been directly affected by violence in the past, these mechanisms functioned at physically and psychologically large distances.

The recent attention to grassroots approaches—often through the use of so-called tradition-based justice and reconciliation mechanisms—entails not only a turn toward more culturally appropriate and homegrown solutions but often also implies the decentralization of the judicial procedure or the reconciliation process to the most remote local level: small face-to-face communities. However, the enthusiasm for grassroots transitional justice processes runs well ahead of evidence that they are effective. Because these processes operate outside the mainstream, knowledge gaps and blind spots exist.[1]

The Rwandan *gacaca* courts that dealt with the legacy of the 1994 genocide are probably the best known instance of this new model for dealing with a history of mass violence. Key features of the modern *gacaca* system were inspired by a customary conflict resolution mechanism also known as *gacaca*—meaning "justice on the grass"—that existed in Rwandan society since precolonial times. Furthermore, the grassroots dimension of the modern *gacaca* lies in the decentralization of the judicial procedure to the lowest levels of society,

a popularization or diffusion of the process among lay judges, and the involvement of the general population. Between nationwide introduction in 2005 and
official closure of the modern *gacaca* system in June 2012, more than 11,000
courts dealt with 1,958,634 cases of alleged participation in the genocide.

These grassroots models of transitional justice—and the *gacaca* courts in
particular—inform scholarly studies and inspire interventions on the ground
globally. This trend will increase because it is convenient to spur ongoing
debates with known examples or assess upcoming programs according to past
experiences. However, despite much attention to the Rwandan way of doing
justice after genocide, the actual functioning of and popular experience with
the court system often provokes controversy. Consider the following diverging
analyses and conclusions.

Although a minister in 2007 claimed that 75 percent of Rwandans are
reconciled (Musoni 2007), others dismiss the reconciliation process, stating
that postgenocide justice in Rwanda consists of a return to feudal structures
and subordination for the Hutu (Centre de lutte contre l'impunité et l'injustice
au Rwanda 2005). In a discussion on the nature of the Rwandan justice system, including *gacaca*, Human Rights Watch (HRW) concluded after three
years of research that the system operates in a political context detrimental to
fair-trial guarantees and that "there is an official antipathy to views diverging
from those of the government and the dominant party" (Human Rights Watch
2008, 2). However, William Schabas, who undertook the same exercise, refuted
most of the Human Rights Watch claims and summarized certain perspectives
on Rwanda as "unrealistic assessments of problems that are more imaginary
than real" (Schabas 2008, 59). In its final assessment of the court system,
Human Rights Watch concluded that "the compromises made in adapting
the customary community-based practice to try grave criminal offenses led to
significant due process violations being built into the system and a degree of
disappointment on the part of many Rwandans" (Human Rights Watch 2011,
130). Government officials responding to the HRW report were quoted as
saying it was "abusive and misleading" and "intended to make a mockery of
Rwanda's efforts to promote justice and reconciliation" (Mazimpaka 2011).

Indeed, the outcomes of the Rwandan way of seeking justice and reconciliation remain contested. This points to an unresolved tension between what
gacaca was supposed to accomplish and what it actually did. This book's ad-
mittedly ambitious aim is to address this tension by clarifying what the courts
did and did not achieve.

According to government sources and academic analysts, from the moment
of its inception the *gacaca* process stipulated five goals: (1) establish the truth
about what happened; (2) accelerate the legal proceedings for those accused of

genocide crimes; (3) eradicate a culture of impunity; (4) reconcile Rwandans and reinforce their unity; and (5) use the capacities of Rwandan society to administer justice based on Rwandan custom. Once the *gacaca* process was well underway on a national scale, these goals were seldom presented as a plan, a project to be implemented, or the objectives of such a project. Instead, they were presented as actual outcomes of the *gacaca* practice.[2] However, goals and outcomes are different things. Only one objective of the *gacaca* practice was accomplished, others were not fully reached, and some were not reached at all.

Examining what the *gacaca* actually did demonstrates how the court really operated, not how it was supposed to operate. Of course, design and practice overlap, and so do objectives and outcomes. However, I find significant differences between the characteristics articulated in the institutional and legal design of the modern *gacaca* court system and its actual operation. Four major findings stand out.

First, although it appeared to be homegrown and based on custom, the modern *gacaca* operated according to a prosecutorial and adversarial logic. When the Rwandan way of doing justice after genocide is evoked, the image of a palaver under the oldest tree in the village followed by people living happily ever after is never far away. This image is wrong. The modern *gacaca* was a court system like court systems elsewhere in that its core was retributive. The system functioned according to typical trial procedures that, at best, established the forensic truth. I discuss forensic truth in more detail later, but it does not have the dialogical, narrative, or healing dimensions that truth-telling processes or rituals of reintegration do. Second, though confession was the cornerstone of the *gacaca* design, once the courts were underway they shifted from confessions to accusatory practices. The confession procedure was supposed to give the *gacaca* process a distinctively restorative dimension: defendants were supposed to receive a reduction in sentence in return for revealing the truth about crimes. In practice, a significant number of the defendants on trial were accused, pleaded not guilty, and were convicted. Third, although the modern *gacaca* is often considered an instance of participatory justice, the general population's participation was rather low. Fourth, several features of the *gacaca* system—for instance, the fact that prisoners were freed only after they confessed—gave the process an almost systemic tendency to find a defendant guilty of genocide-related offenses and to ignore guilt for war crimes and revenge killings.

These developments demand explanation: Why did these characteristics and outcomes emerge once the *gacaca* was implemented nationwide in 2005? What rerouted the *gacaca* process? The difference between design and practice—*gacaca* on paper and its actual unfolding—turns out to result from two mutually reinforcing tendencies: on the one hand, the weight of the Rwandan state;

and on the other hand, the pragmatism of the Rwandan peasantry. These forces shaped the practice of Rwanda's grassroots transitional justice process. Once the court system was underway, a consequentialist ethics animated it: what the court found to be true and just depended on the circumstances and the desired consequences.

This insight helps us better articulate the outcomes of Rwanda's transitional justice process. Because the actual outcomes do not equate with the system's five stated goals, we cannot accurately convey what the modern *gacaca* accomplished by focusing on its goals. A more nuanced view of the *gacaca* experiment allows us to develop a better understanding of what transitional justice is all about—in Rwanda, in grassroots justice systems elsewhere, and beyond.

From Model to Practice

Government sources, legal texts, and policy documents present to varying degrees an overly rosy, numerical, or legalistic picture of *gacaca*. The numerical and aggregate facts are of special interest to a state, as James Scott explains in his analysis of how states see society (Scott 1998, 80). It is indeed striking that state actors' communications about the actual *gacaca* proceedings are dominated by numbers.[3] They convey the accomplishments of the *gacaca* process quantitatively: the number of cases compiled; the number of accused according to category and administrative structure; the number of judges elected, trained, or replaced; the number of judgments pronounced; the number of motorbikes handed out to staff; the number of trauma cases; the number of people killed for participating in the *gacaca* process, for example by providing testimony, and so on.[4] The list is virtually endless.

State actors don't talk only about numbers, of course. They often also refer to *gacaca* legislation. But their discourse about actual *gacaca* practice is almost entirely represented by numerical facts, thus by a process of counting. Government sources have also consistently referred to the five goals of the *gacaca* process stipulated from the moment of its inception, and they have consistently equated these goals with outcomes. General Frank Rusagara, one of the ideologues of the regime, voiced the dominant government view on the modern *gacaca*.[5] In an opinion article published in the government-friendly newspaper, he describes discussions he had on *gacaca* with Rwandan youth in *ingandos* (Rusagara 2006). *Ingandos* are reeducation camps, and I return to fuller discussion of them later. Some of those Rusagara spoke with evoked the retributive or punitive character of *gacaca* (probably based on actual experience) and highlighted the fact that the modern *gacaca* practice was a source of insecurity.

Rusagara said, "This illustrates how the spirit of *gacaca* is misunderstood" and maintained that it is a restorative type of justice. He also said, "The right to security is enshrined in the Constitution under the bill of rights. Therefore, the government, in ensuring security for all, does not favor any one group." In fact, his statement about security is a sort of "magic syllogism" (Cohen 2002, 108), a technique of denial that governments use to counter accusations of wrongdoing. Such statements assert that an allegation cannot be true because the alleged act is illegal according to domestic legislation, the constitution, or ratified international treaties and conventions. According to Rusagara, there can be no insecurity because the law guarantees security. His response obscures actual *gacaca* practice.

Rusagara's response also indicates the approach the Rwandan government has deployed. It has used several strategies to influence outsiders' image of Rwanda and thus also their understanding of the *gacaca* courts. Often this comes down to denial (Reyntjens 2011), at times through magic syllogisms. Recently another strategy became known through the publication of an agreement made in 2009 between the Rwandan government and a public relations firm (U.S. Department of Justice 2011b).[6] The regime's speech acts gained performative force in the outside world through a detailed public relations campaign to create a positive "bottom-up narrative" "to educate audiences about the new Rwanda." This positive narrative seemed to flourish organically, but it actually corresponds with the Rwandan regime's desired representations. "*Gacaca* as a just solution" is one theme the public relations campaign chose to brand worldwide. Other themes were "Rwanda's Miracle: The Healing of a Nation" and "Rwanda's Visionary Leader." The campaign seems to have deployed "offensive and defensive strategies to shape perceptions" through media outlets that have "the greatest possibility to shape opinion."[7] One of the strategies entails "erecting walls of pro-Rwandan data." The public relations firm displayed little concern or reflection about whether they were communicating something real, and they seem simply to have accepted—and sent around the globe—the representation of *gacaca* courts the Rwandan regime presented to them. This is not surprising, given that this PR firm executed a similar campaign for Gaddafi's Libya not so long ago (U.S. Department of Justice 2011a).[8] As Pottier observed (2002, 207), "reality is what Rwanda's political leaders, as moral guardians tell the world . . . it is." This applies to their messages about the *gacaca* outcomes as well. Taking a critical stance toward these types of public relations statements is one step toward a more accurate picture of what is probably the most important transitional justice experiment in decades.

Scholars initially analyzed the "new" *gacaca* system, its legal and institutional framework, the invention and shaping of its contours and objectives, and the model of justice emerging from its first steps almost exclusively from a normative or purely theoretical perspective.[9] Human rights organizations analyzed and criticized the emerging model primarily from a legal human rights perspective.[10] As the *gacaca* system slowly gained momentum, its surrounding framework of intervention, international support, and human rights monitoring also attracted attention.[11]

Most of these studies are primarily legalistic or theoretical because they were almost all written before nationwide implementation. At that time, the *gacaca* laws, policy documents, and—occasionally—interviews with practitioners and policymakers were the only sources available. That said, many studies from this era were, and still are, instructive. Some analyzed the opinion and aspirations of the people of Rwanda regarding the genocide legislation and *gacaca* courts.[12] These first-generation or pre-*gacaca* studies do present a bottom-up and empirically informed perspective, but they represent popular attitudes and opinions before the courts' nationwide implementation.

The fact that many of these studies use the term "model" is revealing. At this stage, the "modern *gacaca*" emerging on paper and in the minds of policymakers, practitioners, and observers was simply that: a legal and theoretical model. McEvoy (2007), following Cohen (2002), describes them as "magical legalism." All these representations of the modernized *gacaca* system have something in common: they are disconnected from the "real world." Like General Rusagara's article, these writings are primarily based on law or law talk.

Close attention to word use and phrasing in these studies neutralizes the magic of the legalism. Specific words—such as "should," "ought," "might," "needs," "could," "seeks," "has the potential," "has the objective," "it is believed," "the prospect is," and the like—reveal that the authors are aware that their studies are conditional or normative or that they make assumptions or predictions. A good example of such careful wording is the study by Daly (2002). Another is Mark Drumbl (2005, 59), who states that "the success or failure of *gacaca* remains unproven and contingent." But when an author uses more definitive language, such as "is" or "will," one is dealing with magical legalism in full force. An example is the study by Wierzynska (2004). Without any insight into actual *gacaca* practice, the author simply states her analysis that a modern *gacaca* court "demonstrate[s] how it helps to promote participation and contestations."

Harrell's (2003) *Rwanda's Gamble: The Gacaca Courts and the New Model of Transitional Justice* was published before the nationwide implementation of *gacaca* and, as the title suggests, assesses the "model" based on the legal and institutional framework emerging at the time. Although informed by the functioning of the *gacaca* court system, Jones (2010), Bornkamm (2012), and Gahima (2013) similarly present a legalistic and top-down analysis of the

Rwandan way of doing justice after mass violence; they consider *gacaca* as only one mechanism among others, including the national courts, the International Criminal Tribunal for Rwanda (ICTR), and cases tried in other countries.

A true understanding of the *gacaca* courts' operation and the social process they generated in the wider Rwandan society became possible only after nation-wide implementation. During the initial pilot stages of the *gacaca* practice, almost no studies were based on in-depth field research, with the notable exception of nongovernmental organization (NGO) reports that followed the *gacaca* activities onsite in the pilot areas and subsequently nationwide; these were written for operational purposes but some provide interesting insights.[13]

Academic studies that focus on actual *gacaca* practice are growing but remain limited.[14] In addition, the Rwandan government as well as NGOs have undertaken impact studies to understand *gacaca* practice.[15] This is a second generation of studies on the modernized *gacaca* court system. The actual methodological approach, the research techniques used, and the interpretative process vary in each of these studies, but the central concern is the practice of the modernized *gacaca* courts. Most of these studies present their analyses either at a very high level or a very low level of aggregation, with the latter applying to studies of the proceedings in one community or the participation of a limited number of people. But even though these studies all focus on practice, they are often in discord regarding essential workings of the court system and its impact on Rwandan society. They often lack a systematic empirical approach, and they do not take into account the fact that the *gacaca* laws, operational procedures, and popular opinion all changed significantly over the years.

A key characteristic of the modern *gacaca* court system was its decentralization to thousands of hills (villages) spread all over Rwanda. These localities look similar from afar, but each has its own demographic, social, political, economic, and historical makeup. Did this give the *gacaca* proceedings a local flavor? Some studies conducted during the *gacaca* process might be more of a snapshot of a particular period in the *gacaca* process or of a particular place where the observations were made. Deeper insights emerge when we take into account the variables of space and time in the unfolding of the *gacaca* activities. Systematic examination of the unfolding of the *gacaca* process in multiple places over time avoids claims based on the idiosyncrasies of unique places, particular time periods, and individuals.

By adopting a bottom-up perspective that focuses on actual practice and popular experience in a systematic way across time and space, this book significantly challenges the arguments and insights presented in Phil Clark's book *The Gacaca Courts, Post-Genocide Justice and Reconciliation in Rwanda: Justice Without Lawyers*. Although Clark has produced the most sustained examination of the *gacaca* courts so far, his analysis fails to move systematically beyond received notions of grassroots justice in general and the *gacaca* courts in particular.[16] Although his book is presented as an ethnography, his findings on *gacaca* are crypto-normative. From the outset, Clark aims at something else, namely "to more clearly analyze what *gacaca* is designed to achieve than most observers—and many participants in *gacaca*—have done so far" (Clark 2010, 4). The focus is thus on the design of *gacaca*, the model itself, not actual practice. Then, as he states several times in his book, Clark wants to analyze *gacaca* "better" than its participants, the Rwandans who actually practiced *gacaca*. Indeed, he repeats throughout the book that a significant number of the practice- and perception-based insights of the population need to be rejected (Clark 2010, 230) or countered (248). The question is whether such an attitude has even a remote chance of generating an insight into the *gacaca* process as it unfolded on the Rwandan hills.

The importance of the local is gaining ground in the domain of transitional justice (Hinton 2010; Shaw and Waldorf 2010) and related fields such as peacebuilding (Hughes, Öjendal, and Schierenbeck 2015). But conventional radar screens do not easily capture signals emitted by grassroots mechanisms and processes. Understanding is impossible without empirical input and conceptual upgrading. Preconceived ideas and assumptions, reigning theories and concepts cannot simply be imposed on a process from the outside. Especially with a grassroots mechanism such as the modern *gacaca* process, physically and mentally moving away from the center of society and adopting a bottom-up perspective captures the voices and practices of ordinary people. The center of Rwandan society develops preferred images and actively constructs, manages, and controls knowledge (Pottier 2002; Ingelaere 2010a). The field of transitional justice operates with preconceived ideas, in an unexamined language, and without awareness that it imposes global models, concepts, and legal, normative, and theoretical concerns (McEvoy 2007). A recent assessment of scholarship on transitional justice comes to the conclusion that in the field "much that is done represents normative beliefs and assumptions that have yet to be substantiated from the perspective of data-driven evidence" (Fletcher and Weinstein 2015, 16).

With these limitations in mind, I cast my own research net wide and deep, and took a primarily ethnographic and data-driven approach. I adopted an "inductive theoretical drive,"[17] striving to discover answers to my initial questions and thus exploring the concepts that underlie this form of transitional justice. My analysis emphasizes anthropological rather than legal frames of interpretation. In the chapters that follow, I detail what I found during my voyage to the heart of the *gacaca* practice.

Overview of the Book

Chapter 1 provides a summary of Rwanda's history with a focus on the events that led to the 1994 genocide and the atmosphere that characterized Rwanda in the immediate aftermath. An overview of the process that led to the adoption of the *gacaca* court system to deal with that genocide follows. I highlight the main features of the court system's design as well as its timing, tempo, and numerical outcome in terms of people processed and convicted. Chapter 2 provides a systematic overview of my research process and techniques, in addition to insights about language, customs, and interpretations. I have elaborated on the notion of *immersion* and the principles of *iteration* and *mixing methods*. I based my study of the *gacaca* courts on the approximately thirty-two months I spent in Rwanda rotating through a number of rural research sites. Besides observing almost two thousand *gacaca* proceedings and the sociopolitical dynamics that accompany them, I used a range of interviewing techniques, primarily the collection of life stories.

The logic of *gacaca*'s basic operational features emerges in chapter 3. This chapter is primarily descriptive but tackles important questions that destabilize the *gacaca* model, specifically how *gacaca* became a prosecutorial process driven to a great extent by accusatory practices rather than confession. I present narratives of trial proceedings as concrete examples of the system's attempts to unearth the forensic truth about the genocide—who did what, where, when, and with whom. I also systematically assess key features of the court system, focusing on the confession procedure, popularization of the justice procedure and the reconciliation process, and the categorization of defendants according to crime.

Some of the insights that emerge raise questions that will only be answered by examining the popular experience of *practicing gacaca*. Therefore, in chapter 4 the focus shifts toward the experience and perceptions of the insiders: the Rwandans who have practiced *gacaca*. Here, I engage available studies on attitudes and emotions accompanying the *gacaca* process and present new primary data on these themes. By looking at the impact of the *gacaca* logic on the social tissue, I establish that a crisis hit the peasantry with the nationwide introduction of the court system and that the peasantry subsequently had a complex experience with the truth.

Having qualified the nature of the modernized *gacaca* process, I turn to why the *gacaca* operated as it did and why the process was accompanied by the observed attitudes and experiences. Penal Reform International (PRI) observed after monitoring the *gacaca* trials that the process was "heavily influenced by its social and political context" (PRI 2009, 4). Chapter 5 aims to contextualize the *gacaca* practice by describing the nature of governance in the periphery of Rwandan society. The state had a heavy influence on some aspects of the *gacaca* process, and authority shaped Rwanda's grassroots transitional justice in a certain direction. Consequently, *gacaca* began to emphasize what I call *Truth-with-a-Capital-T*. And because the political regime and state power operated "from the inside" of people's lives, they affected the nature of participation in the *gacaca* process. This contextualization clarifies tendencies observed in previous chapters, such as the seemingly systemic tendency to foster guilt, for example.

Chapters 6 and 7 contextualize localized testimonial activity in the social environment of Rwanda's hills. They examine why the *gacaca* process shifted toward accusatory practices, why participation was rather low, and why so many people were accused.

Chapter 6 demonstrates how Rwandans adopted a strategic stance toward *gacaca*. The analysis shows that individual motivations and local dynamics observed in the margins of the *gacaca* proceedings influenced to a great extent the outcome of the local process. Participants were navigating a changing social environment, and the unfolding proceedings created feedback loops that structured the nature of subsequent participation. Corruption, score-settling, vengeance, the search for profit, and power plays between individuals and extended families also affected participation in the proceedings, and explain the shift from confessions to accusations and the frictional experience with truth-telling.

Past experiences also structured the modus operandi of *gacaca*. Chapter 7 elaborates on this finding and identifies localized path-dependency that can explain the observed differences from hill to hill. Both the specific histories of local communities and the composition of the collective influenced how *gacaca* operated in the social constellation of local communities (hills), all of which are characterized by their particular demographic makeup, power structure, governance particularities, and existing conflicts. This created the possibility for local inhabitants to forge alliances or to follow a certain strategy as they made accusations or conspired in silence, an eventuality the procedure's designers did not necessarily envision. I examine in detail two hills situated in different regions of Rwanda.

These chapters demonstrate that a rather pragmatic understanding of what constitutes the truth was animating *gacaca*. They also introduce the notion of the *effectual truth* at work in the *gacaca* proceedings: true is that which has the desired consequences given the circumstances.

Everyday action and speech can be "true" in the Rwandan context, and chapter 8 focuses on the strategies and tactics Rwandans employed in daily life in the margins of the *gacaca* activities. This chapter examines praxis—the outward manifestations of the interior self: speech, presentation of self, gestures, interactions and actions—in order to explore the range and meaning of the underlying principles of living together and dealing with violence in the sociocultural context of the Rwandan hills. I argue that "heart" (*umutima*) is a key concept in the sociocultural construction of Rwandan personhood and, as such, in the epistemological framework that animates the Rwandan sociocultural universe. I determine that speech—talking or discourse—is thus not necessarily the same as truth-telling in the forensic sense, an insight that further clarifies the frictional experience with the *gacaca* process. And I assess how pardoning and restitution—acts that are more restorative and have a deeper cultural significance—organized within the modernized *gacaca* practice only to a lesser degree unlock the moral truth and the reconciliatory potential of the long-standing practice on which the modern *gacaca* was based.

The eight chapters of this book reveal the basic operational characteristics of *gacaca* and consider how we should qualify the outcomes of this ambitious process. In the epilogue, I engage with transitional justice beyond Rwanda. Our voyage through the Rwandan grass roots helps us to reconsider key concepts and approaches in the field of transitional justice.

From Genocide to *Gacaca*

Before 1994 Rwanda was hidden in the heart of Africa, almost unknown beyond its borders. On 6 April 1994, however, the aircraft carrying then-president Juvénal Habyarimana was shot down in the skies over the capital, Kigali. This put in motion the campaign of genocidal violence that members of the majority Hutu ethnic group conducted against, mostly, the Tutsi minority but also the so-called moderate Hutu, who belonged to the majority group but opposed the regime in place. In one hundred days, between 500,000 and 1,000,000 people died. These tragic events shocked the world and placed Rwanda on the global map. The country has had the world's attention ever since, in part because Rwanda chose to deal with its legacy of genocide through the boldest experiment in transitional justice ever attempted. The *gacaca* court system adapted—or, more accurately, reinvented—a traditional conflict-resolution mechanism. The modern *gacaca* courts' historical origins, their evolution, but especially the way they were reconceived after the genocide influenced their legal and operational features, the way they functioned, the outcomes they produced, their scope, and their limitations.

The Rwandan Conflict and Genocide

The Rwandan genocide took place in the context of a civil war and an unsuccessful attempt to introduce multiparty democracy. It was the violent apex of a national history in which a long-standing struggle over power and wealth—a struggle grafted onto the Hutu–Tutsi ethnic bipolarity that marks the Rwandan sociopolitical landscape—led to sporadic eruptions of ethnic violence.[1]

Rwandan history is marked by complex sociopolitical dynamics (Vansina 2004; Chrétien 2006; Newbury 2009). Before independence in 1962, the country was a kingdom. In its early history, "Tutsi" and "Hutu" designated not different ethnic groups but different social classes of the same people. Separate ethnic identities crystallized as the result of sociopolitical transformations that started before the advent of colonialism. A king (*mwami*) and Tutsi aristocracy ruled over the masses, who were predominantly Hutu. A Tutsi identity evolved around the wealth and power associated with royal status, while a Hutu awareness developed in relation to, and particularly in subordination to, this other identity group. The colonial rulers further institutionalized, rigidified, and racialized ethnicity by—among other things—issuing ethnic identity cards.

Germany first colonized the country (1897–1916), and in 1919 Rwanda officially became a mandated territory of the League of Nations; later, when the United Nations was founded, it became a UN Trust Territory administered by Belgium. The monarchy was progressively "desacralized" during this period (Reyntjens 1985, 77–93). The year 1959 was marked by a social revolution—an event unimaginable a few years before—which became known as the Hutu revolution. In a wave of successive events between 1959 and 1962, local inhabitants ousted Tutsi rulers from their hilltop communities and elected "burgomasters," predominantly of Hutu origin, to replace them. Grégoire Kayibanda, a Hutu, became the first president of Rwanda. Violence against the Tutsi rulers and their families accompanied these events, and a first wave of Tutsi sought refuge in neighboring countries. A second and larger wave followed in 1963–64, after the Tutsi of the first wave had regrouped and attacked Rwanda from Burundi and Tanzania. Assailants killed a significant number of Tutsi in reprisal attacks, and even more left the country as refugees. These attacks and the violent reaction of the Rwandan regime foreshadowed what was to happen thirty years later. The descendants of these refugees formed the bulk and backbone of the Rwandan Patriotic Front (RPF) and its military wing, the Rwandan Patriotic Army (RPA), which attacked Rwanda in October 1990, seeking an armed return to their country and a share in power.

This attack happened during the reign of President Habyarimana, who had succeeded Kayibanda during a bloodless coup in 1973. The president was the key political actor, but he exercised power in concert with an oligarchy of northern Hutu, members of his clan and his wife's, primarily the latter. They constituted what became known as the *Akazu* (little house), which controlled the state and its monetary privileges (Reyntjens 1995a, 1995b). The entire system aimed to maintain the status quo with respect to the distribution of power in Rwandan society.

Several pressures moved the Habyarimana regime to initiate liberal reforms, among them the war with the RPF and the end of the cold war, which prompted donors to request democratization before economic assistance would continue. Converting to multiparty politics after decades of single-party rule and undertaking institutional reforms while waging a war in an overpopulated country turned out to be a daunting exercise. Rwanda had "settled in a war culture" (Prunier 1998, 108). Violence had become a way of conducting politics, not only on the battlefield but also, with multipartyism gone awry, in the streets of Kigali and in the hills of the countryside.

The insecurity that the political parties caused affected all ordinary citizens during the years of turmoil at the beginning of the 1990s, but the Tutsi were most often targeted. For the simple reason that they were of the same ethnic identity that dominated the RPF, Tutsi citizens were called *ibiyitso* (accomplices of the rebel force) and alleged to be in conspiracy with the rebels. Intensive media and government propaganda portrayed a threat to the established ruling class surrounding Habyarimana as a threat to the Hutu ethnic majority. This propaganda created the perception that danger was coming not only from outside, through the invasion, but also from within, from every single Tutsi citizen living in Rwanda and, by extension, from every single Hutu who was not in favor of the status quo. As the force made its way into Rwanda, stories and reports of the RPF massacring Hutu stirred the imagination and strengthened the fear. Thus, many Hutu believed that the threat had to be eliminated.

In this highly explosive atmosphere, Habyarimana's aircraft was shot down as he was returning from a regional summit meeting in Tanzania. That same night, 6 April 1994, a massive extermination campaign began.[2] Events moved rapidly in the capital. Some rural areas reacted spontaneously to the call for action but others resisted for a long time, at least until outside forces started the killings. The militia, the army, the police forces, and most state personnel drove the killings throughout the country.

Because the sociopolitical context shapes ethnicity in Rwanda, its meaning and function vary over time (Newbury and Newbury 1999). Consequently, Hutu and Tutsi are not born as "natural" enemies. Quite the contrary—despite the outbreaks of violence mentioned earlier, ordinary Rwandan civilians generally live together peacefully. Nevertheless, during the genocidal months of 1994, ethnicity took on a very specific meaning and operated as a dividing force (Fujii 2009, 180). Tutsi were identified as enemies of the state and Hutu as its defenders; Tutsi became categorized as victims and Hutu as perpetrators. However, Hutu who were not in favor of the genocidal campaign, those who were vehemently opposed to the Habyarimana regime, and those who were in some way connected to Tutsi also became victims of the violence.

What is puzzling is how many ordinary citizens, the Hutu peasantry, became involved in the genocidal campaign to track down, pillage, and eventually kill their Tutsi neighbors. A number of factors explain why this call for mass ethnic violence received support: the "fear, uncertainty, and insecurity" that political upheaval and war had caused (Prunier 1998, 108; Straus 2006, 234); the fact that Hutu ideology had pervaded Rwandan society for decades; economic hardship due to land scarcity, economic reforms, and a drop in global coffee prices; and finally the channeling of the call for violence through long-standing hierarchical state structures with few institutional barriers or countervailing forces.

Furthermore, micropolitical matrices and social formations appropriated and fundamentally shaped the violence unleashed at the macro level (Ingelaere 2006).[3] Genocide was shaped from above, but a highly differentiated terrain of local social tensions and cleavages, regional differences, and communal or individual particularities significantly reshaped it. The genocidal violence reflected both the goals of the supralocal forces and factors—mainly the Hutu–Tutsi cleavage that political actors mobilized for political purposes—and their local shadows, namely struggles for power, fear, intragroup coercion, the quest for economic resources and personal gain, vendettas, and the settling of old scores.

The RPF took power on 4 July 1994 and ended the genocide. The defeated government and its armed forces fled to the neighboring Democratic Republic of the Congo (DRC), and a large part of the population followed. The consequences were felt far beyond the Rwandan borders and caused regional instability and insecurity for years to come. Although the genocide machine came to a halt after the one hundred days, violence remained the order of the day. Fieldwork in Rwanda reveals that Rwandans knew a decade of violence between the start of the civil war in 1990 and the introduction of multiparty politics and thus the end of overt hostilities on Rwandan soil in the late 1990s. From 1996 on, after the refugee camps in the DRC had been violently dismantled, the defeated government forces and the Interahamwe militia attacked northern Rwanda from their bases in the DRC. (Interahamwe, which literally means "those who work together," came to refer both to this militia and, later, to all who participated in the genocide.) This came to be known as the war of the infiltrators (*abacengezi*) during which hundreds—probably thousands—of civilians were killed. Claiming that it was difficult to distinguish infiltrators from civilians, the RPF gradually resorted to brutal counterinsurgency strategies to pacify the region.

As the military victor, the RPF was able to set the agenda for postgenocide Rwanda without much constraint. President Paul Kagame, who took office in 2000, has repeatedly indicated that he "wants to build a new country"—a wish that needs to be taken literally. The postgenocide Rwandan regime is characterized by "transformative authoritarianism" (Straus and Waldorf 2011, 5). Liberation from a genocidal order is one of the underlying ideological vectors and legitimization strategies. The regime has instituted a bold social engineering campaign in the postgenocide period in order to translate into practice its vision and ideas. The RPF aims to create the *true* postcolonial Rwanda. In their view, the colonial powers distorted the essence of Rwandan culture, and this colonial mind-set sustained the first two republics. They believe that *Rwandanness* or *Rwandanicity*, not ethnicity, should define relations between state and society, and that building or (re-)establishing this unity of Rwandans goes hand in hand with eradicating the "genocide ideology." They couch reconciliation, an element that had begun to dominate the ideological framework by the end of the 1990s, in terms of unity, and they see the overall objective of justice (in the sense of accountability) for genocide crimes as one of the cornerstones of the regime. They want homegrown traditions derived from the Rwandan sociocultural fabric to replace imported, divisive practices; they see these institutions as part of what they call "the building of a democratic culture," which is in essence "closer to the consensus-based type of democracy" (Republic of Rwanda 2006a, 151).

The choice and installation of the *gacaca* courts fit perfectly into this vision; the RPF presented them as a native, even indigenous precolonial resource and intended them to fight genocide and eradicate the culture of impunity.

Reinventing *Gacaca*

The *gacaca* court system that functioned as the key transitional justice mechanism in postgenocide Rwanda[4] is different in kind from the "traditional" conflict-resolution mechanism also known as the *gacaca*. Although the terminology is the same and the descriptions seem similar, the "old" and the "new" *gacaca* are not identical and are not even on a continuum. An essential change, a real rupture with the past, marks the installation of the *gacaca* courts after the genocide. The "new" *gacaca* courts are in the truest sense an "invented tradition" (Hobsbawn and Ranger 1983). While any "traditional" institution transforms over time due to social change in general, discontinuity prevails in the case of the *gacaca*. State intervention through legal and social engineering designed and implemented a novelty, one that was loosely modeled on an existing institution.

To fully understand the origins and purposes of the precolonial practice of *gacaca*, it needs to be placed in the cosmology of the Rwandan sociopolitical universe of the time.[5] Here, the extended lineage or family (*umuryango*) was the main unit of social organization. It encompassed several households (*inzu*)—the smaller lineages and units of society. Age and sex defined status within the lineage. Only elderly and married men without parents were independent; all others, and especially women, were dependent upon them. The *inzu* lineage head was responsible for the observation of the ancestral cults, and he arranged marriages, paid or received debts, and controlled the collective title on land or cattle. The lineage was the primary source of protection and security. A person had no autonomous existence; the family unit was the guarantor of security.

Political structures were superimposed over the lineages. In the seventeenth century, Rwanda consisted of several smaller territories governed by kings. The king (*umwami*) was at one and the same time the governor of things profane and a link with the supernatural. He embodied power, justice, and knowledge: judicial and political powers were not separated. The *umwami* was the ultimate arbitrator, assisted by the *abiru*, the guardians of tradition. There is a popular saying: "Before something is heard by the *umwami*, it needs to be brought before the wise men." This refers to the fact that the lineage heads, the "wise men," at the lowest units of society addressed problems first. In practice, this initial pass took place in what came to be known as *gacaca* gatherings.

It has become common wisdom that the word *gacaca* means "justice on the grass." In fact, the name *gacaca* is derived from the word *umucaca*, the Kinyarwandan word referring to a plant so soft to sit on that people preferred to gather on it.[6] In precolonial times, groups gathered on such plants to restore order and harmony (Ntampaka 1995, 2003; UNHCHR 1996). There is some evidence that serious cases such as homicide could be dealt with in the *gacaca*, although other sources stress that these types of infractions were normally forwarded to the king's court. Irrespective of the nature of the conflict, the primary aim of the settlement was the restoration of social harmony and, to a lesser extent, the establishment of the truth about what had happened, the punishment of the perpetrator, or even compensation through a gift. Although the latter elements could be part of the resolution, they were subsidiary to the return to harmony between the lineages and a purification of the social order.

Colonialism had a decisive impact on Rwandan society as a whole and thus on the *gacaca* as well. During the colonial period a Western-style legal system was introduced in Rwanda, but the *gacaca* tradition kept its function as a customary conflict-resolution mechanism at the local level. The colonial powers' stance toward Rwandan society was marked by indirect rule: indigenous institutions maintained their functions. Still, the presence of the colonial administrators altered and weakened what existed before their advent. At the judicial level, this is most obviously visible through the introduction of written law and a so-called Western court system imposed over the "traditional" institutions. The latter continued to function but were hierarchically inferior to the new system. The Western-style courts now handled serious cases such as manslaughter. Similarly, the king lost his unique position in the traditional institutions, and hence he and his chiefs gradually lost authority and legitimacy in the execution of judicial powers. This also implied that the legitimacy of the *gacaca* courts waned.

After independence, *gacaca* gradually evolved into an institution associated with state power as state officials were supervising (or taking on the role of) the task of the "customary" judges (Van Houtte et al. 1981; Reyntjens 1990). As the modern state became more powerful, it gradually absorbed the informal and traditional. In that way the institution of *gacaca* evolved towards a semitraditional or semiadministrative body. Some new elements came to the fore: the courts followed certain fixed procedures, kept notes, met on fixed days, and so on. The institution functioned as a barrier so that quarrelling parties would not immediately (have to) resort to the formal court system at the provincial level (*court de canton*). If possible, a dispute was settled at this lowest level of society; this happened with the majority of the cases. If necessary, though, the case would be forwarded to the higher court. *Gacaca* represented both the justice of proximity and a handy mechanism to relieve pressure on the ordinary court system. Despite the introduction of some formal elements and its instrumental relation with the overarching judicial structures, the conciliatory and informal character of the *gacaca* remained the cornerstone of the institution since decisions were to a great extent not in conformity with written state law (Reyntjens 1990, 36).

The possibility of using the *gacaca* emerged in the immediate wake of the genocide, as a United Nations High Commissioner for Human Rights report reveals (UNHCHR 1996). A number of Rwandan researchers and professors working at different institutions contributed research and reflection to this report. Not only did they investigate the nature of the long-standing practice of *gacaca* but they also established through fieldwork that the *gacaca* was already functioning in its semitraditional way in some areas immediately after the end of the genocide (UNHCHR 1996; see also Rose 1995). In these cases, either the local people or the administrative authorities initiated the practice. A letter from the prefect of the province of Kibuye dated November 1995, appended to the UNHCHR 1996 report, reveals that in some areas the administrative authorities took the initiative to support and widely instigate the functioning of the *gacaca* practice they found in some localities. The minutes

From Genocide to *Gacaca*

of a meeting between the residents of a community and a representative of the Ministry of the Interior (MINALOC) in March 1996 proves that the government condoned the informal or semitraditional functioning of the *gacaca*. This support was not part of official policy, and it had no legal and institutional framework. It seems clear that these *gacaca* courts functioned mostly as they had before the genocide, meaning that they dealt with minor disputes within the community.

The fact that the ordinary justice system was virtually nonexistent after the genocide clearly motivated the spontaneous emergence of the *gacaca* activities and the gradual support for *gacaca* by the authorities. The *gacaca* had to resume its former role, relieving the pressure on the ordinary courts. Immediately after the genocide, the latter were not just working slowly, as they had before; they were not working at all. Once they did start to function, they were quickly overloaded with cases of genocide suspects who were filling the prisons.

Meanwhile, a new element came into play in the practice of *gacaca*: genocide-related offenses and consequences. Crimes related to property had long been the main focus of *gacaca*, but such cases committed during the genocide—the destruction of houses, the theft of cows and household utensils, the appropriation of land, and so on—now came before the customary judges and state officials. Observation of current *gacaca* court activities reveals that those accused of looting might dig up documents dating back to the years immediately after the genocide to prove that they had already restored the property they looted or reimbursed the damage they had done. The initial settlement was often struck in the context of a (semi)informal *gacaca* meeting, with the authorities often initiating the action, supervising it, and providing proof (the documents used in the cases brought for the current *gacaca* courts) that compensation had been paid.

The 1996 UNHCHR report states that it was an absolute taboo to talk about killings during the *gacaca* sessions in those initial years after the genocide. People found these crimes too sensitive a matter to tackle. Neighbors and family members seem to have covered up for those who might have taken part in the killing. Nonetheless, the prefect of the province of Kibuye stated in a letter that the *gacaca* meetings should collect the names of those implicated in the violence. Sources in other communities where the *gacaca* functioned at that time also established that people thought it should function as a mechanism to restore order and harmony in society and thus reconcile families and neighbors.

In light of their observations of *gacaca* in 1995–96, their reflections on the origins and nature of the long-standing practice, and the nature of the genocidal violence, the authors of the UNHCHR report (1996, passim) concluded that the *gacaca* institution could play a role in dealing with genocide-related crimes. They made a number of recommendations:

- The violence experienced during the genocide and massacres was of such a gravity that it simply cannot and should not be handled in the *gacaca*.
- *Gacaca* could function as a sort of truth commission with two aims. On the one hand, collecting facts about the atrocities experienced in local communities. Information would be forwarded to the classical tribunals. On the other hand, as a space to reunite Rwandans and to debate the common values they share, a mechanism that helps people to live together and be reconciled.
- Caution should be exercised against too much government intrusion, and the institution should not be subverted into becoming a formal tribunal.

It is clear that the Rwandan government never seriously considered, let alone followed, the recommendations of the UNHCHR report. In 1999, after a period of reflection and a round of consultation, the (then) Rwandan president Pasteur Bizimungu set up a commission to modernize and formalize the "traditional" dispute-resolution mechanism in order to deal with the approximately 130,000 persons imprisoned at that time for offenses related to the genocide—a task the "ordinary" justice system could not accomplish in a satisfactory way. This commission was the result of and worked in the context of the so-called Urugwiro meetings that took place between May 1998 and March 1999.[7] Every Saturday, these "representatives of Rwandan society" held a meeting at the president's office to discuss serious problems facing the Rwandan people. The question of justice and dealing with the genocide was prominent on the agenda, and the participants debated proposed solutions, including the possible use of *gacaca*. Some expressed serious reservations, but proponents countered with arguments in favor. The resulting report summarizes the main arguments of both sides (Republic of Rwanda 1999, passim):

Arguments against:

- Trying crimes of genocide and massacres in *gacaca* would minimize the seriousness of these crimes.
- Can ordinary people who are not educated and acquainted with judicial procedures take care of these serious offenses themselves?
- Family relations and friendships would render the trials partial. It would be very difficult to make people tell the truth, and in some parts of the country there would be nobody left to testify.

- It would be better if the *gacaca* were used as an investigative mechanism providing the classical courts with information.
- Trials by the *gacaca* of accusations of genocide and massacres would create new conflicts and tensions in the local population.
- Would the *gacaca* be in accordance with international laws?

Arguments in favor:

- Letting *gacaca* courts deal with genocide crimes does not imply a trivialization. On the contrary, it would make people deal with the crimes of genocide and other crimes against humanity at the level where they happened. The building of a new Rwanda needs to be done by every Rwandan.
- People are not so uneducated that they cannot be educated. The *gacaca* system should be explained to the population and those responsible trained and assisted by lawyers.
- The danger that the truth might not surface and that partiality might prevail is real, but other participants can give contradictory evidence. This will make it possible to counter these tendencies.
- *Gacaca* would not only investigate but also punish. A truly participatory form of justice would give power to the population to deal with the violence experienced in their midst. After its use for genocide-related offenses, it would be turned into a system dealing with common crime.
- *Gacaca* would accelerate the process of dealing with the backlog of genocide-related cases; it would stop the culture of impunity by singling out those who actively participated in the killings.
- The crime of genocide is an exceptional crime and needs an exceptional solution to deal with it.

A closer look at the list of participants in the Urugwiro meetings where the *gacaca* court system was conceived reveals the involvement of members of the government, members of important state institutions, representatives of the army and the police, and representatives of the (tolerated) political parties. Members of the judiciary and some lawyers also took part in the discussion on justice.

Phil Clark (2010, 55–63) compiled an interesting overview of the genesis of the modern *gacaca* courts from interviews he conducted with key players at the time. He suggests that there were intense debates *within* the RPF. Considering the final modality of the political transition—military overthrow—and because the RPF subsequently dominated all domains of social and political life, it is no wonder that the discussion on the nature of justice in the aftermath of genocide and war did not include many alternative ideas or projects for Rwandan society. The discussion took place among peers, namely the RPF peers, and excluded civil society.

That too is hardly a surprise. Civil society was poorly organized and weak during the Habyarimana regime, although ferment had been bubbling up since the late 1980s. A healthy civil society never had the chance to develop following the genocide because of the new political elite's deliberate choices. The minister of local governance, social affairs, and development in the postgenocide regime, Protais Musoni, described succinctly the Rwandan regime's position on civil society in that period: "There are two debates on the role of civil society organizations in developing countries by international scholars. On one side civil society is seen as a counter power to government and on the other civil society is seen as an effective partner in service delivery and the development process. Rwanda favors the latter approach" (Musoni 2003, 14–15).

Foreign donor countries had a high stake in judicial activities in postgenocide Rwanda and in the *gacaca* court system in particular. Some even called the phenomenon "donor-driven justice" (Oomen 2005). After an initial period of reluctance, most donors came to support the newly created *gacaca* court system out of an awareness that it was the less bad of two possible options for tackling the past—on the one hand, classical (retributive) justice that would not be able to manage and resolve that past, and on the other hand, imperfect, unknown, and revolutionary justice.[8] Once it got underway, assessments of donor influence on the functioning of the *gacaca* process suggest that donors had little sway with the Rwandan government (Gready 2010; Schotsmans 2011; Jamar 2012).

The "Modernized" *Gacaca* Courts: General Features

The report of the Urugwiro meetings makes clear that participants debated and propagated the idea of unity and focused on the need to rebuild the country. It also shows that eradicating the culture of impunity—and instilling accountability—was a common theme underlying the discussions in those years. The word "reconciliation" is hardly mentioned, especially not in the section on justice. The report suggests examining the use of community service as an alternative penalty but only if it can be imposed in such a way as to avoid "disturbing the government's policy of eradicating the culture of impunity" (Republic of Rwanda 1999, 57). The report mentions that the phrase "*gacaca* jurisdictions" should be used to suggest that the Rwandan heritage is a source of inspiration for the new court system, which nevertheless has the same competence and procedures as Western-style courts (the "juris-diction" in the name).

The type of *gacaca* the Urugwiro report describes is the embryo of what was later codified in law, implemented, and constantly adapted.[9] The legislation delineated a modernized *gacaca* system that incorporated three fundamental principles, and these defining features affected the actual functioning of the *gacaca* practice. First, those suspected of genocide and crimes against humanity were to be prosecuted in parallel courts according to the crime committed. Ordinary courts would try the people presumed to be responsible for organizing and orchestrating the genocide; the *gacaca* courts would judge others, the majority of the cases, on their respective *collines* (hills). Second, installing courts in every administrative unit of the state would achieve the popularization or decentralization of justice. The *gacaca* courts procedure was loosely modeled on the traditional *gacaca* with lay persons presiding as judges (*inyangamugayo*) and the (active) involvement of the entire adult population as a "general assembly." Third, confession would increase the amount of evidence and available information. *Gacaca* trials would take place not with evidence gathered by police and judicial authorities but through the testimonials of perpetrators, victims, and bystanders during the trials. The discursive encounter in the *gacaca* sessions would function as the catalyst for the transitional justice process.

Since the nationwide start of the *gacaca* process in 2005, the *gacaca* law changed three times in reaction to the unexpectedly high numbers of accused and convicted.[10] Each time, the general principles of categorization remained the same, but the categories and the sanctions for each category shifted.[11] An overview of these changes can be found in tables 6 to 8 in appendix II. In addition, in the first years of the *gacaca* process, more people were placed in the first category than lawmakers envisioned when they wrote the 2004 law. The changes in the 2007 and 2008 laws, therefore, shifted some of the Category 1 crimes to the second category.[12]

Officially, there were two phases in the *gacaca* process. During the first phase, which took place at the cell (neighborhood) level between January 2005 and July 2006, the system collected information through confessions and accusations in every cell. The *gacaca* system mirrored the administrative structure of Rwanda as it existed both during the genocide and when the nationwide *gacaca* process began.[13] The *gacaca* courts operated at the lowest administrative levels of society: cells and sectors.[14] If someone was alleged to have committed crimes in multiple localities, a *gacaca* court in each locality would judge the person.[15]

At the end of the information-collection phase, the *inyangamugayo*, or lay judges/"persons of integrity" presiding over the *gacaca* court of the cell, categorized the crimes and suspects.[16] Although the elected judges decided how to categorize each person, the information and evidence on the basis of which this was done came from a perpetrator's confession and/or through accusations from members of the general assembly of the court at this level, that is, the entire population of the cell.

In July 2006 the second phase (the trial phase) started. Trials for those placed in Category 2 took place at the sector level. Trials for people placed in Category 3 took place at the cell level. The information collected in the previous phase as well as confessions made by prisoners was used to conduct the trials of the accused and those who had confessed.

The *inyangamugayo* were thus the engines of the *gacaca* process. In October 2001 more than 250,000 *inyangamugayo* were elected (Republic of Rwanda 2001c). These judges were members of the general population, without legal training or experience, and they received a short training on the law and procedures. Because the *gacaca* laws changed between the election and nationwide implementation, not all elected judges presided at the start of the *gacaca* process in January 2005. At that point, there were 12,103 *gacaca* courts in total nationwide, and 169,442 *inyangamugayo* presided over them.

Initially the *inyangamugayo* were, as tradition prescribes, mostly "old and wise men." The *gacaca* law of 2004 stipulates that an *inyangamugayo* shall, among other things, "diligently fulfill" the responsibilities, "remain loyal to the Republic of Rwanda," "work for the consolidation of national unity," and never use the power conferred "for personal ends" (Republic of Rwanda 2004a, art. 9). The "conditions for being a member of the bench of the *gacaca* court" included "not having participated in genocide, being free of the spirit of sectarianism, not having been in prison for more than six months, being of high morals and conduct as well as truthful, honest, and characterized by a spirit of open dialogue or 'speech sharing'" [*sic*] (Republic of Rwanda 2004a, art.14). In addition, politicians, civil servants, security personnel, and career magistrates could not be elected as judge in a *gacaca* court (Republic of Rwanda 2004a, art. 15).

After several months, though, a significant number of these "wise old men" had to be replaced because they were themselves accused of having participated in genocide. By November 2005 approximately 26,700 or 15 percent of the judges had to be replaced for that reason. At the end of the *gacaca* process, this figure had risen to 46,000 judges or 27.1 percent of the total number of *inyangamugayo* (National Service of the Gacaca Courts [SNJG 2012]). These positions were replaced mainly by women, younger people, and genocide survivors.

A modification of the *gacaca* law in 2007 further added the obligation "to be free from genocide ideology" (Republic of Rwanda 2004a, art. 15).

The *gacaca* bench was the most important but not the only organ of the local *gacaca* courts. Apart from the bench there were also the general assembly and the coordination committee. The general assembly of the cell-level *gacaca* courts was composed of all the inhabitants eighteen years old or older (with at least one hundred members present during meetings). The general assembly at the sector level consisted of all the *inyangamugayo* at the cell, sector, and sector-appeal levels. They were required to hold meetings at least once every three months. Every bench had a coordination committee made up of five members. This committee functioned as a management team of the *gacaca* process in their locality.

In time, the coordination committee almost became, literally, the bench of the *gacaca* court. Initially, the law envisioned that every *gacaca* bench would have nineteen *inyangamugayo* (Republic of Rwanda 2001b). In 2005 lawmakers adjusted this to a minimum of seven judges (Republic of Rwanda 2004a, art. 23). They later adjusted it again, to a minimum of five per bench (Republic of Rwanda 2004a, art. 5).

The *Gacaca* Process: Timing, Tempo, and Numbers

The *gacaca* process began with a pilot project in twelve sectors in June 2002. This was soon expanded to a pilot phase in 118 sectors where 751 courts were established. Until March 2005 these pilot *gacacas* dealt only with information collection. At the beginning of 2005, these courts started the trial phase, and meanwhile all other courts nationwide started information collection in mid-2006. From that moment until 2011 the *gacaca* process was operational nationwide. The official closure of the *gacaca* process was announced several times but always postponed. An official closure ceremony took place on 18 June 2012 (*New Times* 2012).

The tempo of prosecution varied significantly throughout that period. The process started slowly in 2006, and the courts dealt with approximately 3 percent of the cases that year.[17] The *gacaca* process did not gain momentum until 2007, when it dealt with more cases than in any other year. In theory, the trial phase would last until all cases had been dealt with. From early 2007 on, though, the government realized that it would take much longer than expected to finish the process, and it took some measures, including increased pressure on the judges, to speed up the trial proceedings. The end of the *gacaca* practice in each sector depended on the specific caseload as well as the efficiency and tempo of the courts.[18] In some places, the practice came to an end during 2007.

The 2007 law made it possible to install numerous courts at the sector level instead of the single court that existed before (Republic of Rwanda 2007b, art. 1). After March 2007, more than 2,000 courts were, therefore, added to the 12,103 already existing. Some sectors had up to twelve sector level courts (excluding appeal courts) functioning at the same time.[19] At the fifty-fifth *gacaca* session in July 2007, the president of the *gacaca* court in Ntabona, one of the field sites where I observed the *gacaca* proceedings, alluded to the pressure the judges were under: "Before we start, I ask anyone who takes the floor to be brief because we haven't come here to tell the story of the past and we must ensure that trials last no more than ten minutes."[20]

Initially there was one fixed day in the week when *gacaca* meetings were held. To speed up the trials, many localities with a great number of cases were obliged to hold two meetings a week. For example, at the Ntabona session mentioned earlier, its executive secretary (an appointed politico-administrative state official) announced that the sector would begin holding *gacaca* sessions two days a week, on Thursdays as well as Tuesdays. All of these measures resulted in judging more individuals a week, more individuals simultaneously, and more of them during each *gacaca* session. A *gacaca* court heard between one and more than ten cases a day. My own observations reveal that while on average 1.45 individuals stood accused during each session in 2006, that figure increased to 3.12 in 2007 and more than 5 in 2009 and 2010.

Estimates in 2004 based on the results during the pilot phase indicated that approximately 750,000 people would stand accused. Statistics provided by the SNJG indicated that by the end of the official information collection phase in mid-2006, 818,564 individuals would be prosecuted for genocide-related crimes nationwide (Republic of Rwanda 2006a). These numbers steadily rose to more than a million (Hirondelle News Agency 2007). During a conference on reforms in the justice sector in June 2008, the executive secretary of the *gacaca* courts announced that the *gacaca* courts were processing 1,127,706 people: 444,455 at the sector level and 612,151 at the cell level (Mukantaganzwa 2008). Although the SNJG was still referring to a 1.1 million "judgments" in 2009 (Hirondelle News Agency 2009), this figure rose to 1,500,000 in its 2011 communications (Hirondelle News Agency 2011a) and, finally, to 1,958,634 cases announced during the closing ceremony in 2012 (Republic of Rwanda 2012). According to the Rwandan government, a total of 1,003,227 persons stood trial in the modern *gacaca* court system (Republic of Rwanda 2012).[21]

Conclusion

On paper, the *gacaca* courts were a blend of retributive and restorative justice with "confessions and accusations, plea-bargains and trials, forgiveness and punishment, community service and incarceration" (Waldorf 2006, 52–53). The tempo with which the courts processed genocide suspects was very fast; the time devoted to the average individual case was very low. The court system did indeed achieve its objective of speeding up the backlog of genocide cases. After 2007, and under pressure, the *gacaca* trials broke all records in quantitative terms. They not only effectively dealt with the approximately 130,000 individuals incarcerated after the genocide but also handled the thousands more who were unexpectedly accused when the *gacaca* courts started operating on the hills in the countryside. The Rwandan way of doing justice after genocide was extremely efficient in terms of speed and cost. The difference with the International Criminal Tribunal for Rwanda (ICTR), based in Tanzania, is telling in that respect. The ICTR indicted ninety-three individuals and completed proceedings for eighty-five accused at a cost of more than US$1.5 billion. Rwandan authorities report that the entire *gacaca* operation cost about US$53.5 million.[22] There was mass justice for mass atrocity (Waldorf 2006), in quantitative terms.[23]

Penal Reform International (PRI)—an international NGO that observed the *gacaca* process with support from international donors—became aware of these extraordinary numbers through their monitoring activities. They asked in 2005, with nationwide implementation on its way, "Is it feasible to handle all the prosecutions for genocide at the same time and within a socially acceptable time frame and with a minimum respect for due process?" (PRI 2005, 52). All in all, the time frame was relatively short, but what remains to be explored, indeed, is the courts' performance in a qualitative sense.

By making changes in the *gacaca* legislation over the years, the Rwandan government showed its openness to adjusting the process. Several changes made the system more effective and efficient, and others incorporated more restorative components such as the reduction of sentence after a sincere confession and the prominent implementation of community service. Still, the modifications came about slowly and were relatively minor. What looks like fine-tuning from one angle seems from another to be disaster management.

Learning "to Be Kinyarwanda"

Various research principles, methods, and epistemologies inform this study of the Rwandan *gacaca* courts and their impact on society in addition to the discussions that are increasingly taking place on how to research and assess the impact of transitional justice (Baxter 2002; Van der Merwe et al. 2009). Scholars often use ethnographic techniques for individual case studies (e.g., Baines 2007) and community studies (e.g., Hamber and Kelly 2005). Nationwide opinion and attitude surveys (e.g., Gibson 2006)[1] or cross-national comparisons (e.g., Olsen et al. 2010) of a number of variables provide a quantified insight into the nature and impact of transitional justice processes.

In order to understand how the *gacaca* was actually practiced, not how it was supposed to operate, I chose an ethnographic and data-driven approach characterized by a "heightened awareness in data collection" (Flyvbjerg 2001, 158). In times of transition, data generation is subject to politicization and needs to deal with widespread distrust due to the legacy of violence or atrocity. Mass violence leaves deep scars on the social fabric. Distrust and suspicion are often pervasive, and the operation of a transitional justice process might aggravate those attitudes, as the Rwandan case shows (Begley 2009; King 2009; Fujii 2010; Ingelaere 2010a, Thomson 2010; Chakravarty 2012). Prudence needs to guide the research process at all levels: presence in the field, data collection, as well as interpretation.

Throughout my research it was paramount to establish and monitor social relationships and increase trust with research participants in an environment of suspicion. I mixed research methods and adopted two research principles—immersion and iteration—to facilitate the generation of broad, deep, context-specific knowledge about the transitional justice process.

Immersion

The notion of immersion occupies an important place in ethnographic and anthropological approaches to research (Emerson et al. 1995, 2; Olivier de Sardan 2008, 51). "Immersion in ethnographic research, then, involves both being with other people to see how they respond to events as they happen and experiencing for oneself these events and the circumstances that give rise to them" (Emerson et al. 1995, 2). Immersion is closely related to the notion of (participant) observation, but although the latter is a research technique, the former is, in my interpretation, a particular approach, a guiding principle structuring a research project. Immersion implies a continued and long-term engagement with the research environment in situ, and thus includes events the researcher experiences or observes when not doing formal research or intending to take notes. It develops a sort of tacit knowledge, where the "interpretation of a given situation becomes almost a reflex" (Olivier de Sardan 2008, 53) that results in a visible difference between the work of a "fieldworker who calls on lived experiences (through immersion) and an armchair researcher working on the basis of data collected by others" (54). This type of knowledge can come only from extended and repeated stays in the field.

The crucial aspect of immersion characterizes my research approach; however, I have never attempted to become, or considered myself to have become, a Rwandan among Rwandans. I do not know what it feels like and how it *is* to have your family exterminated or to be in a Rwandan prison for decades, nor do I know how it feels to personally appear in a *gacaca* court as a plaintiff, defendant, witness, or judge. In the field, I was aware of the fact that I had an international passport, a credit card, and a plane ticket at hand. But I attempted to bracket (not erase) these conditions and move closer to these practices and experiences. Indeed, I am confident that I can now emulate the logics of certain behavioral practices that I studied. As a consequence, I can pass "a test that some ethnographers aspire to, that "if you think you understand the X then you should be able to act like the X" (Olivier de Sardan 2008, 103); hence the choice of this chapter's title, "Learning 'to Be Kinyarwanda.'" In fact, "knowing Kinyarwanda" (*kumenya Kinyarwanda*) means two things (Nkusi 1987, 85).[2] On the one hand, this expression refers to the ability to speak Kinyarwanda, the language of Rwanda, by being familiar with syntax, words, and so forth. On the other hand, "knowing Kinyarwanda" also connotes familiarity with the local customs, the established practices among Rwandans, and also how language is used, when and how to speak, when to remain silent, and the like.

A dimension of "knowing Kinyarwanda" (*kumenya Kinyarwanda*) thus relates to the form of the verbal and nonverbal interactions between people:

the way things go on between Rwandans. This type of knowledge, contextual understanding through immersion, allowed me to navigate the field, which was critical because of the nature of the overall research environment.

During one of my stays in Ntabona, a hill located in the north of the former province of Gitarama, I learned that the former mayor of the area had returned from the Democratic Republic of Congo (DRC) since my last stay on the hill. The man had been mayor for decades before the 1994 genocide. Given that I had been trying to understand the history of the locality in order to better contextualize the ongoing *gacaca* practice there, it was important that I meet him. I realized that he would without doubt be suspicious of any unannounced visit to his place by people unknown to him but also eager to discuss sensitive issues such as the unfolding of the local genocide and the ongoing *gacaca* activities. Maybe he would accept a visit, but that would not necessarily mean he would say anything genuine. The man had lived as a refugee in the DRC for over a decade, which probably meant he had been unable or afraid to return to Rwanda. I had learned that he was not accused in the local *gacaca* trials. His reluctance to return to Rwanda could have been based on fear of the reigning Rwandan Patriotic Front (RPF) and not the fear of being judged for crimes committed. The fact that he returned did not necessarily mean that such a fear had subsided.

It had come to my attention that feelings and impressions of being under constant surveillance were widespread in the population, especially among people who had occupied important positions in the former Hutu regimes, even at the local level.[3] To give one example, in June 2006 I went to visit the former prefect (governor) of a province where I was doing research in order to learn more about the history of the region. The man had occupied his position during the reign of the first Hutu president, Kayibanda. After we talked for some time inside his house, he said goodbye and suggested we could meet again in Europe, where he was planning to visit relatives soon. He stated: "It's better to talk outside Rwanda on these issues because here even the walls have ears."

By observing Rwandans, I had learned that strangers would look for "linkages" to assess and qualify their social relationships. Therefore, I looked for a go-between, someone who trusted me and who had a good relationship with the former mayor. Through key informants in the area, I had built relationships during several visits over the years, and I learned whom the man frequently interacted with and whom he apparently had warm relationships with. I was given a few names. One turned out to be one of the priests of the parish where I was lodging during my stay on the hill. I had developed a good rapport with these priests, and one night, during a dinner with them, I mentioned I had learned that this former mayor had returned. I framed my interest in the man in the general and somewhat neutral discourse I used for my research and explained that I would find it interesting to come into contact with the former mayor. The priest who frequently visited the mayor suggested that he might mention my presence in the parish during an upcoming visit. He would say that I had stayed many times in the parish and had become familiar with the local inhabitants. I had no doubt he would to give a favorable impression of my character and doings. The very next week I was told to pay the former mayor a visit. I did so together with a translator, and the interaction provided me with some insightful information. Does this mean that my interlocutor interacted with me without hesitation? I cannot be absolutely sure. But I have no doubt our conversation would have been different if I had not been first introduced by a trusted friend.

This example demonstrates that the mere experience of navigating the field supplies knowledge about the nature of social relations and about transitional justice processes. By observing Rwandans construct linkages among trusted nodal points in the web of social relations and by reflecting on my attempts to emulate these practices, I became more clearly aware of the nature of the social landscape and of how relationships were being mended or not in the aftermath of mass violence. Other researchers in Rwanda have described such a process as generating metadata that constitute valuable knowledge complementary to the actual data gathering (King 2009; Fujii 2010). However, a researcher taking immersion as a structuring principle will consider the insights it generates as data in and of themselves, as essential rather than accidental to the research process. Moreover, such understanding contributes to putting into action the research strategy conceived beforehand.

When I spoke with sources I was always accompanied by Rwandan field assistants and translators. I chose my collaborators primarily on their ability to interact with the rural population and their skill in navigating the field. I valued these skills as well as the capacity to reside in rural communities over any formal education. They helped me interpret—in the broadest sense of the word—what local inhabitants said and did. This brings me to the other meaning of "knowing Kinyarwanda" (*kumenya Kinyarwanda*): the use of language. I cannot say that I speak Kinyarwanda fluently in the linguistic or grammatical sense, although I am familiar with common expressions and words and can identify the topic of a conversation, especially when it relates to my research. It was not useful at the time to invest in an in-depth study of the language.[4] More importantly, I realized that Kinyarwanda is such a complicated language, both grammatically and as used, that I would need translators to guarantee that I fully understood my interlocutors. Having translators allowed me to focus more on how things go on among Rwandans.

Did the fact that I had only a basic knowledge of the local language constitute an obstacle? Not necessarily. Svensker Finnström (2003, 33–34) regrets having limited knowledge of the local language of the northern Ugandan people he studied, but he nevertheless produced an insightful and widely praised ethnography evoking local understandings and practices of dealing with past violence. A research approach characterized by immersion, and with the objective of unpacking local understandings, does, however, require sufficient attention to language, especially in the Rwandan context. Rwandans tend to speak in proverbs and images. Moreover, phrases in Kinyarwanda can have multiple meanings. Therefore, I attached particular importance to the translation process. For example, often, and always in group discussions, I used two Rwandan translators during interviews. One would translate so I could understand responses in situ, and the other would take notes in Kinyarwanda or French, depending on the type of interview. In order to avoid suspicion and cautious responses, I did not use tape recorders. A third collaborator, based in the capital, Kigali, would later type up, translate, and, if needed, annotate the interviews. I would then jointly discuss phrases with multiple and varied meanings with all my collaborators.

Iteration

I also took an iterative approach to my study of the Rwandan *gacaca* courts. Here, I refer to the notion of iteration in three ways. First, it refers to my successive movement to and from the physical setting of the field, namely Rwanda and the Rwandan hills. Second, it means rotating through multiple locations in the field. And third, iteration refers to a psychological movement: the intellectual reflection on the "field," that is, the topic under study and how it is being studied.[5] Both dynamics, physical and reflective, had the objective—through the very nature of the process of iteration—to progressively embed the research strategy (as well as the researcher) in the field of study.

First, regarding the physical dimension of iteration, my study of the *gacaca* courts is based on the approximately thirty-two months that I have spent in Rwanda since 2004. I made more than ten return visits to Rwanda and spent the bulk of that time in rural areas. When in Rwanda, often for extended periods of six months, I also moved frequently between these rural localities. Danielle de Lame (2005, 25), studying one hill in the period preceding the genocide, asserts that in-depth research will enable the researcher to understand the specifics of the site under investigation, but that a nearby site, another hill, will always remain strange and unapprehended.

By repeatedly moving through different research locations inside Rwanda, I hoped to understand both the breadth and the depth of processes (Barron et al. 2004). Any researcher is faced with two widely different methodological approaches. On the one hand, large *n-studies*, typically nationwide surveys, can establish breadth. By collecting data through survey questionnaires distributed to randomly selected respondents in randomly selected communities, one can infer statistically sound conclusions based on a significant part of the population that represents the population as a whole. Every social setting is marked by idiosyncrasies. The use of large-scale surveys avoids those idiosyncrasies by reducing the complexity of reality, and producing universally valid predictions and statements. But predictions are not explanations, and although predictions and statements are valid for a large population, the data are not rich in detail because they are mostly quantified and collected on the basis of concepts drawn up beforehand.

On the other hand, ethnographic research generates emic conceptions and information that is rich in detail and gives insights into *why* and *how* events happen and processes take place. Ethnographic approaches are able to identify underlying patterns and themes that do not easily surface in a questionnaire, and they are well suited to understanding issues of process. An ethnographic approach can also identify social categories that remain invisible and themes that "fall through" the tight grid of preconceived questions and already-coded possible answers that are common in survey research. Nonetheless, the question of representativeness remains. Why should findings gathered in one place, albeit rich in detail, be valid for a larger population or even for another, similar, nearby place?

These two approaches—broadly summarized as survey versus ethnographic research—do not have to be mutually exclusive. Integration of both viewpoints is possible and results in a better understanding of the topic in question. The idea is to use the best of both worlds and avoid the weaknesses of each.

Figure 1 gives an overview of the interlocking aspects of the depth and the breadth of my research approach. The graph highlights an ethnographic understanding of the four sites in which I lived for longer periods; I studied them in depth through long-standing presence in the field. In these four sites I used multiple research techniques and followed all the *gacaca* activities. I also collected a substantial amount of data, including two rounds of life-story interviewing from a representative sample of the population, and I sporadically observed *gacaca* sessions in a wider range of sites, eleven additional locations in different regions of Rwanda. In these sites the multiple research techniques ranged from surveys to formal/informal interviews, (focus) group discussions (FGD), and observations.

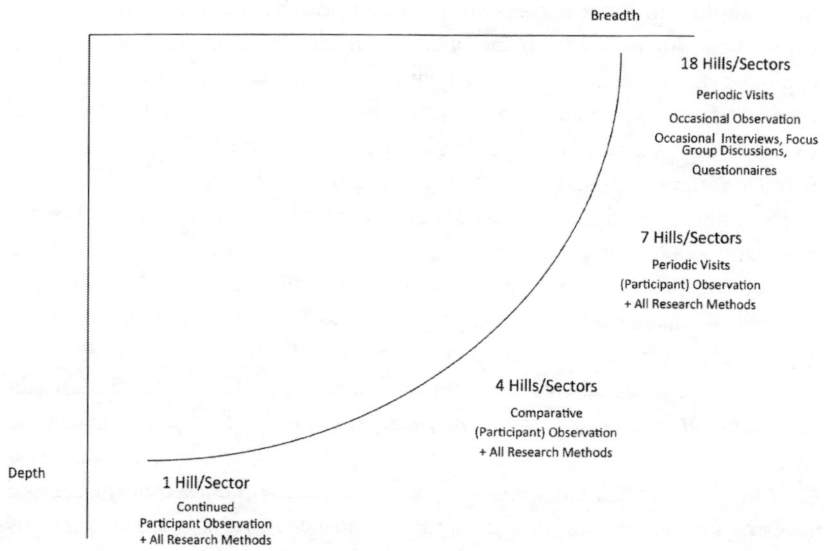

Figure 1. Study breadth and depth

I purposively chose provinces and communities as research locations to maximize variance (Rao and Woolcock 2003) on specific variables, including region, conflict dynamic, historical bases of power, and the like. This approach helped sharpen patterns, made recurring themes emerge, and established findings significant for a wide range of environments.

By repeatedly going back and forth between Rwanda and Belgium as well as between Kigali and the rural research locations, I attempted to deepen my understanding of the changing dynamics and to increase trust between me and the inhabitants of these locations. I returned many times to the same people to conduct interviews, have conversations, or simply spend some time. Numerous return visits to the same location showed them that there was no harm in sharing thoughts and time with me. However, I never considered this process established or taken for granted: I was always prudent, careful not to disturb my relationship with these localities and its inhabitants.

Whenever possible, I resided in the area or very near to the hill, most often in parishes (settlements where priests and nuns live), and took part in local life as much as possible. Most importantly, I continuously walked around, interacting and engaging in small talk; I went to the market, frequented local bars (*cabarets*), played soccer and volleyball with young people in the local playgrounds, and so forth. I brought volleyballs or soccer balls with me several times in an effort to give something to the community, since I was always clear

Learning "to Be Kinyarwanda"

that I would not give any reward, financial or otherwise, to individuals. Giving to individuals could potentially create envy in the population and pollute the voluntary character of the interactions. In order to give back to the community as a whole, I started a small library on one of the hills where I lived for several months. I collected French and English books at home and shipped them to Rwanda during my next return visit; I also collaborated with local schoolteachers to initiate a library service.

Research Sites

Map 1 provides an overview of the research sites. The dots indicate locations where I spent a significant amount of time. I spent more time in the sites with bigger dots and systematically recorded life histories in these sites. Areas marked with a star are locations where I systematically observed *gacaca* proceedings at the sector level and recorded all *gacaca* activities during the trial phase. In the other locations, I observed *gacaca* activities at regular intervals but not systematically.

I defined a research location to be a sector as they existed during the period of the genocide and until the administrative reform in January 2006. I focused on sectors because the *gacaca* tribunals were operating at this level. Moreover, each pre-administrative-reform sector corresponds with the natural horizon, the common action radius of an inhabitant of the Rwandan hills. People interact with other inhabitants, institutions, and authorities at the sector level on a daily basis. Larger administrative units, such as districts, lie beyond the daily horizon.

I started my research on a hill in central Rwanda, in the north of the former province of Gitarama. In 2004, while researching how genocide unfolded at the local level, I lived for approximately three months on that hill and acquired information on the local genocide and the prevailing community dynamics. This meant that I already had access and had established rapport with many of the sector's inhabitants. Having lived in the community before and having gathered information on genocide dynamics would both prove fruitful as I researched *gacaca* practice in the years to follow.

I discuss the research sites in detail in later chapters. Here I provide some basic information on the four sites where I systematically observed the *gacaca* process and the three additional sites where I did not observe *gacaca* but spent lengthy periods of time, conducted two rounds of life-story interviews, and gathered much additional data.

Jali is situated in the north of Rwanda.[6] The sector is located in the heartland of the former regime. Several dignitaries and military personnel in the former regime hailed from this region. During both the years of civil war that started in October 1990 and the genocide between April and July 1994, many Tutsi inhabitants were killed. The sector was also severely affected by the civil war—generally referred to as an insurgency—that ravaged Rwanda, especially northern Rwanda, between 1996 and 2000.

Ntabona and Runyoni are situated in the former province of Gitarama in central Rwanda. Runyoni is located on the main road between Kigali and Gitarama. Although Runyoni used to be a rural community, in the last couple of years it has slowly started becoming semi-urban with the expansion of the city of Kigali. Situated approximately ten kilometers from the center of Kigali, Runyoni was influenced during the period of the genocide by developments in Kigali.

Ntabona, on the other hand, is distinctively rural. It takes approximately an hour and a half by car to get from Kigali to Ntabona. Sector Ntabona is a large hill in the north of the province of Gitarama surrounded by the three rivers that demarcate the sector. The Nyabarongo River is the natural frontier between the former province of Gitarama and the former province of Kigali-Ngali. During

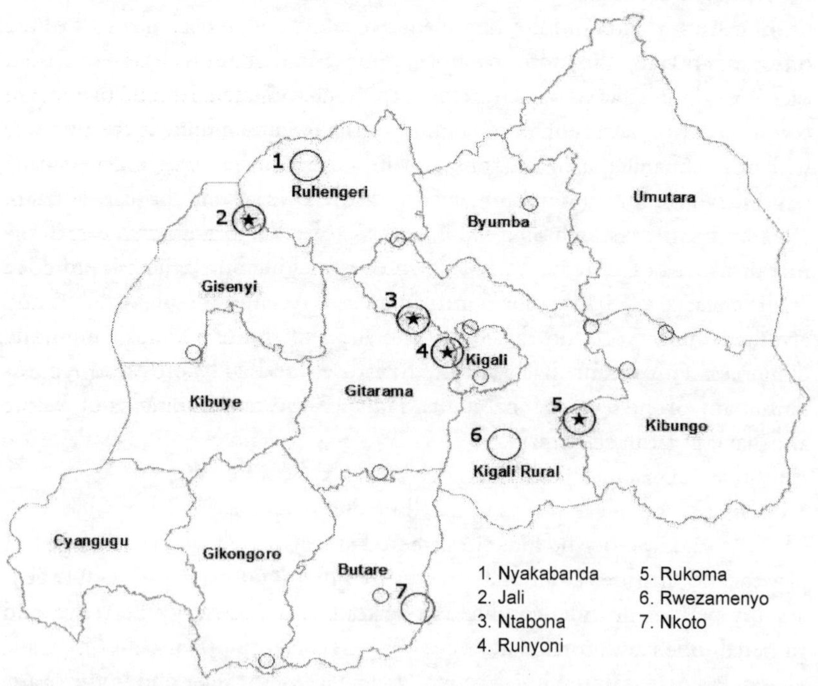

Map 1. Overview of research locations

the three months of genocide in 1994, periods of killing and looting alternated with days of resistance there.

Rukoma is situated in the marshes and along the lakes to the southeast of the Bugesera region (an agro-climatic zone characterized by periodic droughts and harsh living conditions and since 2006 one of seven districts in the Eastern Province of Rwanda). Before the construction of the tar road through Bugesera, it took approximately five hours to go by car from Kigali to Rukoma. In the 1960s the state constructed a so-called *paysannat* in Rukoma to regroup peasants, and it relocated Tutsi from Gikongoro and Butare to this inhospitable environment. During the period of the genocide, thousands of Tutsi died in Rukoma.

I spent significant time in three additional sectors: Nyakabanda, Rwezamenyo, and Nkoto. As well as observing *gacaca* practice at regular intervals in these locations, I collected life stories twice with a stratified random selection of inhabitants, and I organized various interviews and group discussions on different occasions. Nyakabanda is situated north of the former provincial town of Ruhengeri on the slopes of the volcanoes. The sector borders the national park with mountain gorillas and is only a few kilometers away from the borders with the DRC and Uganda. In the early 1990s the RPF twice crossed the sector during attacks on the city of Ruhengeri. The RPF occupied part of the sector in that period, and part was a demilitarized zone. Rwezamenyo is an extremely vast sector located in the center of the Bugesera region. The region is inhospitable due to the climate and soil conditions although the area was home to thousands of Tutsi during the period of the genocide. Currently the sector contains a very high number of so-called old-caseload returnees, Tutsi who returned to Rwanda after the genocide. Nkoto is located southeast of the former provincial town of Butare. It takes approximately two hours to drive from Butare to reach the sector, which borders Burundi. Inhabitants frequently cross into Burundi, and Burundians often come to the Rwandan side. The events in Burundi in the 1990s influenced the dynamics in Nkoto through cross-border contacts. In the region where Nkoto is located, thousands of people fled the start of the *gacaca* activities in 2005–6.

The Mixed-Methods Approach

The adopted research process was necessarily reflective and adaptive, and some phases were open-ended and exploratory. During these phases, I operated in an "unstructured" research mode. Other phases were more focused and characterized by the use of more structured research techniques.

Generally speaking, I mixed quantitative with qualitative and structured with unstructured research strategies to collect data. Social scientists have long debated the epistemological difference and (in)compatibility of quantitative and qualitative approaches. The vision of allegedly mutually exclusive approaches originates in the fact that researchers prefer to use the methodological approach best matched to their skills. Social and cultural anthropology has a particular place in this debate. While the social and behavioral sciences in general aim at reducing the complexity of reality, anthropological, and ethnographic approaches generally aim at depicting the complexity of social and cultural reality. Nevertheless, researchers of all kinds are increasingly expected to adopt mixed-method approaches in order to answer complex research questions (Teddlie and Tashakorri 2003).

I alternated periods of focused qualitative/unstructured research (mainly informal/formal interviews and observations in the field) with periods featuring more structured/quantitative techniques such as survey questionnaires. Finally, I also quantified (coded) qualitative data to bring more structure to apparently unstructured data and allow more systematic analysis. The treatment of the transcripts of *gacaca* observations is a case in point.

After the 2005 introduction of the *gacaca* court system nationwide, my research assistants and I observed a total of 1,917 trials dealing with allegations against 2,573 individuals. When I was residing in Rwanda, I observed trials with the assistance of a translator so that I would be able to follow the proceedings. Another field assistant would record the proceedings verbatim in Kinyarwanda. A third assistant later translated and electronically captured the transcripts. As with interviews, that assistant would also highlight specific phrases in Kinyarwanda that were subject to multiple interpretations. Several collaborators later identified the intended meaning in the context of the trial. Again, my previous navigation of the field and awareness of the need to proceed carefully in the translation process led to this procedure.

When I was not present in Rwanda, a Rwandan field assistant went to the research locations on the day the *gacaca* trials were taking place. These assistants resided in Kigali but traveled to the areas under observation when *gacaca* activities were scheduled. They wrote down every word spoken during the trials in Kinyarwanda. In addition, they took note of important nonverbal interactions during the trials. They also added a field report to every observation of a *gacaca* session that detailed relevant information on events, rumors, and social dynamics observed or established through informal interactions with the inhabitants in the community during that particular day.

In addition to the two Rwandan field assistants, I personally contacted one or more inhabitant(s) of the research sites to request extensive summaries of

Learning "to Be Kinyarwanda"

the ongoing *gacaca* activities. Following the immersion and iteration principles, I had already spent several months in each of the research locations before the systematic observations started. I was thus able to identify trusted and able assistants belonging to the community. Most were young educated people and thus not implicated in the genocide; none were members of the local administration. They wrote observation and research reports on the *gacaca* activities and provided information on the dynamics surrounding the *gacaca* trials. In addition, these people were not personally known to the research assistants traveling to the research sites from Kigali. On the one hand, this procedure established a control mechanism to verify the observation activities of the research assistants. On the other hand, it was a security measure to guarantee the quality of the observations when I was not present on site. Also, an "insider" and an "outsider" to the community could provide complementary information in the research reports, at least with respect to the social dynamics surrounding the *gacaca* activities.

When, in mid-2007, the state introduced a number of *gacaca* courts per sector and the appeal courts began working, it became impossible to record all the simultaneous *gacaca* activities verbatim with the same number of researchers. I consequently adapted the monitoring plan. Since the oversight principles of the previous months had established that all the research assistants were trustworthy, I introduced the inside and outside observers to each other. From that moment, they jointly organized the monitoring activities. Each research assistant focused on one of the *gacaca* courts during each *gacaca* session. They rotated courts in later sessions in order not to follow activities of the same courts all the time.

When more courts were operating than the assistants could monitor, we inventoried all the verdicts in the trials that had not been recorded verbatim. By doing so, we managed to have data on all the *gacaca* activities taking place at the sector level in these research locations. For some trials, however, we recorded only basic information: the act of accusation, the persons involved in the trial, and the verdict. We choose trials to monitor in their entirety not according to a principle but at random.

In total, my collaborators and I recorded 418 complete trials verbatim as outside observers who traveled to the research locations (see tables 9–10 in appendix II). In addition, the research assistants who lived in the communities monitored and provided extensive summaries of 635 additional trials from mid-2007 on. I instructed these assistants to record trial activities in as much detail and as exhaustively as possible, but due to the specific nature of their observing activities and their skills, they did not record some of the interventions in a trial. Therefore I do not consider them complete observations (they are, however, almost complete). In addition, we compiled basic information as well as the verdict for 674 trials we did not observe.[7]

A trial could take place in first instance, in appeal, or in revision, as I will explain later. In all of the research locations as in all other sectors in Rwanda, *gacaca* proceedings were also taking place at the cell level. Since there are many cells in each sector and since the *gacaca* activities at these levels were generally also organized simultaneously on the same day of the week as the sector-level trials, it was impossible to monitor all of these cell-level activities as well. We monitored them only occasionally. Here too, no specific principle led us to select the trial activities to be recorded at the cell level: it happened at random.

Throughout the four locations, we observed a total of 103 property-related trials at cell level as well as forty-five property-related trials at sector level. These sector-level trials were a sort of appeals process for the *gacaca* activities that took place at the cell level. We observed an additional forty-two *gacaca* trials in other locations. These observations took place occasionally and were organized for comparative reasons by situating the systematic observations in the four research sites in the context of ongoing *gacaca* activities in other areas: 1,338 of the 2,573 individuals we observed stood accused at the sector level, and 1,235 of them were involved in cell-level proceedings dealing with property offenses.[8]

The assistants transcribed the *gacaca* proceedings verbatim or summarized them in Kinyarwanda. We did not use any recording devices because the National Service of the Gacaca Courts (SNJG) did not authorize us to do so in the permission they granted. In addition, I preferred not to use such devices since they can create suspicion in the population. The Kinyarwanda version of the observations was subsequently translated into French and electronically captured.[9] The observations in the four research sites resulted in a total of 2,898 electronic pages (based on an estimated 5,800 pages originally written in Kinyarwanda in the field). That is a total of 1,097,172 words.

Time was needed to digest and analyze this much information. With the observations ongoing, I read all the reports the assistants gave or sent me on a monthly basis. With the assistance of a Rwandan collaborator not involved in the monitoring activities, I also occasionally compared the Kinyarwanda version of the recordings with the translation in order to guarantee the quality of both the observation and the translation. This continuous reading of incoming reports as well as my own regular observations in the field made me familiar with the overall logic and the main features of the *gacaca* activities in practice.

Two Rwandan field assistants started coding the observed trials in 2008 under my supervision, and this process lasted until mid-2011. The objective of coding was to bring more structure to relatively unstructured data and thus allow me to systematically analyze the *gacaca* activities. Based on my familiarity with the *gacaca* process, I constructed a set of 171 variables.[10] We coded only the systematically monitored trials observed at the sector level in the four research locations. We did not consider trials observed in other locations or cell-level trials (even in the four locations systematically monitored) in this process of quantification/structuration. We did, however, quantify some aspects of the cell-level proceedings on property cases observed in the four research locations (I present and discuss these results separately). Most of the quantified results are thus based on sector level *gacaca* activities.

An observation is not a questionnaire. A questionnaire is usually completed exhaustively, but an observer cannot manipulate a situation to acquire all the information desired. *Gacaca* trials are not duplications of a preset form. Although they follow a similar pattern, not all trials contain the same information, and the trials did not contain information on all of the variables. Therefore, some information on some variables was simply not visible in the *gacaca* transcript and therefore could not be coded. In addition, some *gacaca* trials were transcribed in their entirety, some were extensively summarized, and for others only basic info was recorded on accusations, people involved, and the verdict. Analyses of the *gacaca* proceedings consequently may have a changing number of total observations (N) depending on the variable.

We could only perform some operations—such as an analysis of the nature of interventions during trials (chap. 3)—with respect to trials that had been entirely transcribed. We based our analysis of certain variables on a total of 418 observations, the total number of trials recorded verbatim with a guarantee that no information was missing. It goes without saying that we could only analyze all interventions during a given trial if we had recorded all interventions during the trial.

We analyzed other aspects of 1,053 trials, a figure that combines trials recorded verbatim and trials recorded as extensive summaries. For example, we could analyze reports from these 1,053 trials and determine whether information-gathering supplementary to the actual trial proceedings had taken place. I had instructed the field observers to record information on a certain number of variables from the start of their observation activities. Therefore, this information was available and could be coded for each case.

The number of observations also fluctuates for a number of other variables. For some variables—such as the number of confessions a defendant made—all we had was whatever information on confessions had been divulged during the trial proceedings. If no information was revealed, we could not of course consider the trial in question in our analysis. The total N is thus lower.

Also, although I had instructed the field assistants to write down the total number of people attending each trial, sometimes, due to human error, they did not do so. They recorded attendance for 927 trials, so we based our analysis on these 927 trials.

I define a "*gacaca* session" as the gathering of a *gacaca* court, even though that is not a legal or regulatory definition. A session can deal with multiple accused and normally does so sequentially, at times in a joint subsession. I considered each individual case as "a trial," and thus a trial is related to an individual. If the cases of two individuals were treated jointly in one subsession, I considered these cases as two trials. The total number of observations I used in the systematic analysis—1,727—thus correspond with the trials of 1,727 individuals. The situation was slightly different with respect to cell level trials, as I explain later.

Life-Story Interviews and Other Data

Over the years, in my voyage to the heart of the *gacaca* practice, I conducted 1,034 interviews with 1,235 individuals, mostly using a life-history format. For each interview, I have both a written and an electronic version, and I have noted time, date, place, and respondent identity.[11]

Life stories are very diverse, and so are the many approaches to life-history research. In its most basic sense, a life story is "the story a person chooses to tell about the life he or she has lived, told as completely and honestly as possible" (Atkinson 1998, 8). Life stories can be long or short and research using life stories can make use of one, a few or many stories. Reducing the length of the stories makes an increase in the number of individuals under scrutiny possible and thus establishes the breadth of the study. One possible life history research design entails doing systematic and structured life interviews in a number of localities and with numerous respondents selected through a sampling scheme. Those who collect oral histories rarely sample their respondents, while those who sample rarely collect oral histories (Varshney 2002, 20). But Varshney has shown in his study on ethnic conflict in India that combining both methods yield innovative findings. Following my research principles, I adopted such an approach.

Because I chose research locations to attain "maximum variance,"[12] the life histories I collected incorporated various indicative dynamics of historical events and state or societal practices. I selected respondents for life-story interviewing based on markers that—to a certain extent—underlie ethnic categories. Ethnicity is obviously an important variable to take into account with

Learning "to Be Kinyarwanda"

respect to a structured selection of respondents. Although Rwanda continues to be ethnically bipolar, with Hutu and Tutsi as the main ethnic categories,[13] local inhabitants have become extremely wary about identifying people through these ethnic markers; instead, they use "new" social categories with refashioned forms of markers to sort or identify individuals without necessarily raising too much suspicion.[14] Local inhabitants distinguish five social categories to identify themselves and others, especially in the context of the *gacaca* activities. I used these social markers in the selection and sampling procedure for the life-history surveys because it was important to understand differences in experience and interpretation of *practicing gacaca*.

Tutsi inhabitants are divided into "genocide survivors" and "old-caseload returnees." In the latter case they, their parents, or even their grandparents fled Rwanda after the so-called Hutu Revolution of 1959 and returned to Rwanda after the end of the genocide and the RPF takeover in 1994. Hutu inhabitants are described as "released prisoners," those "accused in *gacaca*," and those who are "not accused and have never been imprisoned."[15] I compiled lists with the names of all the household heads on the selected hills and asked several groups of key informants to identify every household according to one of these five groups. Subsequently, I selected households within each group through a stratified random sampling format, and I interviewed their heads or another adult member (about seventy respondents in each locality).[16] Those I selected were all more than thirty years old, because I found it wise to have respondents who could remember the period since 1990. I mostly chose interviewees who had lived through the genocide and the period of war in the nineties as adults (eighteen years or older); otherwise their experiences could have been less relevant to understanding the *gacaca* practice.[17] Table 1 gives an overview of the number of respondents and the social categories to which they belong.

Table 1. Life-story interviews

	2007 Wave			2011 Wave			
	Male	*Female*	*Total*	*Male*	*Female*	*Total*	*Total*
Hutu—not accused/no prison	86	65	151	74	58	132	283
Hutu—accused in *gacaca*	81	11	92	52	11	63	155
Hutu—released prisoner	72	1	73	54	0	54	127
Total Hutu	*239*	*77*	*316*	*180*	*69*	*249*	*565*
Tutsi—survivor	39	61	100	34	54	88	188
Tutsi—old-caseload returnee	28	25	53	20	20	40	93
Total Tutsi	*67*	*86*	*153*	*54*	*74*	*128*	*281*
All respondents	306	163	469	234	143	377	846

A pilot study with life-story interviewing took place between January and July 2006, a period during which I was also using other research techniques. I conducted a first wave of life-story interviews between January and April 2007 in the above-mentioned localities.[18] I organized a second wave between January and June 2011.[19] I set out to interview the same people in order to complete their life stories, but the number of second-wave respondents was lower due to attrition (death, migration, imprisonment, etc.).[20] This second wave also made a comparison between two "objective" points in time possible.[21]

Apart from this systematic gathering of life-story data, I had many conversations with inhabitants of the locations under study while living in these areas. I did not formally record these conversations, but at times I made jottings afterward when these verbal interactions had been important in some respect. The example of the former mayor discussed previously is a case in point. Many times, however, I organized formal interviews with individuals. By "formal interview" I mean that I documented the conversation, identified name, time, and date, and have a transcript. The motivations to conduct an individual interview as well as the choice of the topic varied depending on the research phase and the context at hand. For example, I conducted more individual interviews in the exploratory phase of the research in 2006. I might also have contacted a person who had taken part in a group discussion if I thought the person could help explore the research objectives or if I had observed a particular behavior (silence, outspokenness, fear, or the like) in that participant in, and potentially due to, the group setting. In such cases, I would contact the person individually for a follow-up interview on a specific topic; these interviews were mostly informal and aimed at clarifying certain issues. Leaving aside these numerous informal conversations, I have a record of seventy-seven formal interviews conducted throughout the research period in various locations.

I did not consult the *gacaca* records of *inyangamugayo* because I had no permission to do so and, more importantly, because it could create the perception of interference in the unfolding of the *gacaca* process. I wanted to avoid such a perception at all costs because it could create animosity and complicate research activities. With one exception: I consulted the *inyangamugayo* at the local level in 2006 regarding basic numeric data on the genocide and *gacaca* process that they had gathered during the information collection phase.[22] However, I made sure not to consult the archives myself but acted only through intermediaries, namely multiple *gacaca* judges presiding over cell-level courts in the sector. My continued desire to curb suspicion and maintain access to the field informed my reluctance to consult the records myself (or through a

Rwandan collaborator), and my subsequent decision to do so with a minimum of two members of the bench present.

In focus-group discussions (FGDs), I took steps to address their limitations. The group setting—the identity of the participants or the nature of their behavior—can lead to dominance in verbal interaction or guide the direction of the discussion. But a group setting does not necessarily have to be problematic. For example, the presence of many knowledgeable people can guarantee the veracity of solid, factual information, such as the nature and incidence of conflicts in a community. And the group setting is at times also a means to gain insight into the opinions of certain categories of the population. It is important to manage the group discussions well in terms of the selection of respondents, the location of the encounter, and the interaction between the participants. As mentioned previously, the nature of the collective discussion and the behavior of participants in group settings sometimes revealed important nonverbal information.

I selected respondents for the group discussions based on the principle of "snowball sampling," a nonprobability sampling scheme through which one begins by (purposively) sampling one person and then, through this person, obtains a list of persons who have the same characteristics as the initial person selected. For example, for the FGDs I initially selected one person who belonged to the specific group I wanted to interview—genocide survivors, for example—and this person would then provide a list of names of other genocide survivors to be invited for a group discussion.

I strove to have six participants in a discussion group, though at times there were four or up to ten. Given the nature of the group setting and its dynamics, I always made use of the assistance of two Rwandan collaborators: one translated the discussion in order for me to follow and facilitate it, while the other recorded the statements of the respondents.[23] The collaborators recorded Kinyarwanda expressions with specific meanings, and we later discussed them and compared them with the translated statements. All interviews were later typed out and annotated wherever the translation was questionable. As with *gacaca* observations, interviews, and life-history interviews, and for the same reasons, I did not use recording devices.

During the second wave of the life-story interviewing (2011), I added a very brief questionnaire to the interviewing format to gather truncated information that could easily be coded (quantified). I asked every respondent I interviewed during the life-story survey—all of whom I had already interviewed in 2007 since it was a panel survey—a limited number of questions on the appraisal of the *gacaca* courts.

My final research technique, that of observation, is closely associated with immersion. However, that term refers primarily to (participant) observation on the Rwandan social and political environment, while I focused the *gacaca* observations on one institution. Aside from continuous *gacaca* observation activities, I engaged in (participant) observation to better understand life in the particular community by simply being there. Nonverbal communication and observation provided additional information that enabled me to contextualize the data collected through other techniques, and it provided important information and insights in and of itself. The field reports quoted throughout the book illustrate the nature of these observations and how I recorded them. In addition to my own unstructured field notes, I used my Rwandan field assistants' reports to contextualize the trial minutes. They supplemented my own observations, which were particularly useful in understanding the localized practices shaping the *gacaca* process.

Conclusion

The nature of my data and research approach speak to what Aristotle calls *phronesis* in his philosophical works. *Phronesis* is similar to practical wisdom but also has the connotation of prudence.[24] In the aftermath of mass violence and in times of transitional justice, the "field" is riddled with a range of obstacles that demand a practical understanding of how to navigate the terrain. Indeed, Rwandans behave with prudence due to their experience of mass violence and atrocity in their midst. This is no different in other situations after large-scale violence and abuse. As I learned to behave prudently and with great discretion by observing Rwandans' behavior, I increased my understanding not only regarding *gacaca* courts but equally regarding the research process itself.

Such an approach requires intimate familiarity with context. My awareness that I was in an environment of suspicion, of knowledge-producing power relations, and of power-producing knowledge relations informed my *phronesis*-like stance and the research principles and techniques that flowed from it. In fact, the *phronesis*-like character of the research process places the research question at the center of the study and values both subjective and objective knowledge.[25] It considers reality (ontology) to be both singular and plural, and results in a "pragmatically governed interpretation of studied practices" (Flyvbjerg 2001, 140). It implies an antifoundational as well as an antirelativist position, with regard to both the position of the researcher in the research process as well as to the "nature" of the object under study. The situational position of the researcher is inevitable and should not be denied (as in a positivist attitude), nor should it be exalted (as in a subjectivist attitude) (Olivier de Sardan 2008, 97).

The insights that flow from a reflective and adaptive research process are necessary pieces of the puzzle of the ways people deal with past violence. And this is the reason that I followed a data-driven research process and adopted as its structuring device a basic characteristic of the field of study: prudence as practical wisdom.

Gacaca Mechanics

But why you always come hesitatingly when the court summons you?"

Lay judge, Ntabona, *gacaca* session on 24 July 2007

Understanding how the modern *gacaca* actually functioned requires answers to straightforward but fundamental questions: How did the trials work? Did people confess to crimes or did others accuse them? Who participated and was participation high? Were state agents involved? How many people stood trial and who were they? What allegations were lodged against defendants? How many people were acquitted? What were the verdicts and how did the judges reach them? Answering these questions—and others—provides new evidence on basic operational issues that remain little known or that provoke controversy.

We can begin to discern the different dimensions of *gacaca in practice* only by examining the verbatim recordings of concrete cases. One is the trial of Ndambaye, which took place at the sector level, where courts dealt with crimes against humans. The logic of these sector-level trials was different from those at the cell level, which dealt with pillaging and destruction of property. Examining specific cases allows me to introduce the mechanics of the court system at the sector level. Subsequently, I systematically examine all the observed trials and delineate the basic operational procedures of the entire *gacaca* process. This primarily descriptive analysis takes place through the lens of the three crucial features identified earlier: confession, the "popular" or participatory nature of the court system, and categorization of defendants according to crime.

A Trial at the Sector Level:
Crimes against Humans

Ndambaye, a thirty-two-year-old peasant, originates from northern Rwanda but was residing in Runyoni in central Rwanda during the genocide.[1] At the time of his trial he was no longer living in Runyoni but was summoned to stand trial there on 31 July 2007. The session started at 10:20 a.m. Seven *inyangamugayo*, the lay judges, presided over the trials that day; there were fifty people attending the trial, and the session began with one minute of silence in honor of the victims of the genocide.

The trial of Ndambaye took place in a *gacaca* session that dealt with five other accused. Their trials were handled sequentially, but the other defendants on trial that day were accused of being jointly involved in at least some of their crimes. Thus, although the court examined their cases separately, the defendants acted as witnesses in the hearings of the other defendants regarding the crimes they had allegedly committed together.[2]

A given defendant could have committed several crimes, and sector-level courts normally grouped together all crimes that one defendant had allegedly committed in that sector. Information on these crimes may have come from different cells in the sector, but it would usually be gathered together in the accused's file. However, defendants were sometimes put on trial several times for different crimes. This could occur if defendants had committed crimes in different sectors because each sector-level *gacaca* court had jurisdiction only over its own sector. Also, a defendant sometimes underwent a number of trials in the same sector because of either procedural error or inefficient organization by the *gacaca* committees, but these were exceptional cases. Furthermore, many of the defendants on trial at the sector level also had another trial at the cell level dealing with property cases. This, however, was not the case for Ndambaye.

The trials at the sector level were organized according to a prosecutorial logic. During the trial phase the judges summoned the parties in the case—the person who was accused or had confessed, as well as the accuser or victim (often the accuser was the victim, but not always). At the start of the session that included Ndambaye's trial, the president of the court reminded those present of the principles that guide the *gacaca* gatherings and then asked the six defendants as well as three representatives of the victims to approach the bench.

Often the accused were living in the community. Ndambaye came to his trial in Runyoni as a free defendant. He had been in prison previously, but because he had confessed he was released before the start of the *gacaca* process nationwide. Sometimes the *inyagamugayo* had ordered that those accused during the information-collection phase be put in preventive detention to stop them from fleeing. Together with those put in detention in the immediate aftermath of the genocide, they were transported to their home villages to participate in the trial proceedings.

At the beginning of the *gacaca* session, the judges read the compiled case files—a synthesis of the collected testimonies—aloud. In this case, the secretary of the court read the indictments of the persons standing trial. Ndambaye was accused of having killed nine individuals and of being implicated in different acts of pillaging. Each of the defendants' cases was then examined sequentially. Ndambaye was second in line. Generally, the judges began by asking the defendant to respond to the allegations or explain the nature of any confession he or she had made. When his trial began, the judges asked Ndambaye to take the floor and explain what he had confessed. He responded as follows:

DEFENDANT NDAMBAYE: I confess taking part in the attack to hunt down
 Charles. He was turned over to us by the people in Gihembe; I remember that one of them was Nshimiyimana. There were other people
 in uniform but I don't know their name. The soldiers started to hit
 him with the butt of their rifles; we walked on and when we arrived
 in front of Ntama's place, the soldiers forced his head down into the
 muddy water puddles on the road. Charles was wearing a black jacket
 and leather boots. When we passed Birikunzira's place, the soldiers
 snatched Karangwa's club and gave it to me. I hit Charles twice with
 it; he didn't die; we left him there and launched an attack on Nyoni's
 place. Nshimiyimana was leading us.

 At Nyoni's, we found him drinking banana beer from a gourd in
 front of his place along the road. The soldiers took RWF 40,000 from
 him and then they left. Before they vanished, they told Sendasonga
 Vincent, "The rest of the work is up to you," and Sendasonga stabbed
 him once with a lance.

 We started looting; my part in it was that I was among those involved in this attack. The next day, we went to Gakumba's and he told
 us that it was Uwiragiye who finished off Charles and took his shoes.
 We saw him wearing Charles's shoes. It was that morning that we saw
 Karekezi's body; he was very close to where Charles had fallen.

 Karekezi's body was naked from the waist down; about Karekezi,
 this is just information I am providing.

 About the death of Paulin, Uwitije, and Mugaragu: we brought
 them downhill; I don't know where they were found. They were taken
 there by Rukeribuga, Ndamukura Innocent, Munyeragwe, Antoine
 Rwabuzisoni, Gasamaza, Gasake, Nzabandora, and Nemeye. When

they got to where I was, they were bound; I don't know who tied them up. Then I left with those who were going to throw them into the river and as we marched them there, we told them that we were taking them where their colleagues had gone. When we got to the river, Munyeragwe and Rwabuzisoni pushed them in the river; they weren't hit at the river, but I could see that they'd been beaten on their way to join me. My part was that I accompanied those who were going to drown them.

Mbangurika's death: I was very close to Kanogo, and I saw people flushing him out of the bush. I think I recognized Gasamaza, Munyakazi Martin, Rukeribuga, and Munyeragwe among them. We chased Mbangurika. Uwiragiye appeared on his bicycle out of nowhere, and he told me, "If this man escapes, I'm going to hand your mother's breasts to you." So I hit Mbangurika once with my club and he stopped. We took him where the military were; the soldiers told us that they couldn't waste a bullet on this man and ordered us to take him to the river. I was there with Rukeribuga, Uwiragiye, . . . When we got to within five meters of the river, Mbangurika ran and threw himself into the river. My part was that I was with those who took him to the river. I don't know anything else about what happened during the war.

When defendants received the opportunity to respond to the allegations or explain the nature of their confessions, the judges typically asked questions and heard testimony from the defendants, any witnesses, and/or other persons who wished to intervene. Here is a verbatim transcript of the president's questions and Ndambaye's answers:

PRESIDENT: Egide's death?

DEFENDANT NDAMBAYE: I don't know anything.

PRESIDENT: Morukore's death?

DEFENDANT NDAMBAYE: I don't know anything and I haven't even heard anything about him.

PRESIDENT: Is there anything you wish to add to your confession?

DEFENDANT NDAMBAYE: I stole three spoons at Simbizi's place.

WITNESS (FEMALE SURVIVOR[3]): I'd like him to explain to us how Mbangurika could be strong enough to run when he got to the river.

DEFENDANT NDAMBAYE: Going to the river, he could still walk; he'd been beaten, but he could walk; he ran and threw himself into the river.

WITNESS (FEMALE SURVIVOR): Where did you find the club you hit Mbangurika with?

DEFENDANT NDAMBAYE: It was the one I was given when I killed Charles.

WITNESS (FEMALE NO-SURVIVOR/NO PRISON): When Karekezi was disinterred, he was found with clothes on; who dressed him, then?

DEFENDANT NDAMBAYE: Personally, I remember that Karekezi was not dressed; maybe those who buried him put clothes on him.

WITNESS (MALE NO-SURVIVOR/NO PRISON): I was called to attack Simbizi's and I refused; Ndambaye had a club coming from his place.

WITNESS (FEMALE SURVIVOR): Karekezi was in the same hole as Charles; we saw Gaserebuka wearing Karekezi's trousers. The man who spoke just now is Karangwa's father-in-law.

DEFENDANT SIMPARISHEMA: When I saw Karekezi's body in the morning, he wasn't dressed.

[Simparishema is one of the other defendants on trial today.[4]]

WITNESS (FEMALE SURVIVOR): Charles is said to have been the first to be killed in this area; was Ndambaye only taking a walk or was he going to conduct an attack?

DEFENDANT NDAMBAYE: Going downhill, I was going for a walk.

WITNESS (FEMALE SURVIVOR): What time was it when you arrived at Nyoni's?

DEFENDANT NDAMBAYE: We killed Charles at around 3:30 p.m.; we made it to Nyoni's at around 5 p.m.

WITNESS (FEMALE NO-SURVIVOR/NO PRISON): I saw Ndambaye coming downhill with a club prior to Charles's death.

WITNESS (FEMALE NO-SURVIVOR/NO PRISON): Ndambaye, Uziel, and Nshimiyimana were with a soldier. Ndambaye had a club; after looting at Simbizi's, they gave me their loot and threatened to kill me if I didn't take care of it. I spent all day watching over those items.

WITNESS (FEMALE SURVIVOR): Did they loot at Simbizi's after killing Charles?

WITNESS (FEMALE NO-SURVIVOR/NO PRISON): Charles was killed in the morning; they looted afterward.

[The *inyangamugayo* say (among themselves) there are conflicts of interest in this trial.]

WITNESS (FEMALE SURVIVOR): He said before that Mbangurika was covered with blood when he arrived.

DEFENDANT NDAMBAYE: Nobody actually hit him. He was beaten when they were still uphill. When they arrived at the river, he ran and jumped into the river.

Ndambaye's hearing ended here. The exchange between Ndambaye, the judges, and the public was thus very short. The court continued with the hearings of the other accused, and apart from the exchange detailed earlier, Ndambaye did not speak anymore during the *gacaca* session that day. But during the hearings of the other accused, witnesses or defendants referred briefly to Ndambaye and his alleged involvement in the crimes under examination.

At the end of the session, the president announced that the verdicts would be pronounced two days later at the next *gacaca* session. This deferral was somewhat exceptional; normally, the verdict would have been pronounced the same day. After two days, Ndambaye was found guilty. The judges did not explain how they came to their decision except to state that the court did not accept his confession. He was sentenced to fifteen years' imprisonment. Ndambaye announced that he would appeal. The judges told him he had fifteen days to do so. He was immediately taken into custody.

On 15 November 2007 his appeal trial took place in the same sector but was presided over by the appeal judges, thus a different *gacaca* court.[5] During that day the appeal court dealt with four cases, and Ndambaye's case was heard last. The session started at 11:30 a.m. with a minute's silence to honor the victims of the 1994 genocide and to remember its consequences. The president read articles 10, 29, and 71 of the *gacaca* law, and he asked the defendants and the victims whether they agreed with the composition of the *gacaca* bench that was going to preside over the trial. All agreed. Ndambaye's hearing came after the other cases and started at 2:15 p.m.

The appeal trial lasted for about forty-five minutes. The judges read out the indictment and the appeal that Ndambaye had put in writing. The main reason for his appeal was that he was convicted as if he had never confessed to his crimes. Ndambaye claimed that he truthfully confessed to all his crimes and therefore should have received a reduced sentence. During the proceedings Ndambaye admitted to having killed six people but no one else. The court asked released prisoners who had accused Ndambaye of additional killings to help clarify whether he was involved in other killings. To the amazement of the audience, they stated that they did not know the defendant and could not clarify the issue.

When the hearings in the *gacaca* session were over, the judges retreated to chambers to deliberate on the cases they had examined that day. The *inyangamugayo* returned at 5:10 p.m. (after two hours and ten minutes of deliberation) and pronounced their verdicts in public, giving Ndambaye's verdict last. The president announced that Ndambaye was sentenced to twelve years' imprisonment, of which six were to be served as community service, four years in prison, and two years suspended. The president did not explain the decision-making process apart from references to articles in the *gacaca* law. The nature of the verdict showed that the judges had accepted and taken into account Ndambaye's confession. The president of the court asked whether the defendant and victims were satisfied with the result. All parties announced that they were.

Cases of Looting and Destruction of Property:
Trials and Mediation

Most of the cases the modern *gacaca* dealt with took place at the cell level. Approximately 67 percent of the cases, that is, 1,320,554 out of the total of 1,958,634 cases reported by the government of Rwanda, focused on cases of looting and pillaging (Republic of Rwanda 2012).

While trials at the sector level were conducted based on the file prepared against a particular defendant, the logic of cell-level trials was different. At the cell level, the trial proceedings were prepared based on the cases of the victims, not the defendants. At this level the victim was not considered as an individual but as a family, a household. Thus the *inyangamugayo* would make an inventory of all acts of pillaging and destruction that had targeted a particular household. One representative of the household as well as all the persons accused of the crimes committed against that household would be summoned during the proceedings. In a cell in Rukoma, for example, twenty-two defendants were charged with the destruction and looting of the belongings of the Muberuka household.[6] Twenty of them were found guilty of eating meat from the cow belonging to the Muberuka household and were instructed to pay RWF 5,000 each. Two others were convicted of having stolen six cows and were, therefore, fined with the sum of RWF 600,000 in total. The court also decided that one of the latter two had to reimburse RWF 1,153,500 since he was found guilty of having pillaged quantities of beans, nuts, sorghum, maize, and manioc.

The proceedings dealing with the belongings of the Muberuka household followed the logic of a typical criminal trial. They were thus similar to the trials taking place at the sector level dealing with criminal offenses against individuals. At the cell level, however, two options were possible. One was that the parties in the dispute, victim and offender, could arrive at an amicable settlement with respect to the type and amount of restitution. As the *gacaca* law makes clear: "if the author of the offense and the victim have agreed on their own or before the public authority witnesses for an amicable settlement, he or she cannot be prosecuted" (Republic of Rwanda 2004a, art. 51). In such cases, the judges only supervised and ratified the agreement. The second option was a trial.

I observed continuous efforts by the *inyangamugayo* to convince the parties involved to reach an amicable settlement in a very large number of proceedings at the cell level. Often a *gacaca* session at the cell level would start with the judges providing an overview of the cases that needed to be dealt with that day. Subsequently, the judges would verify who had already reached an agreement. The judges would ask the disputing parties to reach an agreement with one of the local *umudugudu* or cell-level authorities as a witness.[7] The authorities stipulated the nature of the agreement in a document that all parties involved would then sign, and they would then send the document to the *gacaca* court as a record of the agreement.[8] Cases where the parties had already taken these steps would not be discussed during the *gacaca* hearings. The judges would only note the agreement and thus identify the modalities of restitution the parties had decided on. In the remaining cases—where an amicable settlement had not been reached—the judges would first encourage the people involved to reach a settlement between them. They generally provided this encouragement before the actual trial proceedings but sometimes also during the trial itself.

For example, on 30 October 2007 we observed the proceedings of the court dealing with cases of pillaging and destruction in Ntabona.[9] At the start of the proceedings—before the actual trial hearings—two of the accused announced they would seek an amicable settlement with the victim in question, an announcement the latter agreed to:

> PRESIDENT: The individuals summoned to appear today may approach, unless anyone wishes to ask a question first.
>
> INTERVENTION BY A YOUNG MAN (MALE NO-SURVIVOR/NO PRISON): I'd like to talk with victim Mukamana Joséphine so we can make arrangements to return her belongings to her. And I also apologize to her because I don't actually want a trial at this level, but I need to return the items looted by a relative of mine whose whereabouts are unknown to me at this time.
>
> VICTIM MUKAMANA: I don't want to ridicule you; we will find an agreement.
>
> MAYIRA (MALE RELEASED PRISONER): I cannot presently afford to compensate for the items looted at Mrs. Mukamana's but I apologize to her. I commit to finish paying what I owe her by 20 February 2008. I ask anyone who has work to do to ask me or tell me where I can find work if they know of any; as a wage laborer or any other work, I'm always available. You all know where I come from [prison] and I'm sick at the moment.
>
> VICTIM MUKAMANA: Maybe you could try to give me part of your field?
>
> MAYIRA (MALE RELEASED PRISONER): I don't own any land; "I'm stuck with a rock."
>
> VICTIM MUKAMANA: This deadline is too far away; you have to do it this November 2007.
>
> MAYIRA (MALE RELEASED PRISONER): I don't know where to find any [resources].
>
> INYANGAMUGAYO: You need to find a way to settle this out of court.

When there was no mutual understanding between the parties in a dispute, a trial took place that followed the same procedures as Ndambaye's sector-level trial. At the end of these proceedings the judges came to a decision on the nature of the restitution. Trial proceedings dealing with property crimes were quite common despite the effort of the judges to reach amicable settlements. In one case in Rukoma, the cell-level court made no attempt to reach an amicable settlement between the parties involved, and it ordered six men to make a payment of RWF 991,400. The court found five of the men guilty of having pillaged household utensils, destroying two houses, and pillaging twelve goats and a pig. One defendant was acquitted.[10]

Our own observations at the cell level reveal that a trial was organized in 71.8 percent of the observed *gacaca* gatherings dealing with cases of looting or destruction of property; 19.4 percent of these gatherings were amicable settlements, and 8.9 percent were characterized by both trial proceedings and amicable settlements. Subsequently, 893 (74.4 percent) defendants out of a total of 1,200 individuals were judged by the court, and 307 (25.6 percent) reached an amicable settlement.[11]

Many defendants stood trial jointly in almost all cases at the cell level. Some of the defendants in a case might already have reached an amicable settlement with the victim(s) while others did not. In such a situation, the two options were at work in one and the same case. For example, the court in one of the cells of Runyoni pronounced a verdict regarding the household belongings of Jérémy Habyambere that were pillaged and damaged during the genocide in 1994.[12] Habyambere was deceased, and his wife, Mukayuhi, represented the household during the proceedings. In total, seventeen of the defendants were found guilty. Sixteen of the defendants were instructed to pay RWF 70,000 each in order to compensate for pillaged and damaged goods with an estimated value of RWF 1,128,000. One defendant was found guilty of having cultivated one of the plots of land belonging to the Habyambere household and was instructed to pay RWF 8,000 as damages. Three defendants were acquitted, and five defendants reached an amicable settlement with the victim. The court heard the latter during the case in order to verify that they had reached an agreement, but they were not mentioned when the verdict of the court was pronounced.

From Confessions to Accusations

The confession procedure played a crucial role in the *gacaca* proceedings, as Ndambaye's case illustrates. The designers of the modern *gacaca* hoped that confession would facilitate the collection of evidence and thus would have made it the cornerstone of the process (PRI 2003; 2005, 21–38). The 1996 law that established special chambers to deal with genocide-related offenses in the classical court system also introduced the guilty-plea procedure (Republic of Rwanda 1996), and the *gacaca* court system retained this element. Through a presidential decree of 2003 one could, in principle, have one's sentence reduced by revealing information about crimes one had committed. A confession that was considered complete and sincere, accompanied by a request for pardon, was the prerequisite for provisional release from prison. This rule fueled confessions in the prison *gacacas*, which started as early as 1998 (Tertsakian 2008, 364–66, 399–422; PRI 2010, 19–21).

In the immediate aftermath of the genocide the entire judicial system had been destroyed, which is one of the reasons lawmakers instituted the confession-and-guilty-plea procedure. It would take decades to judge the high numbers of accused persons; at the same time, the prisons were filled with people accused of genocide crimes. The machinery that would normally investigate the genocide crimes and prepare the cases against the alleged perpetrators had not been functional for many years, and by the time it did become operational it could not deal with the enormity of the task. The confession approach, instituted to collect evidence and prepare case files, continued to characterize the design of the *gacaca* system.

A defendant must "give a detailed description of the confessed offense, how he or she carried it out and where, when he or she committed it, witnesses to the facts, persons victimized and where he or she threw their dead bodies and damage caused, reveal the co-authors, accomplices, and any other information useful to the exercise of the public action" (Republic of Rwanda 2004a, art. 54).

Although the confession procedure began in the prisons well before the actual implementation of the *gacaca* system, the principle was introduced nationwide with the inception of the information-collection phase in 2005. However, confessions made by prisoners did not refer to property-related offenses. Unlike information on violence against humans, information regarding cases of pillaging and destruction of property was gathered once the information collection phase began in 2005.[13] During this first phase of the official nationwide *gacaca* process, which took place at the cell level between January 2005 and July 2006, the system collected information in every cell through confession but mainly through accusation. I observed four tendencies in the data I gathered on confessions.

First, based on an analysis of actual confessions made by 298 individuals in the localities under observation, most of the confessions that did emerge were made either in prison or (late) in the trial phase: 34 percent of the confessions were made in prison and 52 percent during the trial phase; 43 percent of those during the trial phase were additional confessions, thus supplementary confessions to an earlier confession.

Second, in practice, the information-collection phase never ended. During the trial phase, information collection simply continued. The courts compiled new case files based on information that became available during the trial proceedings, including the many confessions that emerged at that time. Thousands of new cases were prepared after the end of the official information-collection stage. A *gacaca* hearing on 15 September 2009 illustrates this practice. On that day Firmin was on trial for the murder of a certain Patrick on 7 April 1994. Firmin denied the charges against him. He was sentenced to fifteen years in prison without any commutation or reduction of sentence because he had not made use of the confession procedure. During his trial, the judges called a witness named Murigande (a neighbor of Firmin) to the bench because they, the judges, had been informed that Murigande had buried Patrick's body. They asked Murigande to explain himself regarding the killing and the burial, but Murigande denied any knowledge of these facts. At the end of the trial he was taken into preventive detention, and the judges instructed the *gacaca* court that had jurisdiction in the cell where Murigande lived to prepare a charge sheet against him.[14]

In some areas, the courts repeated (at a much later stage) the information-collection process that the *gacaca* law stipulated. In Jali, for example, information collection—as an official phase of the *gacaca* sequence—restarted in June 2009. The decision to have a new round of information collection was based on complaints by a number of victims that some crucial information had not been divulged. Considering that new information collections took place in several locations during that period, it seems likely that the SNJG made the decision to organize a new process of information collection where necessary. A day of additional information collection took place in Runyoni at the sector level on 21 July 2009.[15] An SNJG coordinator directed the information collection assisted by two plainclothes police officers. In a sector in the former province of Kibuye, which was not systematically observed, I also noticed a renewed information-collection phase.[16]

Third, the information collection (even at a later stage) was characterized by the extensive involvement of state authorities executing and supervising a task normally allocated to the judges. A booklet distributed to the *inyangamugayo* stipulated that "*nyumbakumi* are specifically charged with the duty of filling those lists [compiling all kinds of information on the local genocide] with the help of the citizens" (Republic of Rwanda 2004b, 9). Although the *nyumbakumi* were and to a certain extent are indeed elected state officials, they occupy the lowest rank of the local administration.[17] Higher authorities generally use *nyumbakumi* to collect administrative data or to pass on (state) policy-related issues to the population in their area. In the Rwandan context, resorting to these state agents during the information-collection stage was natural to a certain extent. There is no reason to believe that using these *nyumbakumi* was part of a malicious attempt to control the *gacaca* proceedings, as some observers suggested indirectly (PRI 2006, 6–18). On the other hand, they are state agents and can be used by authorities higher up.

Fourth, the information-collection phase collected only the *à charge* (accusations) testimonies. The population could only validate information already collected or add more incriminating testimonies. Testimonies *à décharge* (in defense of the accused) were not recorded and were reserved for the trial phase.

During the trial phase (see table 2), only 38.8 percent of the defendants on trial actually confessed to the crimes they allegedly committed. This trend was confirmed at the national level when taking all cases into account. The final government report (Republic of Rwanda 2012) on the *gacaca* process suggests that 31 percent of those convicted at the sector level (Categories 1 and 2 combined) confessed to their crimes. The confession rate at the sector appeal level stands at 30 percent. Remarkably, this final report mentions that the confession rate for those convicted at the cell level (cases of pillaging and looting) stands at 7 percent and 2 percent for appeal cases. Almost all the people *gacaca* processed for cases of theft and destruction of property were thus accused rather than self-confessed. Given that there were more cell-level than sector-level cases, the overall confession rate for the entire *gacaca* process at first instance (that is, before appeal) was only 13 percent. I use the word "only" because this percentage is low considering the prominent role the confession-and-guilty-plea procedure was supposed to have in the *gacaca* system. The majority of the defendants thus adopted a different defense strategy and decided to plead not guilty.[18] The tendency for people on trial not to confess or plead guilty but rather be accused emerged in the pretrial, information-collection phase. According to estimates based on the pilot proceedings at the time, only 5 percent of the pending cases at the end of the information-collection phase resulted from confessions.[19] From the inception of the *gacaca* process nationwide in 2005, there was, therefore, a shift from confessions—the plea-bargaining procedure installed to encourage the exposure of the truth about the past—to accusatory practices. In other words, the *gacaca* system functioned primarily on accusations, not confessions.

Table 2. Defense strategy

	Ntabona N = 276	Runyoni N = 497	Rukoma N = 140	Jali N = 493	All N = 1,406
Guilty plea/confession	44.6%	53.5%	72.9%	11.0%	38.8%

	Ntabona N = 127	Runyoni N = 164	Rukoma N = 85	Jali N = 48	All N = 424
Multiple confessions	32.3%	72.6%	82.4%	58.3%	60.8%

	Ntabona N = 124	Runyoni N = 132	Rukoma N = 73	Jali N = 28	All N = 357
Change of confession	8.9%	11.4%	5.5%	7.1%	9.0%

	Ntabona N = 122	Runyoni N = 308	Rukoma N = 144	Jali N = 48	All N = 622
Acceptance of confession	91.0%	70.8%	61.1%	45.8%	70.6%

Note: "Multiple confessions" refers to those cases where the defendant confessed to different offenses at different times. "Change of confession" refers to those cases where the defendant later altered his or her confession regarding a particular offense. "Acceptance of confession" refers to those cases where the defendant's guilty plea was accepted by the court.

In 61 percent of the cases where this information was available, the defendant, in case he or she decided to confess, had made multiple confessions, thus at different moments in the *gacaca* process (table 2). This reveals that in more than half of the cases, defendants used the confession procedure to some extent. In addition, almost 10 percent of those who confessed subsequently retracted, revoked, or changed their initial confession. This suggests that if defendants used the confession procedure at all, they did so strategically. Thus, participants in *gacaca* adjusted the nature of their participation according to the circumstances and tried to find desirable outcomes.

The defense strategy also changed significantly over time. The majority of the defendants on trial in 2006 pleaded guilty. This dropped to almost 50 percent in 2007 and further declined over the years to end with approximately 10 percent in 2010. The decline in confessions was, however, mostly a consequence of the specific design of the *gacaca* proceedings. The booklet (Republic of Rwanda 2005a, 2) distributed to the *inyangamugayo* in 2005 gave specific instructions regarding the order to be followed in the cases that needed to be tried:

1. Those who confessed, pleaded guilty, and have been conditionally released
2. Those who confessed, pleaded guilty, and have been detained

3. Those who confessed, pleaded guilty, but have not been detained
4. Those who suffer from chronic diseases
5. Those who were aged fourteen years but not yet eighteen years at the time they committed crimes
6. The elderly, at least seventy years of age
7. Suspects who have been detained and have not confessed
8. Suspects who have not been detained and have not confessed.

The objective behind the instruction to adopt this order was probably to create an incentive for people to confess and thus divulge the information needed to conduct trials and identify other suspects involved in crimes. Encouraging people to confess remained a feature of the *gacaca* process. For example, in July 2007 the judges in Ntabona distributed new charge sheets to the attendants of a trial "for those who decided the time was there to confess."[20] In August the lay judges gave the prisoners who were transported to Ntabona (in order to participate in trials) sheets on which to file their confessions. They refused the sheets, saying they had nothing to confess.[21] Not only *gacaca* judges, often instructed by the SNJG, but also other institutions continuously organized campaigns to encourage people to confess to genocidal crimes. In Rukoma, for example, the National Unity and Reconciliation Commission (NURC) sponsored a regional trip for a group of university students who walked among the community to encourage people to confess.[22]

People pleading not guilty were considered less important, at least when it came to prioritizing the sequence of cases. Those pleading not guilty had to stay in prison, and the *gacaca* courts froze the assets of suspects awaiting trial, meaning that they were unable to sell livestock, household belongings, or plots of land (Republic of Rwanda 2004a, art. 39). As a consequence, some confessed to crimes they had not committed. The hearing of Bihoyiki, a seventy-one-year-old peasant from Rukoma, illustrates this phenomenon.[23] Bihoyiki was put in prison in 1995, as were most male inhabitants of Rukoma. Bihoyiki claimed that he had not committed any crime during the period covered by the *gacaca* law. When prisoners were encouraged to confess with the incentive of provisional release from prison, Bihoyiki saw no other option but to confess to crimes he had not committed. He confessed to killing two people with a wooden stick. During his trial the following discussion unfolded between him and the judges:

PRESIDENT: Is your file truthful?
DEFENDANT: No, I lied against myself to be released because it was the only way [*yari amatakirangoyi*].
PRESIDENT: Is there anything you wish to add to what's been read out to you?

DEFENDANT: No, except that I told lies against myself; it was like I was locked in a cave and I wanted out [*nari ndi mu rutare ngira ngo nsohoke*].

Inyangamugayo (TO THE DEFENDANT): You can start your plea.

DEFENDANT: I didn't do anything, except that I saw people die.

Inyangamugayo: You really didn't do anything?

DEFENDANT: Nothing. I have neighbors. You can ask them if I did anything.

Inyangamugayo: You saw people die?

DEFENDANT: Several people were killed, but I never confessed to killing anyone.

Inyangamugayo: In Sake, you said you'd killed a man called Nziherekere, who as it turned out was still alive. Why did you do this?

DEFENDANT: Instead of confessing about someone who's dead, I could do it about one who's still alive.

Inyangamugayo: Well, at least tell us about the neighbors you knew and who died, then.

DEFENDANT: There was only Rutiba who lived near my place.

Inyangamugayo: And who killed Rutiba?

DEFENDANT: It was Barayavuga and Munyankwiro.

[Barayavuga is in exile.]

. . .

PRESIDENT: Does anyone know anything about Biziriko?

[No reaction from the audience.]

In a trial that took approximately thirty minutes and included no witnesses or any accusations against Bihoyiki, and in which Bihoyiki himself explained why he had incriminated himself, the judges nevertheless decided to send him to prison for nineteen years. He had already spent twelve years in prison, so the judges calculated he had to return for another seven years. Because the judges had not accepted his confession, they did not suspend his previous sentence or commute it into community service. Bihoyiki then appealed this verdict, and the appeal court in the Rukoma sector acquitted him for the charges he had lodged against himself and set him free. However, this Rukoma court sent him to prison for another three months because it decided he had committed perjury by confessing to crimes he had never committed. It stated that "he had falsely accused himself."[24]

The substance of the *gacaca* encounters, as the cases discussed so far illustrate, was mostly adversarial, as in typical criminal procedures. The aim was to establish, at best, the forensic truth about who did what, where, and when. The analysis of the actual functioning of the confession procedure shows that *gacaca* trials were conducted on the basis of accusations as much as on confessions. The limited prevalence of confessions in a system designed to encourage them suggests the need to reconsider the whole nature of the system, not in design or as a model but in actual practice.[25]

We should reassess whether confessions made the system work—that is, whether they facilitated evidence gathering—and also whether they facilitated reconciliation. Observers often consider the confession, repentance, and pardon principle as the characteristic that makes the modern *gacaca* essentially restorative and reconciliatory. According to Phil Clark (2010, 325–31), many observers conclude that the modern *gacaca* courts did not (easily) facilitate (interpersonal) reconciliation. And Clark, in fact, comes to a similar conclusion based on his insight into the actual *gacaca* practice (309). What he subsequently does, however, is state that those observers come to such a conclusion because the system itself is wrongly depicted as being, to a great extent, retributive. He considers them as advocacy attempts for legalistic assessments. Clark suggests that these representations of *gacaca* are the result of a particular approach, namely "human rights as retribution" that dominates the transitional justice paradigm. In doing so, he follows McEvoy (2007), who has (rightly) called for letting go of legalism, both in the design and the assessment of transitional justice initiatives. Nonetheless, that these studies, including this one, use the word "retributive" or "adversarial" has more to do with an insight into the actual *gacaca* practice than the adoption of a particular legalistic or human rights perspective. The data challenges this picture of a restorative and conciliatory court system, and it prompts us to question why this shift from confessions to accusations occurred.

Popular Justice

A second key characteristic of the *gacaca* court design was the decentralization of justice; in order to achieve that goal, the state installed courts in every administrative unit of the country, with lay people (*inyangamugayo*) presiding as judges. Lawmakers envisioned the involvement of the entire population, and I needed to verify how this popularization played out in practice.

Cases of alleged rape were an exception to the pattern of popular participation. Initially, sector-level courts were not supposed to deal with such crimes, but the 2008 law decentralized rape and sexual torture to the *gacaca* courts. These cases followed a similar logic as other sector-level cases, except that judges secretly forwarded accusations and testimony about rape cases to the *inyangamugayo* as the *gacaca* law suggested (Republic of Rwanda 2004a, art. 38). The 2008 law clarified specific procedures, prohibited initiating proceedings regarding these crimes "against another in public," and specified that "all formal proceedings . . . shall be held in camera" (Republic of Rwanda 2008a, art. 6). The law allowed only those delegates of the SNJG, security officers, trauma counselors, and members of the *gacaca* court where the complaint was made to follow the proceedings in these cases.

I assume that this provision was meant to protect the social life and psychological state of rape victims and their families. Indeed, the courts often invoked the provision but in such a fashion that cases of rape were easily revealed to the community. In Jali, for example, the case of a rape victim was examined secretly, as required. But before the start of the trial, everybody in the community already knew who was involved: the name of the victim as well as the names of the three defendants. And although the trial proceedings had taken place without any member of the public present, the president of the *gacaca* court summarized the proceedings to the crowd that had gathered nearby, after having pronounced the verdict *in camera*.[26] So even rape cases were public, although the general population did not participate in rape-trial proceedings.

Overall, since its inception and throughout the actual operation of the *gacaca* courts system, most who knew about *gacaca* only from a distance or through the popular media believed that the population had massively participated.

The statistics in table 3 show that attendance should not be overestimated and that the numbers were in fact low. Calculations based on the population statistics of the localities under observation reveal that the "average" *gacaca* trial involved only 4.1 percent of the local population over eighteen years old, which is just 2.2 percent of the entire population.[27] High-profile cases attracted the attention of between 19 percent and 27 percent of the adult population, depending on locality. We cannot, however, use these percentages to make claims about the involvement or noninvolvement of every adult Rwandan since these percentages refer to the "average" attendance in the "average" trial. Different people attended trials depending on the nature of the case under investigation. That means that an important part of the population was involved in the proceedings at some point but not necessarily throughout the entire process. Field observations confirm that often the same key actors were involved in the trials, as I explain in more detail later.[28]

Table 3. Attendance rate at *gacaca* sessions

			% Population 18+	*% Population all*
	Mean	131	4.1%	2.2%
All	Median	120	3.7%	2.1%
N = 927	Minimum	7	0.2%	0.1%
	Maximum	1,200	37.3%	20.5%

Note: Population statistics were gathered on site in 2006.

What is clear is that participation/presence at the *gacaca* trials significantly diminished from 2007 onward to roughly one-quarter of the initial numbers observed in 2006 (see also PRI 2010, 17–18). The first trial in Runyoni attracted a crowd of an estimated 1,200 people.[29] The *gacaca* sessions in the following months continued to attract crowds. In August 2006 there were still up to a thousand people attending the hearings.[30] By mid-2007 the attendance in the same sector dropped to averages of fifty to sixty spectators/participants.[31] The biggest reason for this sudden drop in the attendance rate was that every locality had multiple courts from 2007 onward.

In 2009 and 2010 the average attendance rose again largely because the 2008 modifications of the *gacaca* law resulted in the decentralization of trials for high-profile genocide suspects to the *gacaca* courts. Notorious personalities on trial, interesting cases, or important trials attracted more attention. In Jali, for example, where attendance rates had dropped dramatically since mid-2007, there were about five hundred people attending the trial of a minister in the Pentecostal church at the end of August 2008.[32]

One consequence of introducing multiple courts at the sector level was that some trials took place with hardly any attendants, only participants. Some trials had fewer than ten local residents present during the proceedings. In Runyoni, for example, Mukuri was convicted and sentenced to twenty-five years in prison for having distributed firearms during the genocide. The sentence was pronounced on 14 August 2008 after more than eight hundred trials had been organized in the sector. *Gacaca*-fatigue had set in and other than the judges, the defendant, and those of us there for research purposes, not more than nine people attended Mukuri's trial. Three of those nine people were witnesses summoned to testify in the trial.[33]

The question is not only how many people attended the trials but who actually participated in the trials and how they did so. In order to have an insight into the nature of the participation, we coded 26,912 interventions that were made during 421 trials recorded verbatim. (Tables 11 and 12 in appendix II provide an overview of the number and types of interventions during sector-level trials.)

Attendance does not mean active involvement: 32 percent of the interventions during the observed trials were made by the general public, and most of these interventions came from victims. The *inyangamugayo* or the defendant on trial made most of the other interventions. There were thus three main actors during the *gacaca* proceedings: the accused, the judges, and the victims. The general public played only a minor role.

The average sector-level *gacaca* trial took an estimated one hour and twelve minutes and involved thirty-five interventions.[34] The judges made 50 percent of the interventions in the average trial, the defendant made 18.7 percent, and the general public made 32.3 percent, with 8.4 percent of these an accusation against the defendant (*à charge*) and 4.7 percent in defense of the accused on trial (*à décharge*).[35] Because 19.2 percent of the interventions were neutral means that they did not contain an element of accusation or defense. A limited number of the interventions (0.3 percent) were made by (local) authorities attending the trial.

Some important trends emerge regarding the basic operational procedures of the modern *gacaca* practice. For example, there was no ethnic dominance—sometimes suggested in the literature on *gacaca*—when considering the sheer number of interventions that were made during *gacaca* trials. Participants belonging to the general population of Hutu and Tutsi ethnicity spoke almost as frequently (excluding defendants and *inyangamugayo*). Overall, a number of key actors dominated the *gacaca* proceedings: the judges, defendants, and genocide survivors. The participation of the general population was rather low. After observing pilot sectors and before the nationwide implementation of *gacaca*, PRI (2005, 39) asked whether the process was "participatory justice without participation?" On the other hand, the *inyangamugayo* were, as lay judges, the most important actors in the *gacaca* process. Although "popular justice" is hard to define, many observers consider that one characteristic of this kind of justice is having judges who are members of the general population (Engle Merry and Milner 1995, 4).

Categorization and Sentencing

The principle of categorization by type of offense was the third crucial feature of the modern *gacaca* courts. The underlying objective was to hold accountable anyone who committed acts of genocide and crimes against humanity, and in doing so thus eradicate a culture of impunity. This categorization process was supposed to individualize guilt and differentiate between individuals according to the gravity of the offenses.

The law that established the *gacaca* courts stipulated that the courts had the competence, thus the authority over specific matters, to deal with the "crime of genocide and other crimes against humanity, committed between October 1st, 1990 and December 31, 1994" (Republic of Rwanda 2004a). In addition, "other crimes" ("ordinary crimes") committed during the period that the defendant, public prosecution, or other "testimonies" declared had been carried out with the "intention of committing genocide or crimes against humanity" could also be prosecuted through the *gacaca* courts. The law further specified

Gacaca Mechanics

that a *gacaca* court dealt with the crimes committed on the territory under its jurisdiction.[36]

The law thus leaves room—in principle—to deal with criminal acts that were not directed toward the Tutsi population and/or were not part of the wider campaign of genocidal extermination. In all the locations where we observed *gacaca* trials, Hutu had been killed in the context of the civil war, and political upheaval and generalized insecurity had occurred in the period covered by the *gacaca* law. However, the *inyangamugayo* systematically excluded all crimes under investigation that could not be qualified as acts of genocide against the Tutsi population. A discussion that unfolded between the defendant and the judges during a *gacaca* hearing in Runyoni illustrates this practice:[37]

> DEFENDANT SANKARA: I can also talk about the death of Mbambanyi. He and Nduruma stole the medication of Libakare, a displaced man who lived in Bishenyi, and they also stole RWF 20,000 from him and he had diabetes, so his condition worsened for lack of medication and this news reached Lieutenant Rambagira whom he knew.
>
> [Strong protest from the *inyangamugayo* as the defendant talks about Mbambanyi, who was killed because he stole the diabetes medication of a man by the name of Libakare.]
>
> PRESIDENT: We are here to discuss crimes of genocide committed against the Tutsi, not to try thieves and other criminals.
>
> DEFENDANT SANKARA: Still, Mbambanyi's name is on my indictment, so I'd like to explain how he died.
>
> WITNESS (MALE SURVIVOR): Was he Tutsi?
>
> DEFENDANT SANKARA: No, Mbambanyi was not a victim of genocide; he was not Tutsi. And this man from Butare was no victim of genocide either; he was killed for political reasons.

Having established the identity of these victims and the alleged motives for their deaths, the *inyangamugayo* did not pursue any further information in these cases.

Not only did the *gacaca* courts not prosecute these types of crimes, but people hardly mentioned them. A systematic analysis of 1,053 observed trials reveals that only in a very limited number of trials was there a reference to Hutu being threatened or killed.[38] These few instances all related to particular criminal events that were part of the genocidal extermination campaign and in which Hutu were also killed. Civil war violence, on the other hand, was never mentioned as crime to be dealt with. If the civil war *was* mentioned, it was as circumstantial information in a trial that dealt with genocide-related crimes. In practice, the *gacaca* courts observed have never charged anyone with a crime other than a genocide-related crime (except for charges dealing with violation of the *gacaca* procedures). In fact, the crimes the *gacaca* dealt with were acts of genocidal violence committed against Tutsi.

Moreover, the scope of the law was, in theory, broader than it had been between 6 April and 4 July 1994, the period during which the genocide took place. In the four localities under systematic observation, the great majority of the *gacaca* proceedings dealt with acts of violence that had happened during these three months, particularly during April. In Ntabona and Runyoni, no cases fell outside the 6 April–4 July 1994 time period. In Rukoma, the *gacaca* courts dealt with one case that had happened in 1992, in which they put someone on trial for throwing two Tutsi into a river. In the northern locality of Jali, situated in the heartland of the former regime, the *gacaca* hearings investigated numerous cases that had taken place before 1994. There, 20 of the 176 violent events that generated approximately five hundred trials at the sector level had happened before 1994.[39]

Analyzing the actual scope of charges reveals that the *gacaca* courts did not deal with civil war violence, RPF crimes, and revenge killings by Tutsi civilians, and they barely mentioned such crimes in court. Based on their observations of the *gacaca* process, PRI (2005, 44) refers to a "dangerous unilaterism" in that respect. Indeed, this insight casts doubt on whether the courts actually managed to fight a culture of impunity.

The *gacaca* court's competence—the range of criminal charges it was responsible for trying—was shaped in practice. Was this also the case regarding indictments? To answer that question we systematically analyzed 2,337 charges against 1,524 defendants standing trial at the sector level (see tables 13 and 14 in appendix II). Most defendants were charged with the crime of "participation in attacks in order to kill without attaining this goal."[40] Exemplary in that respect are the cases of Rukara and Ngendo, both standing trial in Jali in September 2009.[41] Both were accused of having played an auxiliary role (being present during the killings) in the murder of a cow herder and his son. In the trial, however, the court decided that these two did not play any role in these killings but were present during the burial of the bodies. They were acquitted. Another frequently used category was "ordinary killers in serious attacks." Munyentwari, an inhabitant of Rukoma, was classified in that category. During his appeal trial, he explained to the court what he had done during the genocide. The following verbatim excerpt from his confession illustrates in his own words what qualified him as "an ordinary killer in serious attacks":[42]

DEFENDANT MUNYENTWARI: I took part in the attack in which Mukama-
  zera, Anselme's wife, was killed, as well as Sabin's wife [Césarie]. I
  personally killed Rukara Magirus with a machete. I almost forgot, at
  Mushoza's: many people died there, and I killed one myself with a

Gacaca Mechanics

machete. I removed sheets of corrugated iron from Musabimana's roof; there were many of us, counting the people from Gatare including Kadirigu and Madonori. I also destroyed the house of Iyakaremye and Rutaganira. We took the bags of beans that were there at Sedori's. I also want to talk about the goats my brother Mudahara referred to. The people of Gatare took the cows and locked up several goats in our house; there were many goats but we only took four and the rest scattered. I apologize for everything I've done.

Comparing the percentages of defendants in the different categorizations over the years makes clear that those who modified the *gacaca* laws intended to shift more people to the *gacaca* process and to lower categories within that process. While initially 11 percent of the accused had to be processed in the ordinary courts, this was reduced to 0.7 percent in the 2008 law (see table 14 in appendix II).

Regarding the alterations or modifications over time, several of these changes made the system more effective and efficient. They were able to alter the system by incorporating more restorative components—the reduction of a sentence after a sincere confession and the prominent place of community service. On the other hand, such modifications could have resulted from the fact that the system had simply generated too many convictions and thus the prisons were in danger of becoming congested again. Emptying the prisons had been one objective for installing the *gacacas* in the first place.

The categorization according to crimes guided the judges with respect to sentencing. At the end of a *gacaca* session, the *inyangamugayo* deliberated among themselves in private and then pronounced the verdict later in public. During the deliberation period, the judges discussed all the cases dealt with during that session.[43] How the judges came to their decisions also remained private. The *gacaca* law suggests that they "shall decide by consensus" or, if needed, by "absolute majority" (Republic of Rwanda 2004a, art. 24).

Table 4 provides an overview of the cases where the defendant was found guilty or acquitted in observed trials at the sector level.[44] Most of the defendants standing trial were found guilty; only 11 percent were acquitted. Overall, the final report on the *gacaca* courts suggests an acquittal rate of 14 percent for the entire *gacaca* process (Republic of Rwanda 2012), including the cell-level trials dealing with property cases.[45]

We noted that the courts organized no trials at the sector level if one of the individuals accused had died since the acts had been committed. At the cell level, however, the pillaging and destruction of belongings was considered to be the responsibility of the family members of the accused, even if the accused was dead, abroad, in prison, in a work camp (and not transported to the locality

Table 4. Guilty verdicts vs. acquittals

	Ntabona N = 307	Runyoni N = 686	Rukoma N = 226	Jali N = 508	All N = 1727
Guilty	46.6%	95.3%	94.2%	91.5%	85.4%
Acquittal	53.1%	0.9%	4.0%	1.6%	10.8%
No verdict	0.3%	3.8%	1.8%	6.9%	3.8%

Note: "No verdict" refers to a particular event during two sessions of the trial in question: for example, the accused died, fled Rwanda, or received a change of categorization.

to follow the trial), or when his or her whereabouts were unknown.[46] We observed many cases in which mothers or fathers, sisters or brothers, children, and even sons- and daughters-in-law represented the defendant during the proceedings at the cell level.

Not only family members of the defendants' families but also people with no "blood" relationship with the defendant could be instructed to repay pillaged or destroyed goods. There are three variations on that practice. First, the courts could oblige defendants to compensate victims for their losses if the accused had acquired goods from a "known" genocide suspect. During a *gacaca* session in Ntabona, the judges summoned someone who had bought the plots of land of people accused of pillaging during the genocide. As the following excerpt illustrates, the person in question was willing, albeit reluctantly, to make restitution for a crime he had never committed:[47]

> *Inyangamugayo*: Anthère, please approach. You were summoned because you illegally bought a field and the people who sold it to you are gone. They should return the property they looted or be forced to compensate from their own estate. So, can you tell us why you bought this field without our authorization?
>
> DEFENDANT ANTHÈRE (MALE NO-SURVIVOR/NO PRISON): I asked you to summon those people who sold me the field so they can be tried and if found guilty I'd be prepared to compensate for them. . . . I'm prepared to compensate only when those accused are here and are found guilty because I don't want to compensate on behalf of someone whose business I'm not aware of.

Second, we found that the courts generally interpreted participation in pillaging very broadly. For instance, a number of people stole a cow from a victim, slaughtered that cow, and gave or sold pieces of meat to more than a few other people who had not helped steal the cow. This followed the normal practice of meat distribution in peacetime. Nonetheless, the *gacaca* proceedings considered all the people who had bought or received meat as accomplices to the act of pillaging. In Runyoni, for example, fifty-one people were accused of being involved in stealing the five cows of genocide victims;[48] most of the defendants had not been involved in the act of stealing the cows but had bought or received meat. Thirty-one of them were convicted and told to pay restitution of RWF 35,000 each. The others were acquitted since it was established they had not received any meat. This broad definition of "participation in pillaging and looting" at least partly explains the high numbers of people who were accused under Category 3 crimes.

Third, when the author of an act of pillaging or destruction was unknown or had died and left no family members or none able to restitute the goods, the court might decide to oblige the neighbors of the victim(s) to compensate for the loss. Illustrative in that respect was a case observed in Jali.[49] In October 2009 the sector court in Jali presided over a property-related case initially tried in one of the cells of the sector. The cell court had decided that it was unknown who had pillaged and burned the house of the Kagano household. No one was convicted of the crime, but Kagano was not satisfied with the verdict and demanded a new trial. Therefore, six of Kagano's neighbors were summoned at the sector level. The judges questioned all of them regarding the pillaging and burning of Kagano's homestead. All said they did not know who had committed these crimes or vaguely referred to a boy unknown in the area. In conclusion and since the court had not established who had committed the crimes, the judges decided to instruct the neighbors of Kagano to pay damages. Each was sentenced to pay RWF 153,330 to compensate for the total estimated value of RWF 920,000. The court explained the decision as follows:

> Whereas the accused do not clarify who looted the accuser's houses, whereas they did nothing to salvage the belongings of their neighbors the Kagano's, and whereas the wrongdoer is one individual against many neighbors. Whereas the criminal cannot be found by the defendants or the court and so that things are clear: he was the one who burnt the houses.

Defendants found guilty at sector-level cases dealing with violence against humans received on average a sentence of 11.3 years.[50] According to specific provisions in the *gacaca* laws as modified over the years, the courts could convert the sentence into 50 percent community service on probation, 17 percent suspended, and 33 percent to be served in custody. Whether or not this happened depended on which *gacaca* law was in effect at the time, whether (and when) the defendant had confessed, and whether the court had accepted his or her confession. The average convict spent 9.25 years in jail, executed 1.4 years' community service on probation, and had eight months suspended on probation.

A large number of people found guilty had already spent time in pretrial detention. The average convict had spent 2.5 years in prison before being sentenced by a *gacaca* court. The longest pretrial detention period we observed was fourteen years, the entire period between the genocide and the trial. The judges would, therefore, deduct the time already spent in prison from the final sentence. Taking that into account, the average verdict implied that posttrial the accused would face 7.75 years of incarceration, seven months of community service, and four months with a suspended sentence. This totals an average sentence of 8.67 more years for the typical convict.

If one received a prison sentence, that person was immediately taken into custody; if that person had already served enough time while in detention awaiting trial, he or she was set free. With an overload of new prisoners congesting the prisons starting in mid-2007, convicts first had to serve a period of community service. Although planners originally intended that the convict would do community service in the sector where the convict—and generally also the victim—lived, most were taken to work camps far away from their home region.[51]

"Only the defendant and parties against him" could lodge an appeal (Republic of Rwanda 2004a, art. 89). There were three means of appeal: opposition, appeal, and review of judgment (Republic of Rwanda 2004a, art. 86): 19.6 percent of all cases tried used one of these means of appeal.[52] But there were differences depending on locality. In Ntabona, appeal was lodged only in 6 percent of the cases compared to 34 percent in Jali. The low numbers of appeal in Ntabona were, however, the result of a dramatic event there that made defendants reluctant to appeal against judgments (see chap. 7).[53]

Conclusion

So far, the basic operational characteristics of *gacaca* have been explained, which allows us to question how *gacaca*'s objectives compare with its outcomes. But before answering that question, we need to deepen our understanding of the *gacaca* process and the people practicing *gacaca*.

Once underway, the *gacaca* process was animated by a peculiar dynamic, which needs further exploration. How exactly was the competence of the courts shaped in practice? What forces prevented people from raising certain issues in *gacaca*? Because people resorted to multiple confessions spread over the entire *gacaca* period, most considered the act of confessing as a strategic process. What motivated people to confess? What strategies did they deploy?

What prevented the general population from actively participating in the court proceedings? What dynamic triggered the sudden surge in the number of people accused? We need contextual knowledge of the Rwandan socio-political universe and more particular information about the localities observed. This is especially true since the operation of *gacaca* varied in both space and time.

4 | Experiencing *Gacaca*

Be without fear and tell us the truth.

Lay judge, Rukoma, *gacaca* session on 22 May 2007

What kind of atmosphere did the sudden shift to accusatory practices create in the local communities where people were practicing *gacaca*? How did the general public experience the changing features of the *gacaca* over time? Did they experience justice and/or reconciliation or did other sentiments accompany the *gacaca* process? I asked these questions in order to gain a deeper understanding of the court system, its impact in Rwandan society, and the experience of Rwandans practicing *gacaca*.

In doing so, I combined two research techniques in seven Rwandan sectors, including the four sectors where we systematically observed *gacaca* trials: life-history interviews that cover the period when *gacaca* was operational in Rwandan society, and surveys that asked open-ended questions on positive and negative experiences with *gacaca*.

Sévérine: A Life Story

Sévérine was born in 1956 in a sector near Ntabona, a hill located in central Rwanda.[1] In 1974 she came to Ntabona to get married. She is currently officially considered as a genocide survivor (*rescapée*) although—at the time of the genocide—there was confusion about her ethnicity, hence the reason why she survived. Her husband was Tutsi, a farmer, but he also had a small shop where he repaired clothing and sold it at markets in the region.

Sévérine related that "after the marriage we had large plots of land. We had a cow and sheep, plots of land and coffee trees, we could charge [fill] a full truck without any problem." The reference to the ability to fill a truck with agricultural produce is her way of saying that her household was wealthy. Her husband had obtained a sewing machine, which allowed him, together with his brother, to secure an off-farm income. In the meantime, Sévérine would cultivate the fields and employ wage laborers. Social relations were good but "because of our richness, we attracted envy and hatred." Together they had three children, born in 1976, 1977, and 1979. Her husband died at the beginning of the 1980s from a disease, she said, and "life became difficult when my husband died. Only when the children grew up did life become better again."

In the early 1990s, Sévérine belonged to several ethnically mixed agricultural associations whose members cultivated sugarcane in the river valley. But due to the war with the Rwandan Patriot Front (RPF) in the beginning of the 1990s and the upcoming polarization of social life during the period when multiparty politics was introduced, Sévérine was excluded from the association. In 1992 a local teacher (who later became a local ringleader in the genocide) would not pass messages from a secondary school in the province of Gikongoro to Sévérine because of her "ethnic identity"—or at least that of her children. One child was consequently expelled from school. In that period, "there was not a single authority looking after us." In addition, when President Habyarimana's plane was shot down in April 1994, Sévérine's children became targets of the violence.

> When I went to cultivate after the plane crash, people started to call me names. Aloys asked where my son was. They said they needed him to participate in the *rondes*, the patrols to maintain security. I told him I would send him, when he came back. A certain day, I saw a large group of Tutsi families who had come to seek refuge in the buildings of the parish. At night a local teacher came knocking on our door asking me to send my children. I did not open the door. They came in a group and I heard whispering, "When you want someone, you will have to proceed very carefully." The next day my son told me they had pillaged the houses of the families of Mazimpaka and Muzindutsi, two Tutsi families. I decided to leave.

Sévérine took the children with her to a neighboring sector, her place of origin, to hide them. Going there she had to pass several barriers on the roads. She was beaten at the barriers several times, and she still has scars from machete blows on her arms. She stayed in her parents' village for about a month. Someone from Ntabona sent messages to the local officials in her village asking that they send her children to the people of Ntabona so they could be killed where they came from. Once this message came to light, the people in her village forced her to send the children back to Ntabona, and Séverine followed these orders and returned. She recounted, "I arrived in Ntabona at night. Rutaganira came to take my children. They transported them to the river. Stanislas took my children at the legs to smash their heads against the rocks. The next morning I went to look for their bodies. I almost turned crazy. The dogs had starting eating the flesh of their bodies."

Stanislas, the man who killed Séverine's children, was twenty years old in 1994. He admits having taken the lead in the killing of her children: "I was sitting in a cabaret [local pub], when Séverine arrived with her children. She trusted these children to one of the local authority figures. Since these local officials had no power anymore, we took the children from him and we killed them. Me too, I was part of the group of killers, I had a big stick and we hit them until they were dead. I did not do anything else [during the genocide], apart from that." Stanislas explains what made him kill the children this way: "I was conditioned by that group; I was young and I followed the others."

After the genocide Stanislas fled the area. Upon his return in 1995 he was put in prison, where he stayed until he was released in 2005. Séverine stayed alone in her house after the genocide surrounded by those, or the family members of those, who had participated in killing her children and looting her house. In 1998 she sold her property and went to live in a resettlement site for genocide survivors in a neighboring sector some three kilometers from her former home and fields. In 2007 Séverine told me, "In 1995 and 1996 they started arresting those suspected of participation in the genocide. Security was then assured. There were always soldiers close to us. I felt represented by the authorities at the time. Even now, but the *gacaca* is a problem." Her most intense social relationships are with other genocide survivors, her neighbors in the resettlement site. She continued:

> Trust means that there is no one running behind you and aims at doing bad. I generally trust people that work together with me and speak the truth. . . . The origin of confidence resides in the possibility to dialogue with others. Being able to talk to someone gives me pleasure and serenity of the heart [*umutima*]. When people talk while smiling, without afterthoughts, it means they have that *umutima*. Did you ever encounter the case when someone did not want to answer your greetings despite your insistence to receive a "good-day"? I have these problems every day. The one who does not salute you, can do nothing for you. He cannot collaborate with you.

In total, 370 *gacaca* trials dealing with 157 violent events against individuals were organized at the sector level in Ntabona. Hundreds of additional gatherings focused on crimes of pillaging and destruction of goods during the genocide. Séverine played an active role in nineteen trials but often attended other trials without intervening. Eleven of the trials at the sector level dealt with the killing of Séverine's children. Seven individuals were convicted not just for the murder of these children but also for other crimes they had committed; three people on trial accused of participating in these killings were acquitted. Stanislas was convicted on 16 October 2006. He had confessed to the crime and pleaded guilty. At the start of the proceedings he declared in front of the *gacaca* bench:

> I was in the center of Ruhoko [a place with bars and shops], consuming banana beer with other people. I saw Séverine arriving with her two children, going in the direction of Ildephonse Habyambare, the *responsable* of the cell [local authority of an administrative unit]. People started crying where we were sitting. They started yelling at these children. They attempted to make sure they would not arrive at the home of the *responsable*. A man called Martin uttered accusations and suggested to kill them and to put them "next to their fellow Tutsi," the accomplices of the Inkotanyi [this word means "invincible" and refers to the RPF]. Ildephonse tried to make sure they were not killed, but those that were stubborn refused to listen to him. Among them were: Kanamugire Jean, Pierre, Kidogo, Munyeneza, Mazimpaka Isidore, and Banyarwanda. These are the ones who made the decision to kill these children. Kanamugire said that those who were going to kill these children were going to receive a banana grove as reward, but that the ones who were refusing to declare their solidarity by staying in the center of Ruhoko were going to be fined with 5,000 Rwandan francs. So I went together with them, to the river, with a club in my hand. We arrived at the house of Germain, the father of Kidogo. Kidogo brought some hoes with which they killed the children. They were buried in the plot owned by Ntampaka, who was also threatened at the time [Ntampaka was Tutsi]. I gave a blow with my club on the head of Mukayuhi Marguerite [one of the children]. I ask for pardon.

Although Séverine had given a different version of the event based on information that was given to her in the years following the genocide, Stanislas's confession was accepted and he was sentenced to ten years' incarceration, divided into five years' imprisonment and five years of community service. Since he had already spent more than ten years in pretrial detention, he was subsequently set free.

In 2006 Séverine also became part of the *inyangamugayo*, the judges presiding over the *gacaca* courts, after other judges had to be replaced because of their alleged involvement in the genocide or affiliation with suspects. She became a judge in the courts that dealt with pillaging and destruction but not in the court that dealt with crimes of murder, the court that had handled Stanislas's case. At the time she was not happy with the way *gacaca* functioned: "*Gacaca* works but not very well. I have lost my children. I saw the people [that took my children] and when I went to give a testimony, everyone turned against me, saying that I was lying. The people that are with me in the committee [of judges] have family implicated. They have relationships with those people. It is their children and uncles [standing trial]." During one of the *gacaca* sessions, one of the inhabitants argued that Sévérine is also responsible for the death of her children, since she had sent them back to the sector herself. Séverine was deeply hurt by this statement and filed a complaint at the district office saying that the people of Ntabona continued to hurt the survivors and tried to blame them for the genocide. She insisted on the presence of so-called genocide ideology (*ingengabitekerezo ya yenoside*).

Although social relationships have been generally strained between Séverine and the other inhabitants since the genocide, the advent of *gacaca* gave rise to some outright conflicts. For example, at the start of *gacaca* in 2006, Séverine and other genocide survivors accused a local teacher of having killed one of their family members who was in hiding in the house of the teacher. Séverine and others accused him of having disposed of the body in his latrine. The teacher claimed he was innocent. For several months, this accusation created animosity in Ntabona, dividing a large part of the population into two camps. Local state officials became involved and gave the order to dig open and empty the latrine. After several weeks of digging and searching, no human remains were found. During these weeks, however, the teacher closely monitored the latrine—he even employed night watchmen—to make sure nobody threw animal bones into the pit. He was afraid someone might do that to settle a score. Several such outright conflicts have surrounded the *gacaca* proceedings in this sector, some involving Séverine, others between Hutu accusing each other in *gacaca*.

Séverine assesses her relationships with others based on mutual help, sharing, and working together. During the period of *gacaca*, she often mentioned that the *gacaca* activities had had a negative influence on others' willingness to help her, work with her, and share with her. Since she has no family members left, it has become difficult for her to organize daily household activities, which the members of a household usually divide among themselves. "Normally there are family members going to the market, others go to cultivate in the fields, fetch water, or gather wood for the cooking stove. For all these things, I need to count on myself." She needs to rely on day laborers to help her. But, she said, "our neighbors that are not genocide survivors don't want to cultivate our fields as day laborers, although I simply consider them as day laborers paid for their daily work as anyone who does that kind of work. Nevertheless, they refuse. They say we [the survivors] have played a role in *gacaca* by putting them or their family members in prison." Finding assistance through others for daily activities is a sign of good or bad social relationships. Help in times of distress is also important. In such cases, Séverine also experiences difficulties in finding support, something she considers another consequence of the *gacaca* activities. "If a sick person needs to be transported to hospital and one needs help, the others [nonsurvivors] refuse their help on the pretext that we are widows of the genocide and that their friends and family members are in prison. They invent reasons such as the fact that [if they would come to our assistance] nobody will remain in their home and if not this one or that one was executing their punishment in prison or through community service [TIG], it would have been possible to transport our sick family member to the hospital."[2]

Since the beginning of *gacaca*, authorities have held several meetings with the population, triggered by allegations made by Séverine and other survivors, to make sure that people leave behind the "genocide ideology." As Séverine mentions, these meetings with local authority figures preaching reconciliation often influence her thoughts and attitudes. "The authorities 'came closer' to both survivors and nonsurvivors to convince us to trust each other since, let's say, 2006, and I have taken my responsibility as well to adjust my attitude, to change positively." "Often the authorities come to play the role of mediators and reconcilers. And apart from my negative experiences with the group of Hutu, there are also some individuals—very few but nevertheless—that put aside 100 Rwandan francs from time to time to help us." Despite her isolation from the community's social life and despite her difficult relationships with most inhabitants, Séverine also has some long-standing friendships, not only with genocide survivors but with some of the Hutu families that live on the hill. These friendships are marked by mutual help, participation in ceremonies, and the sharing of food and drinks.

Séverine also found some relief through the *gacaca* proceedings that dealt with the pillaging of her belongings. If a settlement was reached in one of her claims, the defendant paid her some money to compensate her. "And after that [reaching an agreement], sometimes we go to share a beer in a cabaret [pub])." Since 2010, she also decided to drop some of her claims for compensation as a conscious strategy to influence her social relationships in a positive way. "We [survivors] started to renounce our judicial claims that are a result of *gacaca*, especially regarding restitution since it will make the relationship with the others less tense. The relationship will become warmer again in the future, I think." In fact, compensation through *gacaca* at the cell level can initiate a genuine reconciliation attempt, a major conflict, or both. Séverine experienced both.

In general, reconciliation remains difficult, and sometimes it seems utterly impossible, especially regarding people involved in killings:

> They have killed my children in a brutal way. They have thrown a rock on the head of one. [*Starts crying.*] Those people have committed serious crimes. They pillaged and destroyed my belongings. We are getting old; we don't have any force left. . . . Those people who are in prison don't want me to be alive. They wonder there in prison whether I am still alive or not. The same for their families; the relations are not good. They don't tell the truth. Do you think a prisoner will come here, ask for forgiveness and reconcile? I don't think so. Neither will I. It will not be easy. . . . The state puts a lot of pressure for reconciliation, but I have undergone those actions. The state can do what it wants; it doesn't concern me.

At the height of the *gacaca* process, in the first half of 2007, Séverine told me she did not feel very secure. "Security means that one has peace and that the conversations with others are good, as they were before. Currently, you salute someone and he is not responding. . . . The relations are not good because they [other villagers—Hutu] say that we want everyone in prison so that we [survivors] can stay alone in the country. When you arrive somewhere people stop talking and they whisper, 'Ah, the group [of survivors] that wants to send everyone to prison.'" During a conversation in February 2011, several months after the end of the *gacaca* proceedings on her hill, Séverine had a similar experience. "Often, it happens to me that I am thirsty; so I go to the center [small commercial area with shops and bars] to buy some *ubushera* [nonalcoholic sorghum beer]. But the sellers tell me there is none. They made a collective decision to do so. When I am gone, they start selling and drinking with their preferred customers, their friends, the ones that are not genocide survivors."

On the one hand, she considers her prospects for the future bleak. "If God wants, there can be security. I wish life in the community will be better and with security. During the period of *gacaca*, when I went to the commercial center, I sat down and everyone left. All of that are the consequences of the war and *gacaca*. If *gacaca* had not taken place, the relations would not have been as bad as they are. . . . They put people in prison? Why? Is it going to give back the dead?" On the other hand, since the end of *gacaca* she also has some hope for a future with improved social relationships. "There are some positive changes. And this is thanks to the work of God, who will be the origin of change in the hearts of his children."

Life-Story Narratives

The story of Séverine relates to the theme of popular experience with *gacaca* at the grassroots, the basic level of society. Séverine is a member of the Rwandan peasantry, a term that refers to inhabitants of rural Rwanda and includes cultivators and cattle herders.[3] Séverine lives far from the administrative and political center of Rwandan society, and she seems to be even more disconnected from global dynamics and international trends. Nevertheless, her life story—presented here in an abbreviated form—her interactions with neighbors, and the way she deals both in praxis and psychologically with the violence she experienced are not unaffected by influences from the center of Rwandan society and global dynamics. Her case sheds light on what it means to participate in grassroots transitional justice processes.

We need to move beyond a single case to understand how often experiences like Séverine's occurred. The following sections present the findings of a life-history approach in which a range of Rwandans participated in 2007 and 2011. My objective was to gauge people's experience with the *gacaca* practice in a systematic way. Anthropologists have often used a life-history approach to address two of the field's main concerns: subjectivity and meaning. As Ken Plummer states, "The life history reveals, like nothing else can, the subjective realm" (2001, 20).

But even after I had established trends and identified collective or dominating narratives in the life stories we gathered, I still had the challenge of representing the narrative dimension of the findings. More particularly, I needed to figure out how to retain the rich texture of the narratives and avoid reducing them to singular, anecdotal examples. For example, Liisa Malkki (1995) experienced a similar challenge when faced with the difficulty of representing narratives collected among Burundian refugees: "An ethnographic representation [here] needs to capture, not only the content of the refugees' conceptions of their history, but also a feel for the repetition and thematic unity that characterized the way people told their historicity. . . . The challenge is to find a representational strategy that does not suppress what was the most powerful and striking quality of these narratives: the sense of a collective voice" (56). Malkki's strategy was to create "panels," or passages weaving together multiple narratives but constructed by the author and set apart in the text. Nigel Eltringham (2004, 158–59) builds on Malkki's approach when he brings together thematic narratives from Rwanda's past based on multiple interviews.

I followed a similar but somewhat different strategy by selecting excerpts from interviews to construct narratives about the period when the modern *gacaca* courts were operational, and juxtaposing Hutu and Tutsi narratives to portray diverging and converging experiences. This leads us to consider whether the perception and experience of the same reality may differ depending on the identity of those perceiving it. Because *gacaca* needed to deal with ethnically structured violence, a nonreifying focus on ethnicity is therefore justified.

I call these excerpts or compilations of quotes "collages": they consist of short sentences, explanations, evocations, and the like taken from individual life stories and assembled into a constructed narrative thread. The idea is not to suggest that the Tutsi or Hutu spoke with a single voice. These groups do not even really exist, let alone speak as one (Brubaker 2004). Instead, I use collage on the one hand to represent a dominant theme, an overall trajectory observed in many lives, and on the other hand to safeguard and evoke the existence of multifarious voices within and across the two ethnic categories. Although these voices often talk in unison, that fact does not exclude differences in their midst.

The *Gacaca* Years: 2005–2008

Stability and physical security, being able to cultivate the fields, sleep, and eat was highly appreciated during the initial years of the new millennium, and these "creature comforts" stand in stark contrast to the turmoil of the 1990s. At the interpersonal level, Rwandans often express feelings of trust and security by referring to the heart (*umutima*). Hearts have indeed changed because of the crimes committed, the violence experienced, and the inhuman acts observed. Reconciliation, therefore, is a matter of *umutima*. Hutu and Tutsi would again share the same living area and partake in ordinary village activities in a mode of peaceful coexistence. Rwandans only tacitly explored the "heart" in the years before the installation of the *gacaca* courts. The passing of time with its repetition of everyday practices has an intrinsically healing potential in that respect.

TUTSI

"Before [1994] people shared everything. Today, that's finished. Before, a daughter was given for marriage without verifying the origins of the husband, while this has become a major concern currently."

"The genocide has killed a lot of Tutsi in Rwanda and later, the Rwandan army has equally killed a lot of Hutu. So there is a problem of hatred in the heart of people from all categories [ethnicity]."

HUTU

"The heart of man is far [*kumutima w'umuntu ni kure*]."

"One is confident in others when you can 'read' the heart of the other but since that is impossible, it is equally difficult to be confident in people."

"The face one shows is different from what is in the heart."

"It is difficult to know what is in the heart of the other, so I have to be careful."

Rwandans began exploring "the heart of the other" only in a confrontational, direct, and overtly discursive way after 2005 when *gacaca* courts began to operate in every local community nationwide. Participation in the *gacaca* sessions became the basic means by which one probed the "heart of the other." State-sanctioned speaking and/or listening to "the truth" was an objective of the court system by design, and it could therefore become an important way to increase the level of confidence between parties who had distrusted each other heretofore. In practice, this exercise came to complicate established social relationships. The nature of popular experience that the following collage draws from Hutu and Tutsi life stories confirms this observation.

TUTSI

"*Gacaca* made relationships between people worse."

"They [Hutu] confess only partially; they are not telling the entire truth."

"The *gacaca* judges are not veracious; they are accomplices of the criminals."

"People are not telling the truth [here]. Survivors have become liars in front of their perpetrators and those who confess don't do it from the depths of their heart."

"Our former neighbors don't want to tell us how our family members were killed and who came to pillage our belongings."

"For the Hutu, we greet each other in passing but there is no real confidence. They think I will accuse them in *gacaca* for what the other Hutu have done [in 1994]."

HUTU

"To have confidence you need to be sure people tell the truth, but they don't."

"The victims also need to tell the truth in their testimonies without lying because it 'kills' confidence."

"I have no problem with the genocide survivors but the fact that I denounced my neighbors as accomplices [in crimes during the genocide] has created conflicts."

"A lot of Hutu started fleeing the country since the start of *gacaca*. They are afraid of being accused."

"The inhabitants [of the community] do not trust each other. They are not united; they are not telling the truth. It's the result of the war. Before the war people were united and veracious."

At the height of the *gacaca* process in 2007, when I organized the first life-story survey, the respondents were quite outspoken about the threatening social climate, as the quotes illustrate. When they reflected on that period of *gacaca* retrospectively during the 2011 life-story survey, similar narratives surfaced.

TUTSI

"The *gacaca* discouraged me; I didn't want to work anymore. The people I was accusing were not telling the truth and the rest of the people did not want to stand up for us."

"Some people were terrorizing the survivors who testified and threw stones at their houses at night."

"I was scared of the people who lived next to me."

"I attended trials with released prisoners and others and even with prisoners, there's no trust between people on trial."

"The level of trust fell so much due to the *gacaca*. I testified and they started to threaten me even worse than before."

HUTU

"The *gacaca* attacked us."

"I paid for other peoples' property; I sold everything I had here in the house, all the food."

"At the time of *gacaca*, I was scared."

"People behaved unspeakably, heartlessly."

"My husband was imprisoned on the merits of false testimonies."

"I was tried; I was restless because I was sentenced to community service; I wasn't free."

"I was threatened a lot in *gacaca*, and imprisoned."

"I was jailed again."

"Survivors teamed up and made false testimonies to support their cases, trying to secure higher damages than their property destroyed in the genocide was actually worth."

The research conducted during the initial operational years of *gacaca* (2005–8) highlights a number of "negative" attitudes, emotions, and social dynamics that accompanied the introduction of the court system in Rwandan society: increasing distrust, more conflicts and resentment (Republic of Rwanda 2007a, 2008b; Burnet 2008; Rettig 2008, 39, 43–44; Ingelaere 2009b, 2011a), increased feelings of insecurity and trauma (Brounéus 2008, 2010; Ingelaere 2009b;

Thomson 2011b), and the overarching sentiment that lies or half truths animated the *gacaca* process (Republic of Rwanda 2007a, 2008b; Burnet 2008, 183; Ingelaere 2008, 55–56; 2009a).[4]

Despite *gacaca*—or, better, mostly because of it—Tutsi survivors relived the experience of physical threats and psychological hardships they had suffered firsthand during the 1994 extermination campaign. During the *gacaca* years, Hutu suffered more from an overall climate of distrust, especially due to the denunciation principle on which the *gacaca* courts operated. The nature and functioning of the (local) government structure and personnel seems to have contributed to these grievances.

TUTSI

"Me, I can't trust Hutu; they are angry [because accused in *gacaca*]; they are like animals."

"There are those who still cultivate hatred and others harbor the genocide ideology."

"There is no confidence between people due to ethnicity."

"The government obliges us to live together with them but we know it, they are very malicious people; they can still kill us."

"They can't exterminate us massively, but they can kill us one by one."

"The Hutu dispelled us from Rwanda in 1959; they burned our homes, ate our cows, and did it again in 1973, while in 1994 they have killed almost every single Tutsi. How can I trust people who behave like animals?"

"Nothing is possible to restore confidence in the population; even when you 'boil an elephant in a jug' [*niyo wateka inzovu mu rwabya*], it's over."[5]

HUTU

"How can I be confident when I see that I am going to die in prison?"

"Until now they call us Interahamwe, because we are Hutu."

"The state needs to stop favoring some and punishing others. As long as some feel superior compared to others, there will be no confidence."

"The obstacles for Rwandans are those trials that are unjust. One ought to leave the ordinary peasant who didn't know what was going on [in 1994]. But they do it anyway because they are judging the Hutu (ethnic) group. Is there a Tutsi put on trial? They also killed, but you can't accuse them. In other words, if someone stands upright in his state, you can't do anything against him [*iyo umuntu ahagaze muri Leta ye, nta kindi wakora*]."[6]

"They [Tutsi power holders] can use [make] us [Hutu] as their servile instrument(s) [*bashaka kutugira ibikoresho*]."[7]

"The cry is not combating the drum [*induru ntirwana n'ingoma*]."[8]

When looking back on this period, people I interviewed in 2011 also remembered a loss of intraethnic cohesion due to the *gacaca* practice. The localized practices of testifying, accusing, and conspiring in silence often crossed the ethnic divide and resulted in less trust toward people belonging to the same ethnic category and, almost paradoxically, more trust toward the other ethnicity.

TUTSI

"The Tutsi wanted my field to be confiscated because it was next to the field of one who wanted to take it."

"Survivors started to take money from nonsurvivors to conceal serious crimes like rape."

HUTU

"I started to fear them [Hutu]. I thought they would make up bad things against me to have me jailed."

"The Hutu told lies about me, accusing me of possessing a rifle and manning the roadblock."

In recollection, people also remember that the situation ameliorated once the *gacaca* process was well underway and that some aspects in the operational functioning of *gacaca* had been addressed through changes in the *gacaca* laws. Respondents started to voice more positive appraisals as well, noting issues of pardon, some aspects of truth-telling, the exhumation of bodies of missing family members, the identification of the guilty and the innocent, and liberation from prison.

TUTSI

"They began to apologize in *gacaca*."

"They began to show us where people were thrown during the genocide, where they were buried."

"Trust improved a bit; there are some among them who told me the truth about what happened."

"Change happened in my *umutima* over the course of a year."

"Toward the end of *gacaca*, trust started to emerge."

HUTU

"I'd just won my case; I received a certificate saying I was cleared."

"Over time, trust grew in my *umutima*."

"I came to know the man who wanted me jailed as a Hutu and I learned to forgive."

"A year after prison, the Tutsi came to me looking to renew their friendship."

Experiencing *Gacaca*

The end of the *gacaca* process marked a key change in the lives of ordinary Rwandans. The negative trend in feelings of security stopped, and feelings of distrust leveled out when the *gacaca* activities diminished and, especially, when they ended. In 2011 people evoke the resumption of daily life and the activities by which they measure the quality of social cohesion (*imibanire*): sharing food and drink, the availability of helping hands in the fields and when someone falls sick, marriage ceremonies and festivities. The healing aspects of day-to-day life resumed after the interruption in the *gacaca* years. The practice of everyday life where the humanity of the other is tacitly explored resumed after being short-circuited by the *gacaca* experience.

TUTSI

"*Gacaca* is over and the fear is gone."

"People aren't imprisoned anymore; security has been restored."

"And building trust takes time. I've started to share areas of interest with the Hutu and we share ideas, projects."

"After *gacaca*, we reconciled and I've come to trust them [Hutu]."

"After *gacaca*, they were released and we started greeting each other; we reconciled and it's completely safe now."

HUTU

"*Gacaca* ended; we rebuilt our relation."

"I shared banana beer with survivors."

"Every year, there's something growing in my *umutima*."

"At the end of *gacaca*, the Tutsi had already identified those involved in the 1994 genocide, and their attitude toward the Hutu changed and since then, we've shared drinks at parties without fear and they've become good friends."

"There were weddings between survivors and nonsurvivors."

In Rwanda, as elsewhere, "thin" reconciliation differs from the "thick" version. Cohabitation or "living-with" (*kubana*) is a matter of necessity, which may become less fearful for those directly involved as time passes, but interpersonal reconciliation—*ubwiyunge* or "to reconnect"—is a matter of *umutima* and a state of feeling in social relations. Chapter 8 examines the sociocultural construction of personhood in which *umutima* plays a pivotal role.

Ubwiyunge (reconciliation) should be understood as a process of discrete actions that has the possibility to redefine the nature of "living-with" (*kubana*). For example, when one states that genocide survivors and released prisoners live together (*babana*), it means that they simply do so under pressure of the economic or political circumstances. When one says that they "live together in a good way" (*babana neza*), it implies that they do so in harmony as a consequence of a process of reconciliation. Living-with can also be worse than cohabitation: it can be bad (*kubana nabi*); the latter situation is characterized by open discord and (violent) conflict(s).

Inhabitants of Rwanda's hills assess truth, in the moral sense, by observing and experiencing praxis, especially in and through ritualized exchanges. Action and speech (discourse, conversation, dialogue) can be "true" in the Rwandan context. And speech (talking or discourse) is thus not necessarily the same as truth-telling in the forensic sense, and it differs significantly from the prosecutorial and accusatory truth (and lies) that marked the *gacaca* activities. This does not mean that people have not benefited from some healing dimensions of the *gacaca* activity. Indeed, the ritualized coming together in the weekly *gacaca* sessions had a transformative influence on social relations but not in all cases and places. Some Rwandans make an explicit connection between increased security and/or trust and the functioning of the *gacaca* process. But some evoke the absence of *gacaca* to explain this positive trend. Feelings of insecurity and negative opinions regarding the credibility of confessions remained pronounced near the end of the *gacaca* process (Pozen et al. 2014).

TUTSI

"Since *gacaca* ended, security is back and there's people here at home who apologized to me."

"After *gacaca*, we were safe again."

"At the end of *gacaca*, I wasn't worried anymore; the truth was known; I trusted the Hutu, especially those who'd apologized."

"I forgave them. No one encouraged me to. My *umutima* became clearer and lighter. It wasn't even *gacaca* that encouraged me to; no, it was *umutima* that did and now I'm at ease."

"Trust has improved because *gacaca* is over."

"After *gacaca*, trust improved. The guilty were punished. The innocent were released. I can't read their hearts [*imitima*], but when I see how we share good and bad in our village, I see major change."

HUTU

"When *gacaca* concluded its work, everybody breathed again. Trust improved too."

"*Gacaca* was over. The guilty were punished and the innocent were released."

"There was deep change; toward the end of *gacaca*, the Tutsi understood that not all Hutu were guilty of slaughtering them. Since 2008, I've had good relations with the survivors; I can visit their households to borrow an object or tool; there are no separate groups of Hutu or Tutsi anymore. My Tutsi neighbor recently got married; I was invited but I noticed that there were more Hutu than Tutsi."

"Actually, trust came back after *gacaca* completed its work. The guilty were punished and the innocent were released. People aren't afraid of each other anymore, these days."

"The *gacaca* trials have changed their *imitima*."

The narratives further suggest that trust toward people of the other ethnicity remains weaker than the perceived intraethnic cohesion. The experience of the genocide has made lasting wounds in that respect. Remarkable is the decrease in trust at the intraethnic level, especially on the side of Tutsi, where a rift between survivors and old-caseload returnees seems to be growing. On the Hutu side, released prisoners in particular and others active in denouncing other Hutu during the *gacaca* sessions evoke the lasting influence of these activities in their interactions with people of the same ethnicity.

TUTSI

"I'm scared. Things could change and they [Hutu] could kill again."

"I don't trust them [Hutu], I'm scared of them, they could hurt me; we talk with them but I'm not sharing any secrets with them."

"I have good relations with the Hutu but I don't forget what they've done to the Tutsi."

"They hate me; I fear them and I'll continue to be scared of them; they're very nasty; I'll hate them until I die."

"I trust only the people who hid our people during the genocide; I can't trust people who killed our people."

"I trust them [survivors] because we share the same history."

"The other survivors won't help me even though they know about my difficult situation. They're selfish, defending their families or friends but not survivors living in misery."

"Survivors go too far. We're all Rwandans regardless of which country we came back from as former refugees.[9] It's very unsettling that they still compare us to foreigners after so many years living together."

HUTU

"I forgave all those who stirred up testimonies. We shared almost everything. At my daughter's wedding, there was a mix of survivors and Hutu."

"You can't speak freely; I see some who still cry when they hear people talk about the past. I know that I can't speak freely in front of them. I can't know what's in their *imitima*. I'm sure they're not happy with us. They still have ethnic ideologies. They feel superior to others."

"Many Hutu are like me, part of the big group of day laborers. We share the same fate and they're my companions in fortune and misfortune."

"Among the Hutu, there are people who don't reply to my invitations for ceremonies. Maybe it's because I accused them of participating in the looting or of genocide."

"Those who didn't go to prison treat us like traitors. They say that we disclosed all secrets when we chose to tell the truth in *gacaca*. They don't trust us and vice-versa."

"They [Hutu] are my brothers. I've never mistrusted them. Not once, ever."

What continues to characterize the life of genocide survivors is a sort of existential solitude. The loss of family, children, parents, and friends cannot be addressed by a *gacaca* process, strong intraethnic cohesion, the strengthening of interethnic ties, or anything else.

TUTSI

"We share a very unhappy destiny. Now there's peace ahead of us and our hopes rest on that. The Hutu decimated our families. For those like me who are left without brothers, sisters, or other relatives, meeting any survivor is like meeting a brother, a sister, or a relative."

"I don't have any problems with my neighbors but my personal situation worries me."

"I'm not insecure only because I'm poor but also because I'm alone; there's no one to talk to in order to try and see how to combat this poverty."

Gacaca in Retrospect: Positive and Negative Experiences

By 2011, when I attached a questionnaire about *gacaca* to the life-story survey I fielded in seven Rwandan sectors,[10] the actual *gacaca* practice had come to an end in all these locations. The implementation of some decisions made by the courts was still ongoing (prison sentences, TIG, restitution, etc.). I designed the survey instrument to be as open as possible in order to avoid making any suggestions. It asked every respondent, "In your opinion, what was the most positive aspect/most negative aspect of the *gacaca* process?"

"What is the most positive event/most negative event, fact or act you have observed in the *gacaca* process? Give a concrete example." The first set of questions probed general opinions but were nevertheless open-ended, and the second set of questions necessitated giving concrete examples of a striking element in the *gacaca* practice, both positive and negative. The nature of the second pair of questions counters to a certain extent the overall problem with opinion questions in the Rwandan sociocultural universe. A number of studies highlight the need to differentiate between more global and specific questions (Rettig 2008; Ingelaere 2009a; Pozen et al. 2014). The latter refers to *gacaca*'s actual operation and the former to the general objectives. Overall, given the Rwandan environment, survey research on opinions and attitudes is best complemented and triangulated with other research techniques (Ingelaere 2010a).

Table 5 ranks the most-cited positive and negative dimensions of the *gacaca* process. What is apparent in the table are the consistent differences between the most-cited opinions and the underlying theme in the most-cited examples, especially regarding the positive aspects of *gacaca* and irrespective of ethnic affiliation. Tutsi respondents mostly refer to reconciliation, healing, or unity when talking in general terms about their experiences with *gacaca*, and the most striking examples have to do with the confession-pardon nexus:

TUTSI

"Reconciliation and union of Rwandans."
"The *gacaca* united people."
"The *gacaca* restored 'humanism' [*ubumuntu*] among people."
"Someone apologized to me; I forgive them and my heart is at peace."
"[I especially remember] these two Hutu women who knelt before me and apologized for slandering me."
"There was a man I hadn't seen attack my home and whom I didn't mention when information was collected; he came to me and apologized and even bought me a drink."

Hutu respondents, on the other hand, stress the aspect of truth in their positive appraisal of *gacaca*, but when recalling concrete examples of positive experiences of the *gacaca* process, they highlighted other aspects of *gacaca*. The specific role the respondent played in *gacaca* seems to define the examples that person chose. Liberated prisoners mostly refer to issues of liberation and the reduction of sanctions; the accused in *gacaca* cite examples of accountability— identifying the guilty and the innocent—and the remaining Hutu population mostly refers to confession-pardon:

Table 5. Most-cited positive/negative aspects of *gacaca*

	Positive		Negative	
	General opinion	*Concrete example*	*General opinion*	*Concrete example*
Tutsi				
Survivor	Reconciliation/Healing/Unity	Confession/Pardon	No truth/Lying/False testimony	No truth/Lying/False testimony
Returnee	Reconciliation /Healing/Unity	Confession/Pardon	No truth/Lying/False testimony	Lack of restitution
All Tutsi	Reconciliation/Healing/Unity	Confession/Pardon	No truth/Lying/False testimony	No truth/Lying/False testimony
Hutu				
Not accused/Prison	Truth	Confession/Pardon	No truth/Lying/False testimony	Partiality/No fair proceedings
Accused	Truth	Accountability/Identification innocent	No truth/Lying/False testimony	Partiality/No fair proceedings
Liberated	Truth	Liberation (prisoners)/Reduction sanctions	No truth/Lying/False testimony	No truth/Lying/False testimony
All Hutu	Truth	Liberation (prisoners)/Reduction sanctions	No truth/Lying/False testimony	Partiality/No fair proceedings
All				
Total	*Truth*	*Liberation (prisoners)/Reduction sanctions*	*No truth/Lying/False testimony*	*Partiality/No fair proceedings*

Source: Life-story survey, 2011 (respondents N = 377), coded open question, multiple responses, general opinion (N = 481), concrete example (N = 447), weighted frequencies.

"My husband was released by *gacaca*."

"I spent ten years in prison without a case file and it was thanks to *gacaca* that I was released."

"The man named . . . who confessed to killing twelve Tutsi during the war apologized and the survivors forgave him."

"In *gacaca* I returned the property I had looted and since then I've been at peace."

"I wasn't imprisoned despite giving false evidence several times; the court didn't take it into account."

Overall, respondents most often cite truth-telling as a positive characteristic of *gacaca*, whereas the liberation of prisoners (the reduction of sanctions) is the underlying theme in the most-cited examples. But although respondents most often referred to truth as a positive characteristic of *gacaca*, they also noted the absence of the truth, the practice of lying, or giving false testimony. After years of research on *gacaca*, including more than two thousand interviews with Rwandans, PRI (2010, 21–29) came to a similar conclusion. People of both ethnicities disagree less on that issue than they do on the positive role of the truth in *gacaca* practice. Those who cite the absence of the truth mostly do so when generalizing about the negative aspects of *gacaca*:

HUTU AND TUTSI

"The lack of truth on the side of people who wanted to hide the crimes they'd committed."

"A few wouldn't say the truth."

"Some wanted to steer clear of the truth."

"There were people who told lies."

"There were many perjuries."

"Some people who knew things refused to provide information regarding the genocide."

"Some criminals wanted to provide false evidence so that innocent people would be imprisoned."

"There was the *ceceka* [keep quiet] phenomenon."

"A Hutu who put another Hutu's name on the defendants list simply because he'd refused to buy him a beer in a *cabaret* [pub]."

But when asked to give concrete examples, Tutsi respondents as well as liberated Hutu, the two most important actors in the *gacaca* process, refer most often to difficulties in establishing the truth in the *gacaca* courts:

"Two female survivors testified in defense of people who had killed their relatives; that was following the corruption of survivors."

"A criminal gave false evidence against a survivor. He said that this survivor, too, had killed people."

"*Gacaca* failed to identify the criminals who killed my husband [or] provide information about where they put his body."

"Forcing people to come up with false testimonies. I did so as well against . . . but then, we told the truth when the national *gacaca* coordination came and he was released."

"False accusation against me, simply to help criminals compensate."

Overall, however, most concrete examples refer to an issue of partiality and unfair proceedings as a negative aspect of *gacaca*:

HUTU AND TUTSI

"[At our Seat] there was *emotion* in the court decisions."

"The jury sided with the survivors."

"[I saw a case where] more than thirty people were imprisoned without an opportunity to defend themselves."

"In a few restitution cases, the houses of poor old mothers were destroyed to pay for the corrugated iron their children had stolen."

Conclusion

Throughout the process, the population seems to have continued its verbal support for the prevailing discourse on *gacaca*, saying that it is popular and equitable justice, it brings unity and reconciliation, and the like. Survey results demonstrate that the population expressed its continuing support for the idea of using the *gacaca* court and its general objectives before, during, and after the actual functioning of the court system (Longman and Rutagengwa 2004, 215–17; Pozen et al. 2014; Republic of Rwanda 2003, 2007a, 2008b, 2010). On the other hand, questions probing actual practice as well as more open-ended or indirect research techniques, such as the life-history approach, revealed an additional dimension to the *gacaca* process once it got underway.

The empirical material corroborates and deepens the findings of the studies I conducted in the initial stages of *gacaca*, at the height of its operation in 2007, and even after the end of the *gacaca* process: a detrimental experience with truth-telling activities and a negative perception of the possibility of establishing the truth in *gacaca*. Respondents seem to have developed a more positive perception of this situation with the passing of time.

In his book on *gacaca*, Phil Clark (2010, 195) asserts, "This view of open truth-telling largely reflects the influence of the traditional institution of *gacaca*." Earlier in his book, most probably based on his ethnographic encounters, he states that popular participation in *gacaca* is "a valuable systemic expression of a Rwandan worldview of human identity as communally embedded and 'truth,' both legal and non-legal, as a negotiated outcome reached via communal discussion in public settings" (164). During hundreds of *gacaca* observations, numerous interviews, and simply participating in Rwandan life, I hardly ever sensed that these things actually captured the essence of what *gacaca* was. Clark's statement, instead, seems to be a confusion of goals and outcomes; that is, a frictional dynamic of truth-telling, lying, silence, and sociopolitical forgetting took a prominent place in the popular experience when the *gacaca* courts became operational nationwide.

Because accusations became more important than confession once *gacaca* got underway, the practice developed a peculiar dimension that its designers did not necessarily envision: an adversarial logic and the experience of widespread false testimony. There is thus mixed evidence regarding the status of the truth in *gacaca*: the interplay of truth, silence, and lies was crucial in the experience of the *gacaca* process.

5

The Weight of
the State

We will put you in prison for some time and you will be liberated to tell us the truth.

Lay judge, Jali, gacaca session on 16 December 2008

Understanding the forces that shaped the *gacaca* practice, animated the almost systemic generation of guilt, and created such frictional experiences with the truth requires some context. Key elements in that context include the nature of the state, the nature of governance practice, and the nature of local government entities in the periphery of Rwandan society.

These factors, along with the identity of local authorities, the particularity of their practices, and their connection with state power under the RPF regime have all been documented recently (Ingelaere 2010b, 2011b; Purdekova 2011a; Sommers 2012, 73–94). Rwanda's ruling party, the RPF, created parallel channels of command and control in the countryside, including certain dimensions of the *gacaca* practice, in order to maintain centralized control over the population. But we need to consider other elements besides government structures and governance practice before we understand how heavily state structures weigh on the lives of Rwandans. This weight is tremendous, and it tacitly structured the nature of participation in the *gacaca* process.

Local Governance in Contemporary Rwanda

The Rwandan government instigated a decentralization policy in 2000 (Republic of Rwanda 2001a), partly in response to an analysis of the 1994 genocide that identified hierarchical state structures, which branched deeply into rural life as catalysts of state-sponsored violence (Republic of Rwanda 1999). Major changes came into effect in 2006. Since then, the main administrative entities are districts, sectors, cells, and *imidugudu*. The focus in this chapter lies with the entities below the district level where the *gacaca* activities were taking place.

Districts coordinate and have financial functions; sectors manage and execute development and service delivery; cells deal with "mobilization" and "sensitization" of the local population. In addition, cells contain "agglomerations" called *imidugudu* (pl.; sing.: *umudugudu*). As mentioned earlier, Rwandan rural households used to be dispersed on the hills but are now increasingly grouped in settlements to facilitate access to basic services such as drinking water and electricity.

Figure 2 provides an overview of these local government entities and personnel between 2006 and 2011 when most of the *gacaca* activities took place. It reveals a difference between appointed and elected officials, that difference being an introduced hierarchy, meaning that only those in appointed positions receive a regular salary from the central/district administration. Field observations make clear that the executive secretaries are the most powerful persons at the sector and cell levels. The appointed "decentralized technicians" who assist the executive secretaries receive salaries as well. Most of these appointed

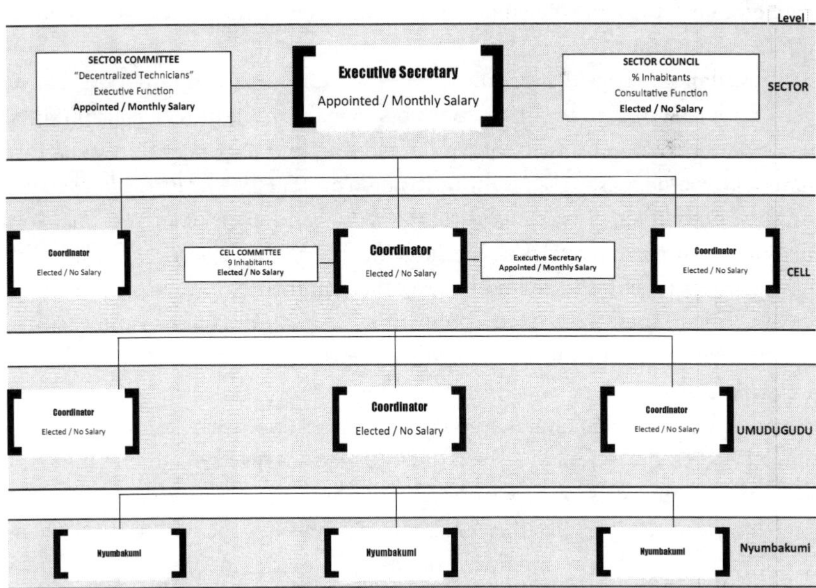

Figure 2. Local government structure between 2006 and 2011

authority figures are educated and dedicated to their tasks. They work professionally and hard, executing policy directives that emanate from the circles that appointed them and pay their salaries, namely higher-level administrative and political entities.

Sector and cell councils or committees of directly or indirectly elected residents complement this government structure. In theory, they are supposed to provide "an important vehicle for the citizens' voice" (Republic of Rwanda 2006b, 2). In practice, however, local elections are not free, and although some popular agency at the local level no doubt exists, the elected officials mostly rubber-stamp the decisions that appointees make (Ingelaere 2011b, 71–73).

The balance between appointed and elected positions has three major consequences. First, appointing people to administrative posts where they have no family or other emotional ties reduces the risks of nepotism and clientelistic politics, namely relationships based on self-interest rather than the public good (Golooba-Mutebi and Booth 2013, 14–15). On the other hand, low-level actors, such as the "heads of *umudugudu*," execute all kinds of administrative tasks without remuneration. In addition, and this brings us to the second consequence of the "design" of this apparatus, the appointed officials' lack of emotional attachment to the areas they supervise means that they are freer to execute unpopular policies and, at times, go against the well-being of the local population. The third consequence of introducing a hierarchical structure of appointed and elected positions is that the main direction of accountability is upward.

Policymakers consider accountability and performance as important norms accompanying decentralization: "Both policymakers and providers [should] be accountable to citizens, who should have strong influence over the availability and quality of services" (Republic of Rwanda 2006c, 9). The Rwandan version of accountability in governance is called *imihigo* and refers to a traditional vow of bravery in the execution of a task (OSSREA 2007, 17–19). Through that vow, authorities commit themselves to other authorities to reach a number of development targets in a given time period. Evaluation exercises and ceremonies regularly measure and announce progress.

This dynamic does not mean that there is no popular agency, a point I return to in chapter 6. This architecture, nonetheless, has constraining dimensions because the executive secretaries and decentralized technicians are appointed and thus cannot be voted out. Moreover, they are accountable to the higher authorities who pay their salaries and thus have the power to fire them if they decide they have underperformed in the execution of their tasks. Even President Paul Kagame has begun to wonder whether the development outcomes that the appointed officials report during *imihigo* evaluations reflect genuine progress on the ground. They seem "too good to be true" (*New Times*, 3 October 2013).

Purdekova (2011a, 482–87) has fleshed out this hierarchy of appointed and elected authorities by stressing the importance of lateral structures. These emanate from the hierarchical backbone when administrators co-opt numerous people into their ranks by giving each of them a little bit of responsibility in a certain domain, for example by having them represent youth or women, or by serving on community policing committees, electoral committees, and the like. As the following interview excerpt shows, being given a task can change a person's relationship with the administrative structures of power. The respondent in this case was a Hutu woman, living in southeastern Rwanda, who became a "companion of pregnant mothers" in her locality:

> I'm very well represented because my husband was released [from prison], my authorities listened to me when I explained about the looting [in *gacaca*], and now they're giving me some administrative duties. Coaching all pregnant women in my village, it means that my authorities take care of me.

She feels incorporated in the authority structures and "very well represented" despite the fact that she also expresses in her life story a sense that these very same structures of power treated her unjustly, especially in the context of the *gacaca* proceedings:

> They started accusing me too in *gacaca*, of many things. They said I'd destroyed their houses for firewood but that's not true. They made me pay for myself and for my husband. . . . A lot of things have changed in my life since 2000, especially because of restitution in *gacaca*. I have given a lot of money to survivors' families who said that my husband had looted their homes or eaten their cows; they were lying and my husband didn't loot anything, but I still paid and I'm still paying now. I started paying back in 2002; I've paid for seven families of survivors. . . . My husband was released but I had to pay a lot of money; I was under a lot of pressure from the authorities. They [the authorities] accuse me a lot and force me to pay a lot of money. I've paid the amount they wanted.[1]

Such incorporation "offers a number of the dispossessed and disempowered just a little authority over the rest" (Purdekova 2011a, 483). People in similar roles survey and assess each other according to their alignment and compliance with the center. In fact, incorporation into the power structure gives other "authority" figures the means to assess those "incorporated" according to the standards of the reigning order. It is a process of *imposing accountability* toward the center.

The nature of governance depicted here results in far-reaching surveillance activity. When a vertical power structure incorporates a sufficient number of people, albeit in a limited way, a spontaneous horizontal dynamic of surveillance is enhanced.[2] This type of surveillance happens not only at the very local level of neighborhoods but also within the administrative ranks. In the wake of the territorial and administrative reforms of 2006, an informant explained the "new" administrative structures to me:

> Four people are part of a committee at the level of the district: the mayor, the executive secretary, and two vice-mayors. In addition, there is the military commander of the region and the head of the police. The way the system works is a bit like the CIA. All are sent to monitor the actions and objectives of the others. These people are busy with those kinds of things while the "technicians" are executing the work in the field. In this way all these people are kept "busy" in the countryside. And after some time they are all replaced.[3]

This quote and the reference to the CIA also suggest the experience of information control that lies beyond the dynamic of ordinary surveillance. Information control has two complementary components: information dispersion and information gathering. The first has to do with sensitization, and the second is simply espionage. Both are instances of intelligence activity, which a contemporary handbook on intelligence defines as "secret, state activity to understand or influence foreign entities" (Warner 2009, 9). I suggest leaving out the word "foreign" in this definition, especially in the Rwandan context. Later I discuss the mechanisms of information dispersion—such as *ingando* and local-level meetings—deployed to foster a "rehearsed consensus." But here, I depict the dynamics of information gathering that lie beyond the surveillance detailed earlier, focusing particularly on how this dynamic interacts with the *gacaca* practice.

An intelligence network operates in the background of the administrative apparatus. Given the secretive nature of the activities such a network undertakes, it is a great challenge to research this network. Entry points are the rare occasions when this background activity manifests itself during fieldwork. What is important here is that one grasps the impact of this background network and understands how it is felt throughout Rwandan society. This invisible dimension shapes speech and action in the visible realm, including the nature of participation in *gacaca*. And indeed, during my years of fieldwork, there were a number of events that underlined the existence of this network.

Near the end of May 2006, I spent a few days in a rural sector in northeastern Rwanda. The objective was, as usual, to understand the *gacaca* practice in that particular community. The atmosphere was tense: a police officer had killed a young man in the local *cachot* (jail) a day or two before our research team arrived. The killing and our arrival happened to coincide, and our presence aroused suspicion with the state officials and security personnel. During conversations with the local population I learned that the young man had been arrested under the pretext of illegally producing *kanyanga* (a strong liquor similar to Uganda Waragi). A number of genocide survivors told us that the murder was ethnically motivated. The young man was Hutu, and the survivors told us that most people of Hutu ethnicity were unwilling to divulge information on the genocide during the *gacaca* process. They suggested that the police officer killed the man because of these circumstances.

Despite the tensions (and partly because of them) I continued doing research. At one point I wanted to organize a group discussion with a number of *inyangamugayo*, the *gacaca* lay judges, on the topic of the local history of the community. The objective was to learn from them the overall dynamics of what had happened during the genocide in their local community and how they experienced the functioning of the *gacaca* activities. As usual, I made sure that there were no "authority" figures in the group. Again I explained the overall research objectives, verified their consent to participate, and explained the modalities of the interview. It took a very long time to explain the nature and objectives of the research, and I noticed that the participants were uneasy. A couple of minutes into the discussion, I asked, "Can you explain what happened here when President Habyarimana's plane was shot down?" I posed the question simply to facilitate the discussion and to introduce a time marker to structure the open-ended debate on the localized genocide dynamics.

Immediately one of the participants stood up and left. A bit later he returned with another man, who simply took a seat in the group. I asked him why we had the honor of him suddenly coming to assist us. He stated that he wanted "to listen in." I told him that it was not possible since I had selected a group of *inyangamugayo* and that he was not part of these *gacaca* judges (I usually used such a technical reason to explain how I selected respondents). Not only was this often a legitimate reason from a purely methodological point of view but, in doing so, I could also generally avoid "authority" figures being present during interviews and at the same time avoid suspicion. He immediately started a litany about the necessity of being there in order to verify whether what was said was in line with the "current policy of the government." When I asked him why he was the one who needed to do so, he explained that he was an "intelligence agent." I told him that if he was a good "intelligence man," he would find out what we were going to talk about without having to be present during the discussion. He seemed taken by surprise and left. During the remainder of the discussion, I talked about topics "in line with the policy of the government" at the time. The day the discussion took place was also the last day we conducted research in that area in that period. The tension and surveillance were simply too intense to continue in that spot at that time.

This example illustrates, first, the tensions on the Rwandan hills with the arrival of the *gacaca* courts. These tensions were visible in the life-story narratives presented in chapter 4. But this example also shows that intelligence agents—generally referred to as *maneco* in Kinyarwanda—are present to check whether things are aligned with government policy. In this case, the agent came to verify whether our "talk" on *gacaca* was aligned with directives from the center, and so it is not difficult to imagine that such verification of alignment also occurred with regard to the nature of Rwandans' participation in *gacaca*. Or, better, awareness of the existence of this intelligence network could have influenced the nature of participation by the ordinary citizenry. Both the dispersal of centralized "authority" through dense layers of administrative structures along with the semihidden surveillance apparatus deeply affected the grassroots transitional justice process of *gacaca*.

"Authority" Animating *Gacaca*?

This insight—that the Rwandan state apparatus has dense layers with both visible and invisible dimensions—leads us to expect that the "weight of the state" on society and the lives of Rwandans is high.[4] To verify this, we need to ask how the weight of the state in Rwandan peasants' lives can be made explicit in a systematic way. The physical presence of authority figures at *gacaca* meetings and the nature of their involvement in the process also needs further scrutiny. The extent to which "authority" is present in the lives and minds of Rwandans also needs verification.

During the initial stages of *gacaca*, in both the information-collection phase (2005–6) and during the start of the trial phase in 2006, the policy was that everybody needed to attend the *gacaca* activities. Local officials ordered security personnel to close shops and schools on the days *gacaca* meetings were held. Sometimes those who failed to be present at the *gacaca* meetings were penalized. For example, after a cell-level *gacaca* session in Jali on 13 February 2007, one of the cell authorities took the floor and addressed the population:

> You are asked to continue to attend the activities of the *gacaca* court. I ask you why you have refused to appear in *gacaca* these last few days. I tell you: appearing in *gacaca* is mandatory for anyone eighteen or older. I take this opportunity to also tell you that we've had a meeting with the people in

charge of security. The decision is that you will be fined for failing to appear in *gacaca*.[5]

In March 2006, during the information-collection stage, the *gacaca* judges fined two men because they had not attended an earlier session.[6] We also noticed at times during that period that state officials took attendance at the meetings. The authorities then might deny service delivery on other matters to those who were absent. These are examples of fines not provided by law, actions that are in violation of the *nulla poena sine lege* (no crime/penalty without law) principle. This effort to force the population to participate in the *gacaca* meetings diminished over time, starting around the middle of 2007. On the one hand, this change happened because of complaints about the forced nature of the participation. On the other hand, the change happened because (starting in 2007) *gacaca* proceedings were held in many locations on various days of the week. It thus became impossible to force attendance or keep track of it. During the judgment phase that began in 2006, in 13.4 percent of the observed trials a state agent was present during the meetings.[7]

Thus, the presence of government personnel was low or greatly diminished during the actual trial phase. Moreover, there is no reason to assume that such a presence automatically influenced the *gacaca* process. In fact, security personnel attend trial proceedings all over the world. We also did not observe systematic attempts to influence the proceedings. Nevertheless, the analysis presented so far suggests that the multilayered presence of authority figures who are mainly accountable to the center is deeply felt in Rwandan society. As a way to analyze the presence of state authority in the lives of Rwandans, I returned to my systematic life-story approach and collected the stories of 377 Rwandans—all peasants—living in different regions of rural Rwanda.[8] I gathered these life stories between February and May 2011 as the second wave of the survey initially conducted in 2007.[9] Life stories contain a combination of factual and interpretative, objective and subjective information. They are also a social commentary. Exploring this "subjective" realm in relation to the "objective" context is paramount if we are to move beyond mere observation of the administrative layout and the presence of state agents.

The following list presents the findings of a simple word-frequency count executed on the entire body of life-story narratives covering the period from 2000 to 2011. The most frequently used word is "land," followed by "children," "authorities," "house," "problem," and "cow." Given the way the authorities functioned, the mere presence of the word "authorities" in these narratives reveals the omnipresence of central power, not only at the local level but also in the consciousness of Rwandans.

1. land	8. *gacaca*	15. female
2. children	9. household	16. neighbors
3. authorities	10. family	17. harvest
4. house	11. money	18. genocide
5. problem	12. prison	19. production
6. cow	13. poverty	20. war[10]
7. health	14. work	

Rwandan peasants mention "children" almost as many times as they refer to "authorities." Ironically, the RPF presents itself as *umuryango*, the "family." Given that almost all local authority figures are RPF members, "RPF authority" appears to have penetrated the intimacy of the household and thus functions as a sort of Freudian *Über-Ich*, animating Rwandan peasants lives as much as land, children, the household, daily problems, and cows. Through the structures and governance practice already identified, authority is present in *all* areas of Rwandan life: education of children, cattle breeding, cultivating, heritage distribution, commercial activities, and the like.

This insight suggests that few Rwandan peasants are "uncaptured" (Hyden 1980) by state authority. Understanding the nature of this "capture" is more complex. For example, ranking word frequencies does not imply any positive or negative evaluation. The words, and thus the issues the words refer to, should simply be considered on their mere presence in the life of the peasantry. Peasants have referred to *gacaca* in a positive, negative, or neutral sense, in the same way that they may call a harvest or production good or bad. And, although the word "problem" often has a negative connotation, its high frequency can be due to both encountering problems as well as solving problems. The same is true for the reference to "authorities." A different analysis is needed to fully explore such multiple connotations; it suffices at this point to conclude that "authority" is one of the most important variables in peasant life. A closer examination of interview and life-story narratives will deepen our understanding of this presence.

To further strengthen the suggested intricate connection between authority or the state (*Leta* in Kinyarwandanized French), the process of reconciliation, and the *gacaca* practice, following are several lengthy excerpts from an interview with a genocide survivor.[11] Albert lives in Runyoni in central Rwanda; although he survived, his children were killed during the genocide. I had a lengthy conversation with him on 21 February 2007, at the height of the *gacaca* process.

Q: What's your opinion about the *gacaca* trial phase?

A: I've just learned about the court decisions, but does a court decision bring a child back? Are they going to give me my brother back? I lost my mother; are they going to bring her back? People will serve community service. That's for the state. I'm a Rwandan myself, but reconciliation with someone who shed blood? How do you make your peace? You watched the court session yesterday. What's the point for the victims?

Q: So the purpose of the *gacaca* isn't reconciliation?

A: You can't patch up when there's blood involved [*ntabwiyungebwo mu maraso*]. As you've seen, there are things happening elsewhere.[12] They haven't changed their bad ways. What I see is that the defendants and their families are even more set against you after their trial.

Q: The *gacaca* actually makes things worse?

A: Many people say that relatives have been imprisoned, but many are released too. The *gacaca* didn't make things worse; these people have always been angry. When you jail someone, they're annoyed. And since you're asking the question yourself, didn't you hear about people taking to their hoe?[13] If it was one of yours, you'd be unhappy too and you'd cry. Killing people only because of their ethnicity!

Q: So, what should be done with people who killed?

A: They did what they did. It's done. Back there, in court sessions, we're forced to relive unhappy times. . . . It was the state that committed the genocide. Now it's the state organizing reconciliation. But when we organize community service, it's for the state. What's done for people who have lost? Nothing. Only revisiting the horrors of the past.

Q: What should the state have done for the victims?

A: As you can see, when someone lost their family, the state should help them rebuild their life. OK, there's support for survivors. But how many survivors actually benefit? My house was destroyed. I rebuilt it myself. Community service? What's in it for us? The state should at least do something for the victims in addition to sentencing convicts to community service for the government. We have to go through what happened all over again.

Q: Has your case been tried yet?

A: Yes, ah, ah, yes! It was in . . . I lost children there. There was a trial; I was asked: "Is there anything you wish to add?" What could I possibly add? There's no compensation for my children. What could I add? My brother was mentioned yesterday, that he was thrown in the toilet hole. I listened to that and I attended, to no avail. I heard that people were bundled together with ropes and then thrown into the river. Or that they were cut up with machetes first. What use could there be in knowing such things?

Q: The authors of those crimes, the killers of your children—what was their sentence?

A: Three children were killed there. But there was no verdict because a suspect raped one of my children. So he'll be tried in an ordinary court. He's been released pending trial. Maybe one day he'll be jailed. There's many people like this. Some deny; others confess. It changes all the time.

Q: Did the truth come out of *gacaca*?

A: Overall, there's no genuine truth. They missed the truth. People say, "I was on the road and I was forced to do this or that." But they all had their own way to be involved at the time.

Q: Has restitution started?

A: Not yet, except if you've asked for restitution of a goat or a cow. In my own case, four cows haven't been returned yet. My little brother and his entire family were killed, and I'm awaiting compensation for that. For two other brothers, I also have to supervise compensation on behalf of their surviving children.

Q: The people who looted are still there; will they compensate?

A: The one who took my cows was in prison before. He asked his wife to sell part of his plot. He was released and now he's disappeared. He fled. I don't know if his wife will compensate. About my little brother, the man who did it is dead. His wife is still there. I don't know if she'll compensate.

Q: Did you first learn what happened to the children in *gacaca*?

A: I learned about it before, back when they were killed.

Q: So it's not good to remember those events?

A: They explained how the children were killed. Why? What's the point? I was asked if there was anything I wanted to add. What could I add? I saw it with my own eyes.

Q: Can you live together again with these people?

A: Even if they come, I won't share anything with them.

Q: What should be done with these people?

A: It's a difficult issue. They could work for me to replace my sons whom they killed. And it's not only me; I'm old but I'm a man. There are old women without children now. What's life for these old mothers?

Q: What's your overall opinion of government action in recent months?

A: About the state, I have nothing to say. The state is organizing reconciliation without consulting us, without consulting the wise men. The state does what it wants. The state decides what needs doing. People implement state decisions and afterwards it's said: "See, it is you who did this [not the state]." The state says "do this" and you applaud. You just saw it here; when the state says "do this," they do it. The *umuganda*, the *gacaca*. If someone comes up with another scheme [plan] in the future, people will do it.

Q: What scheme? If people are told to kill again, they will do it? Despite the experience of the past?

A: People do as they're told [*abantu ni banyamujya iyo bijiye*].

The Weight of the State

Q: Still, people talk about governance and democracy. Isn't it remarkable compared to other regimes?

A: What has changed is that there's security. There's a quiet period. But peace is not a given.

Q: Why?

A: Habyarimana, too, said that there would be peace and reconciliation, but then our children were killed. You sleep at night and if you get up in the morning, it's good [*ni ukubara ubukeye*]. It changes all the time. Everything changes here on Earth. The priest says that things revolve in eternal succession, so . . .

Q: What would it take for the past not to repeat itself? If you were a leader?

A: God himself can't prevent those things. If I was a leader, I could ask people not to do things like that again. But changing people's heart [*umutima*] is difficult. They did bad things.

Q: Have you always thought that it could all happen again or is it something you realized at some point?

A: These things have happened regularly since 1959. The leaders say there's peace. In 1973, for instance. Still, you saw what happened in 1994. How long has it been since 1994 that we can claim that it will never happen again?

Q: If it happens again, where will it start?

A: I don't know where it usually starts. Maybe with the authorities or from abroad.

Q: Where did it start in 1994?

A: In 1994 they claimed it was the attack of the Inkotanyi [RPF]. But were they attacked in 1973 too? The idea of eliminating people had been there for a long time.

The conversation with Albert reveals the experience of an extremely state-driven reconciliation process. Albert is obliged to participate in *gacaca* even though he does not see the benefit for himself; it even complicates his own processing of the violent experiences of the past and his relationships with his neighbors. In addition, his statement reflects an interpretation of the alternation of power in the course of Rwandan history and its repercussions for ordinary people both during the genocide and in its aftermath.[14]

The *Gacaca* Competence in Practice

Looking again at how actual practice shaped the courts' competence, or matters over which they had authority, further illustrates that the working of state power *from within* created an intricate connection between state and society.[15] The court system did not handle some crimes that fell within their mandate, as we read in chapter 3. Why did the *gacaca* process exclude certain crimes in practice? Why did the court system not even debate these crimes? Indeed, Rwandans experienced multiple forms of violence apart from the genocide against the Tutsi: there was a civil war between 1990 and 1994, revenge killings by civilians and the RPA/RPF following the genocide, and an insurgency war between 1995 and 2000 that provoked brutal counter-insurgency tactics. Many civilians, and especially Hutu, died during these violent events. The ruling RPF was responsible for a significant number of these crimes.

The *gacaca* courts did not refer more often to RPA/RPF crimes toward the end of the *gacaca* proceedings and in fact rarely mentioned these crimes.[16] On the contrary, the courts did mention the crimes at the beginning of the *gacaca* process during the so-called information-collection phase. At that point, the population was not yet familiar with the functioning and scope of the modern *gacaca* courts. In at least one case—in a locality that was not systematically observed—an older woman raised this issue in a subtle manner.[17] During an introductory session on the upcoming activities of *gacaca*, someone asked what types of crimes *gacaca* could deal with. One of the local authority figures explained to the audience that only genocide-related offenses could be raised. The area where this happened is situated in the north of Rwanda, in the former province of Byumba, which was particularly affected by the civil war in the period preceding the 1994 genocide. The woman subsequently took the floor and told the authorities present that during the civil war soldiers of the RPA had gathered a number of young men in the area, including her five sons, and said that they were going to hold a meeting. She said that since that moment her sons had not returned, and she wanted to know how long that meeting was going to last. She wanted to get her sons back. It was obvious to the other inhabitants who knew the history of their region and to the authorities as well that the RPA had killed these young men. The woman did not receive a response, but everybody including the authorities grinned on hearing her question. It was clear that people were not supposed to raise such issues during the upcoming *gacaca* proceedings. In theory, *gacaca* could deal with all crimes that happened within the time frame stipulated by law. In practice this was not the case.

Evoking any of these issues during the *gacaca* meetings or venting frustration and discontent regarding the (perceived) partiality of the courts (a common experience, as chap. 4 shows), this practical delimitation of the court's scope turned out to be a dangerous exercise. During the genocide commemoration in a northern sector in 2006, a number of inhabitants were put in prison after asking when justice would come for family members who were lost in the period between October 1990 and April 1994 as well as during the war with the infiltrators after the 1994 genocide.[18] In fact, no one was killed in the sector during the genocide since there were simply no Tutsi inhabitants living there. The *gacaca* process lasted only a couple of days, and two people who had possessed firearms had been put on trial. The sector, however, had been severely affected by two RPA incursions before the genocide and even more during the war with the infiltrators. Many people had died at that time. These issues were not dealt with during the *gacaca* process. When some inhabitants mentioned this issue during the genocide commemoration in April 2006, they were accused of harboring the "genocide ideology" and were subsequently incarcerated.

Such actions and continued zealous attempts at sensitization and reeducation shaped the competence of the *gacaca* courts and other dimensions of the *gacaca* practice. When Danielle de Lame conducted fieldwork in Rwanda in the late 1980s, she noticed that all public gatherings—whether festive religious events, ritualized public drinking activities, or "politico-private" gatherings—"serve to transmit meaning, provide the instruments of memorization, and create consensus" (2005, 303). What she saw as a cultural predilection for consensus was, of course, encouraged and enhanced after the 1994 genocide as part of the massive effort to restore order and maintain security. Sensitization campaigns, commemoration ceremonies, speeches by dignitaries, and reeducation programs—the so-called *ingando* and *itorero*—are intended not only to eradicate "genocide ideology" but also to promote a specific image of Rwanda, a desired representation. *Ingando* is not just about reeducation as much as it is about political indoctrination (Mgbako 2005), social control (Thomson 2011b), and the reproduction of power (Purdekova 2008, 2011b).

Through observation in an *ingando* for demobilized rebels and through analyzing several diaries, which participants had been asked to keep during their various stays in *ingandos* throughout the country, I noticed that a range of strategies gave performative force to the ideas propagated during the teaching sessions that addressed particular topics, such as the modern *gacaca* courts. In the physical setting of the camp, normal activities were suspended and participants had to wear military fatigues that stripped from them the outward manifestations of their individualities. Another strategy was the use of songs. The themes of the songs tacitly underscored some ideas propagated during the reeducation sessions, and the act of singing became a mnemonic device supporting the teaching activities. At night and at the end of every teaching session, the students collectively sang songs, many of which were quite militaristic. As a result, one of the enduring consequences of participation in *ingando* has been the adoption of a sort of self-censorship (*kwibwiriza*). One of these songs indirectly dealt with the *gacaca* by addressing the *gacaca* objectives of unity and reconciliation:

> I will be at the Rwandan frontier with the eyes fixed toward those
>   approaching
> The one transporting the basket of peace, unity, and reconciliation,
> I will show him my smile and will let him pass
> The one presenting himself differently,
> I will stop him and I will force him to change opinion,
> Oh Rwanda, I love you.[19]

The song raises the issue of responses to different opinions, and it implies there are good and bad Rwandans (or even visitors to Rwanda): it seems clear that people with certain opinions are not welcome in Rwanda. The only acceptable opinions are those the *ingando* sessions propagate.

Omnipresent state structures and agents made clear they would permit only the government-produced version of the violent past and regime-condoned understandings of present experiences. The continuous state reactions to the slightest sign of nonconformity made people adopt a similar stance on things, a "rehearsed consensus." I refer to this phenomenon as *Truth-with-a-Capital-T* (see also chap. 9). Many aligned themselves with this type of truth emanating from the center in their reactions toward others and also, often tacitly, in reactions toward themselves. In the course of the *gacaca* process, authority was at work through self-surveillance and self-censorship. This is, however, not solely a Rwandan phenomenon. Foucault (1980, 131) argues that "each society has its regime of 'truth,' its 'general politics' of 'truth': that is, the types of discourse which it accepts and makes function as true; the mechanisms and instances which enable one to distinguish true and false statements, the means by which each is sanctioned; the techniques and procedures accorded value in the acquisition of 'truth'; the status of those who are charged with saying what counts as true."

Because people did not bring up issues such as war crimes and revenge killings *in public* does not mean that they forgot about them.[20] During a private conversation with a number of Hutu men in the north of Rwanda, they shared the following thoughts with me:

(1) We are talking now about the genocide, the genocide against the Tutsi. Don't you hear talking about it on the radio all the time? In that period, there were Tutsi killed and Hutu killed. But on the radio there is only talk of the Tutsi killed, the genocide against the Tutsi. Did you hear talking about a Hutu killed? I don't think so. What is ambiguous is the fact that during *gacaca* reunions one only talks of the Tutsi that were killed.

(2) When you mention that Hutu were killed as well, they reply that the Hutu were killed because of the war. But the Tutsi as well, they were also killed because of the war! When you hear these things, you start doubting: "Are the Hutu not the same human beings as the others?"

(1) They say that Tutsi were killed by the Hutu and the Hutu by the war. So, they started the war. Were there two different wars?[21]

In the south of Rwanda, similar experiences were prominent during the initial stages of the *gacaca* process in 2006:

(1) The *gacaca* is a problem. The survivors have lost the members of their family, but the Hutu also. And in the *gacaca* talk goes only about the genocide survivors. First we had massacres [*itsembatsemba*] from one side. [Later] all lost [family] members.

(2) When the plane [Habyarimana's] crashed, the Hutu rose up, but after the arrival of the Inkotanyi [RPA], we have had reprisals. They also killed. The authorities say only people from one ethnic group were persecuted. The survivors say it as well; they refer to bad governance. . . .

(1) In the *gacaca* it is impossible to recognize that the Hutu have been victims as well. We asked that question but those in charge of *gacaca* don't want to accept. "The Hutu were killed by the children of the Tutsi. It was vengeance because their parents were killed." This is what the *inyangamugayo* say.

(3) They say we can only accept the persons killed because of the massacres [*itsembatsemba*] against the Tutsi.

(1) The problem of the Hutu that were killed does not exist.[22]

After the *gacaca* process came to an end in 2011, these experiences and the frustration and sorrow resulting from the impossibility of mentioning them in the *gacaca* practice were still pronounced. A female inhabitant of Rukoma, an area where many people were killed when the RPF took power, recalled during a life-story interview conducted in 2011:

At the time of *gacaca* I really felt insecure because I remembered the death of my first husband, the father of my three children. Soldiers of the Inkotanyi [the RPA] took him on the road. He was with my three brothers; it was in 1995. The soldiers imprisoned them; the next day we went to look for them at . . . Upon arrival, only one of my three brothers was still alive; the others were already dead, my husband and brothers. During the period of *gacaca*, I did not feel at ease; one did not talk about my folk although they had done nothing wrong during the genocide. They as well, they were killed because of their ethnicity.[23]

In the northern region, where many people died during the war with the infiltrators, the supporters of the regime that had carried out the genocide mounted an insurgency from the neighboring Democratic Republic of Congo (DRC). These activities and retaliation by the RPA, the security forces of the new government, resulted in thousands of deaths. These issues could not be raised during the *gacaca* proceedings, and this experience marks the recollection of participation in *gacaca*.

> During the information collections by the *gacaca* courts, the genocide survivors confused the remains of bodies of their family members with those of bandits and the Hutu victims of the 1994 war. They did not want to believe us when we tried to reveal to them this damning truth and they accused us of adopting Hutu strategies of *ceceka* ["keeping quiet"] or giving false information to protect our criminal brothers. Many unjustified imprisonments followed the distrust of Tutsi that we would be ardent to divulge that information. Such an information was unacceptable to the political authorities as well as the judicial ones, the National Service of the Gacaca Courts [SNJG].[24]

These quotes testify to ideas, experiences, and opinions that exist but which people cannot air openly because the laws on genocide ideology and other reeducation activities heavily shape public narratives. The only individuals I observed challenging this *Truth-with-a-Capital-T* in public and with impunity were those considered mentally ill. In the Rwandan countryside, the mentally ill often continue living in the community; they are not locked away in asylums or clinics. In March 2006 I attended a rather peculiar *gacaca* session in Ntabona and noted it in my field diary:

> The *gacaca* meeting was a sort of final session in the information-collection phase and directed by the *gacaca* coordinator of the area. Contrary to the typical information-collection session that took place at the cell level, this session gathered all inhabitants of the sector. The idea was to clarify some particular issues that posed problems before the actual trial phase would start. I did not really understand, initially, why they were organizing this meeting. Why not simply send the information collected in the respective cells to the sector level and await the trial phase to verify the veracity of that info? Based on the proceedings, however, I learned that the meeting was primarily motivated by the idea that some information had not been divulged. The *gacaca* coordinator clearly directed the proceedings toward the testimony of the genocide survivors. I assumed that they might have alerted the coordinator and the authorities about attempts to leave out certain "facts," dynamics to protect some people. Or maybe they wanted to put their own issues on the agenda as well? In any case, while the *gacaca* coordinator and the local officials directed the meeting, they were assisted by someone with a mental illness. This man (approximately forty years

old) acted as a sort of master of ceremonies and was known to most of the inhabitants. At the start of the meeting he was greeted by many; they called him "*nshuti*," friend. He shook hands with many; people smiled when they saw him. He did not portray the behavior so characteristic of the other inhabitants of the hill, the behavior that typifies most social life and interactions in the Rwandan hills in general. To the contrary, he was outspoken, loud in speech, pronounced in his gestures. He carried a wooden stick that he used to intensify his gestures. At times he used the stick to rhythmically hit the ground or to point in the direction of someone addressed by the *gacaca* coordinator. Nobody attempted to stop him. His behavior and verbal interventions were accepted by all. Actually, given his mental illness and the acceptance of his "deviancy" regarding prevailing norms of conduct, he was able to express what others could not. In addition, his comments created cathartic moments to diffuse and release some of the tension that clearly lurked in the meeting. When he did so, the other attendants would start laughing, clap their hands, or click their tongues. When a female survivor said that she was ready to die to hear what had happened to her children, he said, in astonishment: "What are you saying? You want to die? Why would you? You know we are all going to die one day?" When the *gacaca* coordinator urged people to tell the truth, he said: "Yes, speak. You, Hutu, you have people in prison. Speak, you might be able to get your friends and family released from prison." And when someone was describing the circumstances of a particular crime and invoked the shooting down of President Habyarimana's plane to situate the crime in time, he walked to the center of the meeting ground, waved his stick in the air, and yelled: "Yes, yes, we of the RPF, we shot down Habyarimana's plane." Everybody, including the *gacaca* coordinator and the local officials, laughed loudly.[25]

Conclusion

A dense web of administrative structures, a semihidden network of intelligence agents, and continuous reeducation and sensitization activities mean that Rwandans are continuously monitored and that they also constantly monitor each other and themselves. This apparatus has roots in long-standing practices of authority and state structures. What is most important for our perspective here is that this apparatus was rebuilt and refurnished by the time the judgment phase of the *gacaca* process began nationwide.

This institutional environment penetrates the intimacy of individual consciousness to the extent that it fosters continued self-surveillance and self-censorship. A Rwandan always monitors his or her alignment with directives from the center in all domains of life, including the nature of participation in the *gacaca* process. "Authority" (meaning RPF authority) dominates peasant consciousness and, as a consequence, many align themselves with the reigning regime of Truth, the *Truth-with-a-Capital-T*. State agents' active involvement diminished over time, but the dynamics to increase self-surveillance have been enhanced over the years. State power or authorities did not have to remain actively involved to guide participation in *gacaca* and key elements of the *gacaca* practice, such as its scope. That happened from within.[26]

6

Navigating the Social

Can you bring us four people that can testify in your defense?"

Lay judge, Jali, *gacaca* session on 20 May 2009

The *gacaca* trials were conducted through verbal testimony—confessions, accusations, and witnessing. Throughout the entire *gacaca* period, many people resorted to multiple confessions, which suggests that they considered confessing to be a strategic move. Many also looked at testimony in strategic terms. *Gacacas* were designed to discover objective truth, and according to that benchmark, much testimony was partial or false. Riding the system, score-settling, and the search for profit as well as silence or nonparticipation were widespread. A pragmatic truth, not the objective truth the court designers envisioned, dominated the *gacaca* practice.

Several forces motivated these partial or false testimonies. By observing testimonial practices and gathering contextual knowledge, I began to understand why the dynamics of the *gacaca* activity shifted from confession to accusation, and, finally, to see that "the truth" was not only important to Rwandans practicing *gacaca* but also problematic. In what follows, I use the notion of "effectual truth" to evoke these situations where truth is equated with utility.[1] The "truth" emerging in *gacaca* was defined by the circumstances and the desired outcomes, and those desired outcomes were often different from the court system's stated goal of finding the objective truth on genocide crimes. False and partial testimonies further illustrate how *gacaca*'s design differed from its practice, and they show that the outcomes cannot be fully equated with its objectives.

Overall, the material presented so far suggests that—if we take the "objective truth" or "forensic truth" underlying the court system's design as a benchmark—we can categorize *gacaca* testimonies as sincere, partial, or false, in complex combination. A "sincere testimony" was made by someone who explained everything he or she had done or knew about the past. These people—plaintiffs, defendants, or witnesses—were often grappling with their own consciences and wanted to be reconciled with themselves and, if possible, also with others. "Partial testimonies" were those where people told an aspect of the truth about the past that the general population often already knew. People who gave partial testimonies avoided accusing others not already accused, and they could also keep silent on issues not many others were aware of. In the best-case scenario, those who had decided to make sincere testimonies refuted the partial testimonies. The phenomenon of partially testifying often created a tense atmosphere in the *gacaca* proceedings. Many times, people tried to persuade the sincere testifiers to retract part of their testimony. "False testimonies" were exactly what the name suggests: false. The person testifying simply lied.

A genocide survivor's testimony during a trial in Runyoni illustrates that people sometimes told an aspect of the truth about the past often already known to the general population. When a defendant explained the circumstances of the killing of a male inhabitant of Runyoni in 1994, the survivor replied:[2]

> WITNESS (MALE SURVIVOR): This man is lying. There's no truth in what he's saying. He's telling the truth about what everybody knows because he knows there's no escaping it. Let him tell the truth about what he did or his confession should be rescinded.

In order to understand the dynamics the various types of testimony produced, we need to situate the *gacaca* process in the Rwandan sociocultural universe, one element of which is the notion of *kumenya Kinyarwanda* or "speaking (knowing) Kinyarwanda" (see chap. 2). Since the *gacaca* process hinged on verbal encounters between parties in dispute, it is worth remembering that speaking Kinyarwanda refers not only to the ability to speak the language but also to the use of language, to mastering the codes of communicating (Nkusi 1987, 85). This entails knowing when to speak, when not to speak, how to speak, and what to speak.[3] Related to these Rwandan ethics of communication is the notion of *ubwenge*. *Ubwenge* can be considered an essential form in the local social imaginary. The elementary forms of the social imaginary define—in a tacit fashion—how things go on between people and the expectations people have of each other (C. Taylor 2004, 23). I return to this Rwandan social imaginary in chapter 8.

Ubwenge is a complex notion incorporating a range of elements. In the broadest sense, it refers to intelligence/knowledge that results in self-controlled public acts. But it also refers to elements of wisdom and trickery, caution, cleverness, and prudence. It is the capacity to gain a clear understanding of situations and the capability to surround oneself with a network of profit-generating social relations.

This long-standing practice still has force in contemporary Rwanda. Johan Pottier (1989, 475) documented how the nature of communication, including silence, highlights existing social hierarchies in the context of a development intervention in the 1980s. The following excerpt from an interview with a prisoner accused of participation in the genocide illustrates the horizontal dynamics of *ubwenge* in the context of *gacaca*. It shows how people navigated the space of *gacaca* in order to achieve a preferred outcome for themselves and not necessarily the outcome the designers of the court system envisioned.

The accused appeared as a free man before the *gacaca* court in his village, as did another man accused of similar offenses. The court acquitted the other man but sentenced the first one to a year of incarceration. Having observed their trial, I went to visit him in prison to find out why he had been convicted and the other defendant acquitted, given that he was apparently convinced that the second man was guilty as well. His statements touch on the complex connection between intelligence, "truth"-telling, lying, and forging alliances. It is a phenomenon related to the localized setting of the *gacaca* tribunals, but it is also a consequence of the specific nature of communication in Rwanda.

> Q: During your trial, there was also another man who was acquitted although he had been in attacking groups [chasing persons during the genocide]. What is the difference between you and him?
>
> A: Even when he has been declared innocent, he is not innocent before God, maybe in front of human beings.
>
> . . .
>
> Q: But why did you receive a prison sentence and the other man was acquitted?
>
> A: It depends on the approach [of the trial], the intelligence [*ubwenge*]. I could have received a sentence much higher than one year. I looked for people that could give testimonies in my favor. He has done the same. It depends upon the relations. One can ask someone to come and testify in favor of your innocence but even better is to approach the victims.
>
> Q: So you give them something?

A: It varies according to the type of relationship; you share something with
them in order to make them participate in the debate.

Q: Even if what they come to say is not true?

A: Well, the idea is to diminish the sentence, even if it means deflecting the
"truth." The people you try to persuade in your favor try to direct the
trial, even if it means bending the "truth."

. . .

Q: So for that other man that was acquitted, did part of the "truth" related
to his case not surface?

A: The "truth" between Rwandans is something that is not close [not easily
forthcoming]. It is far. No matter what situation you are confronted
with: if you end up in the judicial services, on the level of the ordinary
justice system, for the unity and reconciliation between families, even
within households, there is no "truth."

Q: Why?

A: Between Rwandans, before there can be "truth"? A Rwandan being satisfied with another Rwandan: impossible, and therefore you bend the
"truth" in order to defend your own interests.

Q: So for the case of the person that was tried together with you, has the
"truth" been spoken or not?

A: Difficult question. I'll think about it. [*Silence.*] . . . Ok, he, it is a person
that participated [in the genocide], I am absolutely sure. . . .[4]

This example illustrates that communications—confessions, accusations, and
witnessing in general in the context of *gacaca*—often depended on their use-
fulness. *Ubwenge* speaks to the notion of "maneuvering," as Michael D. Jackson
defined it (Jackson 1998, 26), namely as the ways "in which persons vie and
strategize in order to avoid nullification" in the complex sociopolitical environment of the Rwandan hills. Many *gacaca* participants practiced *ubwenge* in
order to reach the most optimal outcome in the given circumstances.

Score-Settling

Many issues could prompt participants to use *ubwenge* as they
navigated the *gacaca* system. For instance, conflicts prevalent in the community
influenced many trials and required a particular way of navigating the social
environment. The *gacaca* courts frequently settled two types of such conflicts.
On the one hand, inhabitants or even family members might have conflicts
that had no, or hardly any, relation to the genocide but were instead contemporary or long-standing. The courts took on such conflicts under the guise of
allegations of participation in the genocide. On the other hand, people tended

to try to settle conflicts through the *gacaca* process, conflicts that had emerged because of the *gacaca* process or—in the broadest sense—the postgenocide justice process. These "meta-conflicts," as I call them (Ingelaere 2011a), motivated accusatory practices in their turn.

Consider the following case, which I observed in Jali.[5] The case was in itself somewhat peculiar and attracted wide attention in the community since it also involved corrupted lay judges. A Hutu woman was standing trial for having been involved in the persecution and killing of a Tutsi woman. Both women had the same husband. The trial was unusual in that the Tutsi woman was not killed during the genocide but during the so-called war of the infiltrators in 1997 (which falls outside the scope of the *gacaca* courts). Since his marriage with his second wife, the Tutsi woman, the relationship between the husband and his first wife, the Hutu woman, had deteriorated. The man had seven children with each of the women. The husband accused his first wife of having befriended Hutu rebels, who had infiltrated the region in the second half of the 1990s, and asking them to kill her rival, the Tutsi woman. In the first trial, the Hutu woman was convicted. On appeal, and after the SNJG intervened and explained that the *gacaca* courts were not supposed to deal with such crimes, the narrative changed: the husband as well as other witnesses testified that the Hutu woman had already attempted to kill the Tutsi woman during the genocide but had failed to do so. Based on these allegations, she was sentenced to nineteen years in prison. In the meantime, two of the judges approached one of the children of the Hutu woman and suggested that the children pay RWF 400,000 (US$720) in exchange for a favorable judgment.[6] The children actually paid, but they also reported the corruption case to the police. The judges were caught in the act and imprisoned.

Because the Tutsi woman was killed in 1997, the *gacaca* courts should not have dealt with the case in the first place. The attempt to refocus the case on appeal to persecution during the genocide was a clear attempt to settle a domestic problem between the husband and his first wife under the guise of a genocide crime. This was especially obvious once the appeal trial revealed that during the genocide, the Hutu woman was living in Jali, while the Tutsi woman was living in Kigali. The testimony of killers sent from Jali to Kigali—which was not referred to during the first trial—was rather unconvincing and only thinly concealed the actual conflict.

A trial in Ntabona exemplifies attempts to settle conflicts emerging from the postgenocide justice process.[7] Indeed, the *gacaca* fueled conflicts in the population, and those conflicts reentered the *gacaca* arena under the guise of accusations of participation in the genocide. A freed prisoner explained that people in prison would sometimes falsely accuse those who had played a role in their imprisonment. In other words, those who had given evidence regarding the involvement of others in the genocide would be accused in turn as a sort of revenge.

> WITNESS (MALE RELEASED PRISONER) MUGABONAKE: In prison, we tried to accuse Mathieu and Rekeraho because they, too, had us put in prison. [*Laughs from the audience.*]

Gacaca created constant feedback loops that informed the nature of participation. Initially, *gacaca* unsettled and threatened Rwanda society, as we saw in chapter 4. Participants had to navigate a complicated, ever-changing environment. Social navigation "highlights motion within motion; it is the act of moving in an environment that is wavering and unsettled. . . . We move in social environments of actors and actants, individuals and institutions, that engage and move as we move along" (Vigh 2009, 420). In Runyoni, for example, a defendant even suggested during a trial that he might have falsely accused someone and that his accuser was getting even with him:[8]

> INTERVENTION BY BANYARWANDA (DEFENDANT): What I see is that it's some kind of revenge because I personally testified against him. But it doesn't matter, it's tit for tat.

Trials fueled by underlying conflicts were thus actually about something other than trying to find the truth about what actually happened in 1994. This situation was a source of distress for genocide survivors who, although they were not involved in the intrigues, were eager to find information about their deceased loved ones. A genocide survivor suggested to the *gacaca* judges in Runyoni that they punish one of the other genocide survivors:[9]

> WITNESS (FEMALE SURVIVOR): Mukakimenyi and everyone behaving that way should be punished: she knows very well that she lost people during the genocide and when it's about her people, she's given every opportunity to make her case, but when it's about our people [she refers to her family members], she sides with our executioners to prevent the trial from running smoothly. It's time she was punished because the local *inyangamugayo* don't dare touch her although she routinely does this.

With the *gacaca* process gaining momentum, it became clear to all the participants involved that underlying conflicts in the population were actually informing many of the proceedings. Participants made remarks revealing such an awareness during numerous trials. For example, on 1 November 2007 during a trial at the cell level in Runyoni, the president of the court asked the following question of the defendant:[10]

Navigating the Social

PRESIDENT: And what if you're exposed as having had any part in this?

DEFENDANT SIMBIZI: If another witness says no, apart from Mr. Banyarwanda, who could be seeking revenge because I accused him of looting in two different places, I'll admit it.

During the same trial another defendant also remarked that there were multiple testimonies *à charge* necessary before he could accept his guilt:[11]

PRESIDENT: Can you tell what your part was in looting Buhangwa's place?

DEFENDANT RWAGAPFIZI: I was never at Buhangwa's and I didn't loot anything there.

PRESIDENT: And if a witness can be found to testify against you?

DEFENDANT RWAGAPFIZI: If one can find at least four witnesses testifying against me, I'll have to admit it too.

[*Laughs from the inyangamugayo.*]

During another session of the same trial, a different defendant on trial for pillaging of belongings expressed a similar concern regarding people who testify with specific intentions:

DEFENDANT UWIMANA: These people are lying; I never wore these clothes.

PRESIDENT: And if we manage to establish that you lied to the court?

DEFENDANT UWIMANA: Except if people who hate me testify, if I'm guilty, I should be punished under the law.

In cases like these, defendants asked to have multiple witnesses *à charge* because they believed that while a person with a particular grudge against them might resort to false accusations, it would be hard to gather so many witnesses for such a project. Fear of being condemned based on the testimony of one individual was widespread, especially since it could mean that a score was being settled. In Jali, for example, a trial around which there were rumors of a conflict between the defendant and the sole accuser provoked serious discontent and discomfort in the local population. After the defendant was convicted, the population speculated that the judges had been unwilling or unable to identify the underlying conflicts and take them into account during their deliberations.[12]

Although the public had a general awareness that underlying conflicts often permeated trials, we did not observe systematic attempts by the judges to identify these conflicts. Occasionally, however, they did. In Ntabona, the judges were aware that defendants might organize themselves, potentially together with witnesses, in order to falsely accuse others. At times they tried to identify these practices, as the following example illustrates:[13]

<blockquote>
PRESIDENT: Aren't there other people who helped you have these people wrongfully condemned?

DEFENDANT RENZAHO: We lied about them. Rekeraho came to help from where the children were hiding; he did not go with us to the river.

PRESIDENT: The people you're trying to clear now, other people are accusing them. So, wasn't there a meeting to agree how to have them wrongfully condemned?

DEFENDANT RENZAHO: There was no meeting; I accused Rekeraho of being there; about Munyaneza, I heard from others; Gasamagera and Kanyabyoba are my witnesses; about Habarurema, I lied. I apologize and I have nothing to add.
</blockquote>

In Runyoni, on one occasion the judges inquired as to whether and why the defendant distrusted one or several of the witnesses:[14]

<blockquote>
PRESIDENT: And if we find that you're trying to confuse the court and this audience, what will happen?

DEFENDANT ZIKAMABAHARI: If two or four witnesses come forward and confirm the charges, I'll admit.

PRESIDENT: Who among the witnesses can't you trust?

DEFENDANT ZIKAMABAHARI: There's Fidèle Samputu, who testified against me at sector level; I can't reach an agreement with him. These very people were there: Banyarwanda, Ndahayo, Rutaboba, Bizimana.

PRESIDENT: Do you have a problem with Samputu?

DEFENDANT ZIKAMABAHARI: Yes, we had a dispute over some land before the war.
</blockquote>

And so the lack of trust was based on a conflict between the defendant and one of the accusers. Participants dragged land problems in particular into the *gacaca* process with the objective of settling them under the guise of a genocide crime. More than anything else, land animates peasant life (see chap. 5). In Jali, a defendant explained to the judges that they should consider the fact that the primary and, actually, sole witness giving testimony *à charge* in his case was someone he had had a serious dispute with over land in 1989.[15] The dispute had passed all the judicial echelons up to the Tribunal of First Instance in the provincial town nearby. At the time of the *gacaca* court session, the dispute had already been settled in favor of the defendant on trial. In that particular case, the *gacaca* judges acquitted the man on trial, taking into consideration the underlying conflict with the accuser.

During an appeal trial in Rukoma, the female defendant declared that she had lodged an appeal because she was convicted based on the testimony of someone "who was not her friend for a long time," as the following exchange between her and the judges revealed:

Inyangamugayo: Why did you appeal your sentence?

DEFENDANT KAMPIRE: She accused me of looting her wrap but then she changed her story and said they were clothes.[16] The woman from whom I bought this wrap is here. The woman who accuses me hasn't been my friend in a long time.

Not being someone's friend is, of course, a euphemism for being someone's enemy. At times, the judges even asked questions about the nature of the actual actions that had taken place between people on trial in order to gain an insight into the nature of their testimonies during the *gacaca* session. An example from a trial observed in Jali is revealing in that respect.[17]

Inyangamugayo: Is Maringo your neighbor?

DEFENDANT: Yes.

Inyangamugayo: Do you invite each other over when you have something to drink?

DEFENDANT: Yes, I invite him and he invites me too; I have witnesses to that.

Inviting someone to share beer is a strong token of well-established and friendly relationships between people in the Rwandan sociocultural universe, especially in the countryside. Hence, the judges put this question to verify whether the testimony could be trusted.

The Search for Economic Profit

Cases (sometimes even courts) where *inyangamugayo* were systematically involved in corruption were commonly referred to as the *mutuelle*. This word refers to a system of health insurance (*mutuelle de santé*), which is compulsory in Rwanda. People need to contribute an amount of money every year to gain access to treatment in health centers and hospitals at reduced cost. Similarly, especially near the end of the *gacaca* process and at the cell-level courts dealing with property offenses, it became common knowledge that one had to contribute to the *mutuelle de gacaca* by "giving something" to the judges. That way, one would receive favorable treatment during the proceedings, and false testimony would be more easily accepted.

Especially during trials taking place at the cell level and dealing with property offenses, defendants often attempted to implicate others not involved in the crime under investigation by using false testimony. Restitution was a collective effort: all the people involved in the looting or destruction of property needed to compensate part of the total value. It was thus in the interest of the actual perpetrators to have many others found guilty of the same crime in order to reduce their own share of the restitution.

This practice can be considered a sort of "search for profit" in the negative sense of the word, namely by diminishing costs. More typical of these searches for profit were cases where someone falsely testified because money was given to him or her, or other deals were made within the population. The *inyangamugayo* were not involved in this form of corruption, but it could have had many sources and taken various forms.

Another manifestation of the search for profit were cases where genocide survivors provided incorrect and excessive estimates of the goods pillaged or destroyed. They did so with the objective of receiving more compensation than they were entitled to. We observed this especially near the end of the *gacaca* process. In Jali, for example, a case dealing with the pillaging of goods went to appeal near the end of 2009.[18] The defendant's wife had lodged the appeal. Her husband had been convicted for his involvement in genocide crimes at the sector level, crimes to which he had confessed before dying in prison. Since his death, and six months before the cell-level trial dealing with the property offenses, he was suddenly accused of having pillaged goods worth the excessive amount of RWF 61,940,000 (USD 111,604). As his wife explained during the appeal trial, her husband had never been accused of pillaging until after his death. Only near the end of the *gacaca* process, and with her husband deceased, did these claims surface. It was clear to most of the inhabitants of the community that these allegations were an attempt for quick gain because the defendant's family was quite wealthy. The judges also believed that the allegations were based on motives other than seeking justice, and they acquitted the defendant and his family. The judges did not punish the accusers for perjury.

In several other cases dealing with pillaged belongings, we observed that people were obliged to pay a second time for goods pillaged or destroyed. It was common practice to organize restitution in the years following the genocide, sometimes by using *gacaca* meetings for this purpose, sometimes under the supervision of local state agents, and sometimes in simple agreement between victim and perpetrator (see chap. 1). At times, the *gacaca* sessions dealing with property crimes at the cell level would refer to these previous actions and explain that restitution had already taken place. The victims occasionally acknowledged that fact even when no written documents could be produced as proof. In most cases, however, written proof was required if the victim denied that restitution had already taken place. Such proof could not always be provided:[19]

PRESIDENT: . . . You, victim Muligo, can you tell us what your problem is with Kijyambere [defendant]?

Navigating the Social

VICTIM MULIGO: I didn't reach an agreement with him, but he should tell us who else [was] with him.

DEFENDANT ISIRAHINZE (KIJYAMBERE): Honestly, I returned a window to him and it was in September 1994, but he didn't give me a receipt because it was at the time of the *abakada* so I gave him a window and RWF 2,000 without a receipt, and it was Mr. Muligo himself who came to my home to ask.[20]

PRESIDENT: Can you provide any tangible documentary evidence supporting this?

DEFENDANT ISIRAHINZE (KIJYAMBERE): At the time, we didn't draw up a receipt.

INTERVENTION (MALE SURVIVOR): No, this defendant is lying because at the time, looted property was handed over to the police here at the office and submitted to the *abakada*.

INTERVENTION (FEMALE NO-SURVIVOR/NO PRISON): I know this Muligo [victim]; immediately after the war, he visited all districts, going from house to house, loading up all the property that was in the districts, and he was alone and he took it all to Kigali.

INTERVENTION (IMPRISONED MALE): Can this Kijyambere [defendant] tell us if anyone was present at the time of restitution?

INTERVENTION (MALE NO-SURVIVOR/NO PRISON): At my place, the house was full of capital goods but this Muligo [victim] came and loaded all my property in a vehicle and there's nothing left.

PRESIDENT: Is there anyone here who was a *responsable* [local official at cell level] at that time?

INTERVENTION BY KARENGERA (FORMER *responsable*): I went with Muligo [victim] to Gahima's and Ndahiro's to recover property, except that he didn't give any receipts, but he told the authorities.

In this example, it is difficult to discern who is actually lying and thus searching for profit. It is true that written documentation of restitution was scarcely ever provided in the immediate wake of the genocide. Conversely, a person accused of pillaging might have been tempted to claim that they had indeed compensated the victim in the past and thus hide behind the fact that no written documents existed. In this case, however, at least some witnesses testified that there was no written documentation and, moreover, that the victim was himself somehow involved in pillaging others after the genocide. Despite this "evidence," the judges found the defendant guilty and ordered him to pay RWF 36,000 for his part in the restitution.

Similarly, genocide survivors were at times tempted to accuse people other than the ones who had pillaged them during the genocide. They did so to make sure they would actually receive restitution. In Runyoni, for instance, it was an open secret that a male genocide survivor had accused people who were not involved in the pillaging of his shop.[21] During the genocide, one of the Interahamwe leaders had forced open the door of the shop and subsequently instructed some street children and vagabonds to loot the property. Since the latter were unknown to the community and in any case not present at the *gacaca* process, the genocide survivor decided to accuse others who were still living in the community and had sufficient means to compensate him. The court accepted the accusations and sentenced a number of inhabitants.

The search for profit was also evident in certain cases referred to as "buying hills" (*kugura imisozi*), a popular expression. This figurative phrase referred to a tactic that those already accused in *gacaca* adopted if they were willing to accept responsibility for all or many of the crimes committed in a certain locality (hill) even though they had been involved in only some of them. The accused person received money, livestock, cattle, or other valuables in return for accepting all the blame and the punishment that went with it. The person who provided the goods did so in an attempt to avoid being sentenced, and he or she was the one people referred to as "buying the hill." This meant that the person was buying a favorable judgment by influencing the inhabitants of a particular hill. In Runyoni, it was rumored that a certain Niyonzima had "bought the hill."[22] Niyonzima, a wealthy merchant living in Kigali, was accused of being an accomplice to the rape of a woman. The woman had initially testified that she had been raped by several men, including Niyonzima. During the trial, one of the defendants confessed to being the sole perpetrator. Nobody raised the involvement of anyone else, including Niyonzima.

Nonparticipation and Silence

Participation in *gacaca* was rather low (see chap. 3), and the most obvious reason is that probably only a limited number of inhabitants were aware of the issues particular trials were dealing with. Nevertheless, local residents could have been present or could have made "neutral" interventions during the trial, but there must have been other reasons as well. For example, many local people were not concerned with the *gacaca* process in the first place. They considered it to be an issue of the main actors: the accused, the victims, and the judges. If they were actually present during a trial, they were simply physically present without necessarily intervening. Three other reasons explain low levels of attendance in the *gacaca* process: unwillingness to "denounce one's own blood," fear, and, finally, disappointment. These latter reasons can be considered as strategic as well.

An important reason for limited involvement in the *gacaca* process was not wanting to "denounce one's own blood." This was generally manifested through expressions such as "keeping quiet" (*ceceka*), "not touching oneself in the stomach" (*kutimena inda*), or "not denouncing oneself" (*kutivamo*). In these cases, these people did indeed have information on the cases the *gacaca* courts were investigating but preferred not to divulge it. There was thus no false testimony, there was simply *no* testimony. "One's own blood" can mean many things: it can refer to household or family relations but, equally, ethnic belonging. Some people opted not to testify against members of their family but did testify against others with whom they had no family relations, even though they belonged to the same ethnic category (in most cases Hutu). This could be the case for (Tutsi) survivors as well. Some survivors did not want to testify against people (Hutu) on trial who belonged to their extended families. Sometimes the refusal to testify was simply based on ethnic belonging: a Hutu does not testify against a Hutu.

All of these refusals were not necessarily the result of the intrinsic valuation of household, family, or ethnic affiliation. On the contrary, they often happened for one very pragmatic reason: the person was afraid of the (social) consequences that might follow the denunciation of a relative (in the broadest sense of the word). This is fully in line with how social navigation is conceptualized: "we act, adjust and attune our strategies and tactics in relation to the way we experience and imagine and anticipate the movement and influence of social forces" (Vigh 2009, 420).

Chapter 4 portrayed some of the security concerns people raised on both sides of the ethnic divide. It can be detrimental for one's economic and social existence when trouble arises in relationships with the those who are an essential part of and support one's existence. In Jali, a woman decided to reveal the truth only after she had been put in prison for three months for refusing to testify. When the judges asked her why it took so long for her to testify, she replied that she did not want to denounce her neighbors:[23]

> *Inyangamugayo*: Why did you not identify these accused the moment we were looking for that information during the information collection at the cell level?
>
> WITNESS (FEMALE NONSURVIVOR/NO PRISON): One tells the truth; one accuses one another when the time has come. During the cell proceedings [information collection] I stayed silent because I did not want to betray my neighbors.

Another reason why the general public made little effort to attend and participate in the *gacaca* proceedings was fear of what might happen after providing testimony or after the end of the *gacaca* process. In certain localities it was common practice to put someone who had provided testimony on the list of those suspected of participation in the genocide. The judges reasoned that providing information on a particular crime implied involvement in that crime or, in the broadest sense, the genocide.

For example, by the end of the *gacaca* process in Jali, the whereabouts of the bodies of several victims were still unidentified.[24] It was an open secret in the community that at least some knew where the bodies were buried. No one wanted to provide information on where those bodies had been thrown, despite attempts by *inyangamugayo* and local officials to make people speak up. Entire neighborhoods were put on trial and punished in an attempt to find the truth.[25] Nobody spoke—not because no one knew but simply because they were afraid that if they testified about the burial sites, they would be accused of having had something to do with the killings. The strategy that the judges and the local officials adopted in 2011, after *gacaca* had come to an end in Jali, showed that it was generally known that people could testify but did not want to. The officials suggested to the population that they go at night and place bamboo sticks on the spots where the bodies were located. If they did so, the bodies could be recovered without anyone revealing they were aware of these locations.

Another reason people were reluctant to provide testimony in the *gacaca* proceedings was fear that *in the long run* it might turn out to be detrimental, either to the person giving the testimony or the people it might involve. In the minds of many—it is difficult to assess—the general policy of the regime could suddenly change or the regime itself could change. For example, the interview with Albert, the genocide survivor living in Runyoni (quoted in chap. 5), revealed his uneasiness with state policies and his suspicion regarding the promise of long-term stability.

A final reason for limited involvement was disinterest, disappointment, and frustration. Some Hutu were disappointed by the excessive and violent reaction of the regime after the genocide, when people were killed in an extrajudicial manner or arbitrarily put in prison. They considered the *gacaca* courts as a continuation of this policy. Also, the *gacaca* courts did not deal with killings by Tutsi civilians and the RPA (see chaps. 3 and 5). And that action discouraged some from participating in *gacaca* because they had no stake in doing so: they could not find any justice for themselves or their losses. Or, as we saw in chapter 4, they simply considered the *gacaca* system to be a form of institutionalized injustice because it did not deal with these crimes.

Among survivors there was also a degree of nonparticipation. While some survivors may have decided not to participate in the *gacaca* proceedings to avoid the trauma of bad memories, some may also have been disappointed but for different reasons. Other survivors loathed the leniency of the *gacaca* system and considered the punishments as a sort of amnesty. Because the government had already pardoned the perpetrators who had confessed, those survivors did not consider it useful to testify against others or against those who would be pardoned soon and, in any case, might return home at short notice. The story of Sévérine is a case in point (see chap. 4): Sévérine decided to abandon some claims in *gacaca* so as not to further complicate the social relationships on her hill. For some survivors, testifying against a defendant was useless because it was not going to bring back their loved ones, it was not going to bring them any material compensation for their loss, and it might even generate bad relationships with the accused and their families with whom they had to live on a daily basis.

Conclusion

In the *gacaca* process, Rwandans were not simply renegotiating imposed categories of ethnicity, guilt, innocence, and the like, and neither were they solely seeking justice and truth as generally conceived of in the transitional justice paradigm.[26] Local testimonial practices, including silence, reveal that communication—designed to be forensic truth-telling in *gacaca*—was to a great extent used to serve other goals than finding justice for crimes of genocide. The actual *gacaca* practice reveals something similar to what Sally Falk Moore discovered when studying the act of witnessing in Tanzanian courts during the colonial era: "Witnesses often testify (or fail to appear) with the idea of helping to construct a story favorable to the person to whom they owe a partisan account, either because of kin relationship, or for favors done in the past, for favors anticipated, for fear of displeasing, or the like" (1992, 38).

The field of transitional justice generally does not equate truth with utility or recognize *effectual truth*. But *gacaca* testimonial practices reveal that consequential ethics dominated that process. Not only the strategic use of the confession procedure but also the widespread existence of score-settling, search for economic gain, and other (so-called) vices characterized the *gacaca* activities in the Rwandan hills to an important extent.[27] The practices here echo Machiavelli's ([1532] 1998, 61) advice to rulers that vices can be virtues:

> And furthermore one should not care about incurring the fame [i.e., infamy] of those vices without which it is difficult to save one's state; for if one considers everything well, one will find something appears to be virtue, which if pursued would be one's ruin, and something else appears to be vice, which if pursued results in one's security and well-being.

The nature of participation in the *gacaca* process was shaped by these motivations and particular localized circumstances (as chap. 7 demonstrates), at least until *gacaca* participants reached the limits of maneuverability due to the weight of the state itself shaping autonomous power in a certain direction (chap. 5). And in fact, this vertical shaping also influenced the nature of the testimonial activity similar to the horizontal dynamics described earlier in this chapter. People aligned their practices of finding justice and truth-telling with the understandings of these notions propagated in the center of society. It was in their interest to do so. The resulting truth is more of the pragmatic type: it is that which is useful in the given circumstances.

A Thousand Hills,
a Thousand *Gacacas*

Did your wife ask you to kill her because she was Tutsi?

Lay judge, Ntabona, *gacaca* session on 15 July 2006

Alignment with the center does not exclude autonomous dynamics in the periphery. And these types of social activities are more than simply reactions to the "weight of the state," as some analyses of social dynamics in rural Rwanda tend to suggest (Ansoms 2009, 193–212; Thomson 2013).[1] Indeed, although the state and authority shape life to a great extent, Rwandans are not machines who execute a plan designed in the center, and neither do they (always) (un)consciously resist such plans. There is always "a sense of agency in the face of disempowering circumstances" (Jackson 2002, 15). Autonomous dynamics emerged in the space of the *gacaca* process. Chapter 6 on social navigation demonstrated that the self-governance Rwandans exercised by practicing *gacaca* was close to *virtù*, in the Machiavellian sense, in which basic survival and the increase of well-being in the short and long run dominated.

In fact, although undisputable trends emerged in the systematic analysis of trials throughout the sites under observation, variation in the nature of the proceedings among research sites was one of these trends. "Navigating the social" did not depend only on the individual choices of the litigants; the localized and historical social constellation of the community also shaped such endeavors. Socially navigating the *gacaca* process was influenced not only by feedback loops and assessment of future well-being; it was also contingent on past experiences and events that had carved out specific trajectories in particular places. Throughout the country, the unfolding of the *gacaca* practice was dependent on these very particular community characteristics and histories. This chapter juxtaposes the *gacaca* dynamics in their sociohistorical context in two of the research sites: Rukoma and Ntabona.

Rukoma

Rukoma is an isolated hill (or sector) in southeast Rwanda, surrounded by marshes and near the border with the former provinces of Kibungo and Kigali-Ngali. Before the construction of the tar road through Bugesera, it took approximately five hours by car to go from Kigali to Rukoma. After the social revolution of 1959, the Tutsi living in other parts of Rwanda—mostly Gitarama and Gikongoro—were deported to this area known for its harsh environment. They were settled in a smallholders' collective farm called a *paysannat*, which the government had constructed in the 1960s. At the time, the hill's only inhabitants were a few Hutu families. The assassination of President Habyarimana in 1994 caused panic in Rukoma, and both Hutu and Tutsi families assembled in the central square. There was an attack from a neighboring hill, and Hutu and Tutsi inhabitants fought together to repel it. Three days later, a member of Parliament who was born in the region and who was also a Protestant minister with connections at the highest level of government explained that "it was an ethnic war." He told the Hutu they must stand aside from the Tutsi or they would be killed too. Most followed those orders.

Mostly young men, members of the Interahamwe militia, assaulted Tutsi with traditional weapons such as machetes and spears even though they were still assembled in public places, including schools and churches. Some of their Hutu neighbors—who defended the Tutsi at first—either stood and watched or joined the aggressors after they were *sensitized* ("encouraged") to take an active part, but other Hutu refused to separate from the Tutsi. There were rumors that the Tutsi had killed the president; the Tutsi then fought the attacks also using traditional weapons. Rukoma was known for its large Tutsi population, and this attracted attackers from neighboring sectors for several days. A large group of Hutu refugees from Burundi also raided the hill to kill, steal, and rape, and they encouraged others to emulate them. These Hutu lived in a nearby camp, having fled Burundi in 1993 after that country's first elected Hutu president was killed, which caused violent outbursts.[2] Later, Interahamwe militia groups arrived, accompanied by soldiers who were ferried to the area in buses and jeeps. The militia and soldiers carried modern weapons, which broke the resistance of the Tutsi. Finally, a boat carrying groups of attackers crossed the nearby lake en route to the hill. It is worth noting that the attackers left the area at night and came back in the morning, which allowed the persecuted Tutsi to leave their hideouts at night to look for food in empty fields.

In less than a month, 12,758 Tutsi inhabitants were killed.[3] On 5 May 2004 Rwandan Patriotic Army (RPA) soldiers arrived in the area and put an end to the genocide against the Tutsi: the Burundians went back to Burundi, and the soldiers who belonged to the regular Rwandan army also left the region. All Hutu inhabitants fled, either to the marshes—like the Tutsi had done before them—or to neighboring countries. Members of the RPA tolerated mass revenge-killings against the Hutu and, in the Rukoma area, committed massacres against the Hutu. The number of Hutu killed in these circumstances remains unknown. Originally, the population of the hill totaled 14,984 inhabitants, 90 percent of whom were Tutsi—an exceptionally large proportion for a Rwandan hill—due to enforced internal displacements in the years that followed the Hutu revolution. In all, 538 Tutsi survived the genocide, of whom 292 still lived in Rukoma in 2005 when the *gacaca* process began.

In Rukoma, the genocide was unimaginably devastating. Since 1994 the predominant feeling in Rukoma has been a desire for revenge against those (Hutu) who stayed (alive). Rather than a trend visible only in current *gacaca* sessions, it is a feeling that permeates and defines all social relations and every aspect of daily life. Some genocide survivors occupied the houses of Hutu families exiled to the Congo in the aftermath of the genocide. They did so after their own properties were destroyed, and the return of these Hutu families caused additional animosity. In the years after the genocide, the state instituted a policy called *villagization* whereby all families had to live together in *imidugudu* (small towns or agglomerations) rather than in their scattered hillside dwellings.[4] Local NGOs built housing for those genocide survivors in direst need of shelter. When the local village for genocide survivors was built, local authorities required the Hutu to destroy their own houses and move to "the roadside." They received no help or materials, which further fanned ethnic discord, and the people perceived that the authorities were favoring only one ethnic group. Living conditions reinforced separation. The first phase of the *gacaca* activities simply unfolded according to these existing dynamics.

Although many Hutu admitted taking an active part in the extermination campaign or pillaging activities, or many simply confessed to being present during the month of April 1994, most Tutsi victims are known to have died with the help of "strangers" to the hill: Burundian refugees, soldiers, Interahamwe militia, and others who came with the express purpose of killing and ransacking. These individuals were (and are) unknown to the community or they simply disappeared afterward. So the accused in *gacaca* were those who were still there by the time the information collection began in 2005.

Mistrust pervaded social relations when *gacaca* first arrived in the community. And if this gloomy—yet realistic—depiction of a sinister atmosphere of mistrust were not enough, there were more killings and atrocities as the *gacaca* process unfolded. In late 2006, at the height of the process, a Hutu who had admitted taking part in the genocide killed a young Tutsi survivor. The murder weapon was, again, a machete. The motive—a dispute over a cow—was unrelated to the past, that of ethnic belonging, or to the *gacaca* trials, but it was, nevertheless, explained to the outside world by evoking the pervasive "genocide ideology." In revenge, a group of Tutsi genocide survivors killed at least ten Hutu, half of whom were children, and also ransacked and burned more than thirty houses. Subsequently, the terrified Hutu fled. The army stepped in, and the Hutu were guaranteed safe return. Even though the Hutu, the police, and the administrative and judicial authorities knew the names of the avengers, not one of them was arrested or tried. On the contrary, officials accused a few Hutu of not providing security to genocide survivors and jailed them on the pretext of harboring "genocide ideology." The initial murder and the spontaneous acts of revenge that followed were rare open displays of the rampant tension between those belonging to the two ethnic categories, tension that had remained invisible because it had had no public outlet. The reaction of the government and judiciary showed once again that not only in the Hutu mind-set but also in actual practice in Rukoma not everyone was equal, whether in the eyes of the law or in front of the *gacaca*. In the week that followed this massacre, the *gacaca* carried on with its work.

As a consequence, a great many Hutu inhabitants of Rukoma considered themselves "enslaved tools" in Tutsi hands and used phrases referring to feudal times, for example, "they can use us like their tools" [*bashaka kutugira ibikoresho*]. In the experience of the Hutu inhabitants, the Tutsi were now the "rulers" and powerful; this perception affected Hutu participation in *gacaca*. During *gacaca* sessions in Rukoma, nobody mentioned the murders the RPA committed after the genocide.

In Rukoma, all *inyagamugayo* except for those in one area—the cell where the Hutu live—were Tutsi survivors. This situation did not help legitimize the courts in the eyes of the Hutu. Attendance records from hundreds of court cases in Rukoma also revealed that on average, Hutu made only half the interventions that the Tutsi did, although the reverse is true in the other three localities that we systematically observed.[5] In addition, 72.9 percent of the defendants standing trial in Rukoma pleaded guilty, while only 38.8 percent did so on average in the four research locations.[6] Observations and conversations in Rukoma revealed that Hutu accepted almost any accusations because they were afraid of being jailed on charges of contributing to the so-called

A Thousand Hills, a Thousand *Gacacas*

genocide ideology. Especially in the initial stages of the local *gacaca* process, judges generally did not adhere to any of the court procedures and operated under intense pressure from the many genocide survivors who attended trials and whose numbers far exceeded the total Hutu population. Sometimes, the population simply did not accept the court's decisions, nor did the judges easily accept confessions.

The path-dependency and social context of local communities influenced the proceedings in many cases; this was often the result of certain powerful actors who were involved and who could mobilize a multitude of people along historical and social fissures. Numerous *gacaca* trials would then deal with actual genocide crimes as envisioned, but false testimony would shift the essence of the proceedings, and so it was not about the crimes in question but about something else.

These types of power struggles informing *gacaca* proceedings often resulted in a sort of "eternal litigation," which was possible because of so many provisions to appeal verdicts. The trials organized to deal with the case of Rwaziyabagabo in Rukoma is a case in point. More than twelve *gacaca* sessions dealt exclusively with Rwaziyabagabo's case, and he had six trials. He had two initial trials, once when he was placed in Category 2,[7] and once after he had been recategorized into Category 1.[8] This recategorization was, in fact, a sort of retrial because the second trial dealt with the same allegations—it was an attempt to reopen the trial without a legal basis to do so. He had two appeal trials, one for each categorization,[9] followed by two different *gacaca* courts from neighboring areas, each of which retried him for the Category 1 crimes.[10] Each time, one of the parties perceived the verdict as unfavorable to them and asked for a retrial.

Article 23 of the 2004 *gacaca* law stipulates that when "all the Seat members are objected to or disclaim competence, the help of persons of integrity from the nearest *gacaca* Court having the same competence is requested" (Republic of Rwanda 2004a, art. 23). Although lawmakers incorporated this provision as a solution to the problem that might arise if all the judges turned out to be "incompetent," in practice and especially near the end of the *gacaca* process the "spirit" of this provision was often evoked to restart the hearings of cases with "particular difficulties." This provision was used in the case of Rwaziyabagabo, by both himself and his accusers.

Such a sequence of eternal litigation happened only when the two parties involved in the trial (defendant and plaintiff) were both powerful actors, often due to their extensive networks. And generally these eternal litigations were based on an underlying conflict between the parties on trial. Such a trial was ultimately a test of strength and a show of force, and resembled what Gravel

(1968a, 167) observed in the 1960s regarding gatherings dealing with conflicts in the population at the time:[11]

> These gatherings were also often an occasion for trials of power. . . . These trials would normally be interpreted by us of the western world as contests involving rights governed by customary law. But, I repeat, the contests were seldom contests of rights. They were, rather, contests of power. . . . What counts is that the locus of relative power has been pinpointed. But the play for power is perpetual and it is most likely that, in those cases where two litigants are not greatly differentiated in power, the loser eventually regroups his forces, creates new alliances, thereby shifting the locus of power.

This was also the case with the many sessions and re(trials) dealing with the allegations against Rwaziyabagabo. He had been a powerful merchant in the area before the genocide, and his family continued to wield considerable influence at the time of the *gacaca* process. Moreover, although Rwaziyabagabo might have been involved in a number of acts of violence during the genocide, the conflict that actually informed the proceedings was over Rwaziyabagabo's wealth and especially about a house, now occupied by one of the genocide survivors, which Rwaziyabagabo had owned before the genocide. It was a *gacaca* case informed and fueled by an underlying conflict, a common phenomenon aimed at reshaping the balance of power at the local level.

The reason the struggle surrounding Rwaziyabagabo spread through the local *gacaca* trials and seemed to last forever was that both parties were matched in strength. If this had not been the case, a power struggle could still have underlain the actual *gacaca* activities but would have been settled immediately and without notice. Overall, the nature of doing *gacaca*—whether finding justice and reconciliation, settling scores, searching for profit, or keeping silent—hinged on the extremely localized balance of power. From this perspective, *gacaca* proceedings in Rukoma were to a certain extent organized as collective vengeance (I distinguish vengeance from the practices of score-settling discussed in chap. 6). In the case of Rwaziyabagabo, though, the *gacaca* proceeding was score-settling with a vengeance, so to speak.

How can we understand this? Most attempts to settle scores occurred within the Hutu population. Hutu would accuse other Hutu of involvement in the genocide in order to get rid of a long-standing enemy, an annoying neighbor, an untrustworthy husband, or an avaricious parent. If genocide survivors were involved in this practice, they were generally motivated less by a conflict with a particular person and more by a desire to inflict harm on the Hutu population in general. In other words, survivors attempted to settle scores for what "the Hutu" had done to them and their families during the genocide. When Tutsi misused the *gacaca* system, they did so to achieve *generalized* vengeance, and survivors used false testimony with the aim of having as many Hutu convicted as possible. On the other hand, Hutu pursued *general* vengeance—against the system, the regime, or the local Tutsi population—by not participating in the *gacaca* proceedings but instead by keeping quiet, "*ceceka*" (see chap. 6).

Field observation in Rukoma indicated that tension and the vengeful stance abated over time, in particular after the *gacaca* law was again amended in March 2007. At that time, sentences became less arbitrary and harsh than before because they were lighter by law, punishment for breaches of procedure during trials was more clearly defined, and judges received additional training. Following these regulatory changes, the mind-set of some of the judges also changed, and they came to view the *gacaca* as an instrument of reconciliation (rather than of punishment) as well. Previously they essentially used it as a tool of organized vengeance. With *gacaca* proceedings completed fifteen years after the genocide, more encouraging signs of interethnic contact emerged in Rukoma. But trauma, distrust, fear, and frustration are still lurking below the surface of Rukoma's daily life.

Ntabona

The social situation in Ntabona is in stark contrast with the situation and prospects in Rukoma. Mistrust existed in Ntabona too, and daily relations were fragile in the wake of the genocide. But different genocide dynamics had been at play in Ntabona, in the north of the old province of Gitarama. Ntabona, like Rukoma, is distinctively rural. It takes approximately an hour and a half by car to get from Kigali to Ntabona, a large hill surrounded by three rivers demarcating the sector. The Nyabarongo River is the natural frontier between the former province of Gitarama and the former province of Kigali-Ngali. Due to war with the RPF and the introduction of a multiparty system in the early 1990s, the atmosphere in Ntabona had changed long before the genocide, and the community had become increasingly polarized along ethnic lines. Still, even after Habyarimana's plane was shot down, things remained calm in Ntabona. Four days later—as in Rukoma—Hutu refugees displaced by the conflict with the RPF in the north attacked the sector from a nearby hill. Initially, the Hutu wanted to bully rather than kill the Tutsi population of Ntabona. The *bourgmestre* (mayor) and the population raised the alarm and repelled the attackers, killing a few in the process. Tranquility returned, but a small group of "ideologues" arrived later with a former FAR

(Rwandan Armed Forces) soldier and well-trained Interahamwe militia who started to terrorize the community. They targeted the local Tutsi as a symbol of the larger and more abstract concept of *Tutsi-as-the-Enemy*. But it was not until two weeks later that their actions intensified and wholesale killing of Tutsi began, something that happened because the balance of power on the hill had shifted. The *bourgmestre* who initially opposed the killing spree lost power at the behest of the national authorities, and the Interahamwe leader who took control of the hill filled the resulting legal and administrative vacuum. He formed groups of attackers (*igitero*) comprised of ordinary peasants to hunt down and kill Tutsi.

The general feeling among the population—Hutu and Tutsi alike—was that those resorting to violence were "a group of bandits" interested only in thieving and taking power, as confirmed later when many heads of Hutu families appeared on "death lists."[12] These Hutu were united by family or other ties; they were the local "rich," occupying positions in the state administration or earning a living outside of farming. Their behavior can be interpreted as ambivalent: they were concerned with their own safety, and they did not resolve to kill the Interahamwe leader until they personally became victims of violence.

The hill was soon restored to its previous calm until another Interahamwe leader supported by the national authorities arrived, at which point the "natural order" or balance of power changed again. The group that had been busy ransacking and hunting Tutsi found an incentive in the discourse of the national authorities, which invited the population to share out Tutsi land. This economic incentive provided considerable encouragement for people to take part in the attacks. And some became involved for highly personal motives, for example a teacher who led a raid against a Tutsi family that had refused him their daughter's hand many years before.

In Ntabona, the genocide was not a linear event; rather, periods of resistance alternated with episodes of absolute violence. The Tutsi—as well as many Hutu—were the victims of this violence. The RPA occupied the area on 4 July 1994. Hardly any Hutu fled the hill; there were no revenge killings but many incarcerations.

In 1990 the population of Ntabona was 2,930, including 245 Tutsi, of whom 128 were murdered in the months spanning the genocide. Another 30 died seeking protection in neighboring hills. At the various roadblocks set up in Ntabona, 55 Tutsi from other areas were murdered, and 58 houses were destroyed. After the genocide, 64 people were jailed and charged with taking part in the killings. Most had to await trial in jail for more than ten years. Out of 87 genocide survivors, only 31 have remained in Ntabona, and the others have moved to towns or the new shelters built for them by the state.

A group of women who had lost their husbands and children during the genocide moved in together toward the end of the 1990s. Séverine, whose life story was presented in chapter 4, is one of them. These widows lived as a group in a reintegration village some distance from their former homes. In fact, the village brought more separation than integration since they now lived among themselves and at a considerable distance from their former neighbors, even though it increased the women's (perceived) sense of security. They lived in a state of severe impoverishment, having lost their possessions and their ability to rely on family—the traditional recourse in times of hardship and need. In 2003 they saw released prisoners, those who had confessed in prison, return. The women were scared: some of these prisoners had been jailed at the request of the widows in the years following the genocide. Seeing their seemingly unconditional return, the women feared for their lives.

Female survivors who came to live in this reintegration village preferred to keep to themselves, a small group of widows who had faced the same traumatic events. Relations with the Hutu were extremely cold, and they were not very good with the Tutsi wives of Hutu men either, mostly due to their own officially recognized status as genocide survivors and its potential benefits, namely some support for housing or children's education through the fund for genocide survivors (FARG). Some of the Tutsi wives of Hutu did not receive this kind of official status and therefore had no recourse to those benefits.

A number of female genocide survivors have refused to leave their dwellings on their hill of origin, likely because many survived the genocide . . . thanks to Hutu protectors. While many of them are widows of Hutu men whose extended family and friends took care of them, there are also Tutsi families that were saved by Hutu inhabitants. This remarkable phenomenon convinced them to stay in their remote enclosures. Hutu families who saved Tutsi during the genocide acted as a beacon in the sea of suspicion in the postgenocide era. Such a phenomenon was totally absent in Rukoma.

In Ntabona, communication, broader organizational structures, and social positions all shaped how *gacaca* unfolded. Take the case of Boniface. Boniface used to be a local official in Ntabona during the former regime and also in the genocidal months of 1994; he was considered one of the ringleaders of the local genocide. He resigned from his post after the genocide, but he remained a rich merchant. He influenced the *gacaca* proceedings, and not many wanted to testify against him. Although it is unclear whether he also used overt coercion to manipulate the proceedings, his position as a wealthy person controlling food distribution and employment made direct pressure unnecessary. Some released prisoners managed to accuse him in the information-collection phase, but during his actual trial he was acquitted simply because nobody testified against him, not even the genocide survivors. One does not (easily) confront the powerful even if they are only slightly higher up in the social organization.

The example of Silidio, who also lives in Ntabona and changed his confessions after release from prison, is a case in point. In 61 percent of the observed cases in our study where such information was available, the defendant had made multiple confessions at different moments in the *gacaca* process. Moreover, people on trial who had previously confessed often retracted, revoked, or changed their initial confession. Silidio, a freed prisoner residing in Ntabona, changed his confession after the *inyangamugayo* read his confession aloud at the beginning of this trial:[13]

> PRESIDENT: Is there anything you wish to add to your confession?
>
> DEFENDANT SILIDIO: There's something about the people who were with me [during the genocide] that I wish to change. These last few days, I've been listening to the radio and I've heard clarifications about the categories of people who committed crimes, and I've realized that there are at least four people in my confession who're innocent. Uwimana Gérard: I didn't see him in the attacks except that he was at Damascene's when we went there looking for children to kill, and he didn't follow us on our way down to the river. Kanyabyoba: I didn't see him in any attack either; he was where he was because Habineza forced him. Where it says that he threw a baby in the river, he didn't actually mean to. Habineza had just thrown the tall girl and he started threatening Kanyabyoba, who had to throw the baby to save himself, but then we had to stop him from throwing himself in the river next too. Rutiganira Gaspard didn't do anything. Habimana Marcel: I can't accuse him because he was persecuted too. However, as we were taking the children, a young boy may have escaped, he fled and we let him. . . . I don't know who killed him.
>
> PRESIDENT: Why did you mention all these people when you knew they were innocent?
>
> DEFENDANT SILIDIO: I mentioned their names because at the time of my confession, we were told to mention all the names.
>
> PRESIDENT: Did you believe them to be accomplices?
>
> DEFENDANT SILIDIO: Before I heard this clarification, I thought they were.

Silidio, with whom I spoke many times individually, changed his confession because of particular difficulties he experienced after his release. A number of the people he had accused while in prison had never been incarcerated but learned about the nature of his confessions. Social pressure, intimidation, and potential resort to bribery made Silidio "slightly" adjust his confession. This type of behavior further illustrates the previous discussion of social navigation

A Thousand Hills, a Thousand *Gacacas*

in the context of the *gacaca* process: "people act in and shape their social environment in constant dialogue with the way the social environment moves and the way it is predicted to 'act' upon them and shape the circumstances of their lives" (Vigh 2009, 433). Thus, shaping these future life circumstances resulted in exercising *ubwenge* and the emergence of the *effectual truth* in *gacaca*. Whatever statement resulted in an increase in physical or other well-being was considered true as long as sufficient social forces shaped and sanctioned it as "the truth" at that particular time and place.

Aside from the strategic confessions mentioned earlier, which would perhaps leave out crimes that the wider community might not know about, I also observed a related strategy. In certain areas, people tended to blame the dead or those who were absent, either in prison or abroad. People deployed this strategy both during the information-collection period and the subsequent trials.

In one of the cells of Ntabona, local residents killed one of the Interahamwe leaders during the genocide after that leader started harassing the local Hutu population. Many Tutsi had already died before that event. During the *gacaca* proceedings, the inhabitants of the community were inclined to blame the leader and some prisoners, absent from the community, for all the killings and other actions that had taken place during the genocide. In particular, those who had been local state agents and the wealthy people of the cell during the genocide attempted to do that very thing. As important actors on their hill, even in the postgenocide era, they managed to define the overall narrative about what had happened during the genocide, and they gave the murdered Interahamwe leader a prominent role. Because these important actors were so influential, the ordinary population largely followed their lead and talked about the genocide within the framework laid out for them. Although the Interahamwe leader had, indeed, played a significant role during the genocide, rare testimony—often by prisoners returning to the community to testify—suggested that the overall picture was more complex, with at least some indirect involvement of people within the power network during the genocide. None of them, however, was convicted for genocide crimes.

In Ntabona as elsewhere, the *gacaca* was subject to the so-called path-dependency due to its very design: the embedding in small face-to-face communities. Nevertheless, numerous eyewitness accounts of *gacaca* sessions in Ntabona showed that they generally operated as the organic laws envisioned and as the SNJG instructed. The *gacaca* bench included Hutu and Tutsi inhabitants, and it often followed procedures, although procedural error was also rampant in Ntabona. Everyone seemed to be participating as planned. Still, intense radicalized ethnic awareness characterized the information-collection phase. Terror crystallized in the face of the inability to defend oneself or others against accusations. This feeling abated when the trial phase started and the court allowed statements from all sides. But even though the same people had until then been systematically cited as genocide leaders, others who had thus far tried to dodge their responsibility were now slowly admitting their role in past atrocities.

In contrast to Rukoma, Tutsi (42.3 percent) intervened in *gacaca* almost as often as Hutu (57.7 percent), even though the former were a minority in the community.[14] In addition, there were almost as many interventions *à charge* (10.3 percent) as *à décharge* (9.2 percent), a situation that was significantly different in Rukoma (where the corresponding figures were 10.7 percent vs. 3.7 percent).[15] The acquittal rate in Ntabona was also very high (53.1 percent), whereas the average rate of the observed trials stood at 10.8 percent. All of these trends were to a certain extent the result of the history of social relations in the community.

As in Rukoma, though, there were also murders in Ntabona after the *gacaca* had started. A local judge—a Tutsi survivor of the genocide and president of the local sector-level *gacaca* court—was killed. Security forces rounded up a group of *gacaca* convicts who had appealed their sentences and had been released to await new measures in the hills. The armed forces killed several in revenge and left their bodies on the hill with the message: "This is what happens to the beasts who learned to kill (during the genocide)." None of them was involved in the murder of the *gacaca* judge, which most likely resulted from a family dispute—a scenario that the police never seriously investigated. In fact, the judge, who was the president of the sector *gacaca* court, was killed by his own son, as several trustworthy informants—including members of the family—confirmed to me in the years following the killing. The son in question fled to Uganda about two years later when he realized that some members of the family, probably motivated in part by family tension about property, intended to divulge the secret to the police.

The revenge murders caused panic and unvoiced anxiety among the population, especially among genocide survivors who believed that the Hutu thought *they* were the ones who had enticed the security forces to exact revenge. The killing of the *gacaca* judge was announced and widely discussed on the national radio as a clear case of "genocide ideology" lurking in the Hutu population. Approximately three weeks after that murder, a delegation of government officials and members of parliament came to Ntabona to visit and support the victim's family (including his son, the murderer) and to lecture the population on the need to eradicate the genocide ideology. The delegation said that every inhabitant of Ntabona "had to watch the genocide survivors as him or herself."

No further violence occurred, calm returned, and the fragile *gacaca* process resumed. But Ntabona's population had understood "the order of things": the government delegation had reinforced the alignment with the center, and that alignment resulted in a certain way of participating in the *gacaca* activities. From then on, very few dared challenge a verdict as the victims of the reprisals had done before. This sequence of events explains why there were so few appeals in Ntabona compared to the other localities under observation.[16] It also underscores again how the actions and presence of state agents that abundantly populate the dense layers of Rwanda's administrative structures tacitly influenced the way people participated in the *gacaca* proceedings.

Soon thereafter, most prisoners left prison to do community work, some of them on the Ntabona hill. This helped assuage resentment among the Hutu, who had seen many men disappear into prison since the *gacaca* started. Their return sparked new issues though. Some determined denouncers of genocide perpetrators—whom they had thought would remain locked up—were now seeing their return. As we saw with Séverine, some of those genocide survivors subsequently decided to reduce the number of their appearances as witnesses providing testimony. They found some solace in the fact that the cell-level *gacaca* granted them damages to try and punish looting and other material crimes, which were often settled out of court through mediation. Slowly, a few survivors returned to the local cabarets, where victims and killers now sometimes share a beer.

Conclusion

Everyday life dynamics as well as local strategies and histories reshaped *gacaca* in diverse ways in different localities. Scholars have documented the rerouting of national programs in localized social textures in the context of a wide variety of phenomena. Referring to the Rwandan case, Pottier (2002, 207) remarked on the implementation of a housing policy and land (re-)distribution: "Whatever the national guidelines on repossession prescribed, and they allowed for local interpretation, [this] locality's dominant moral discourse would construct its own guidelines." Timothy Longman (1995) made a similar observation when studying local dynamics in two sectors during the genocide itself.[17] I also observed that *gacaca* affected social interactions, and social interaction affected *gacaca*. By comparing Ntabona and Rukoma we can discern many similarities. In both communities, people participated to a significant degree, as the design of the court system envisioned. Because they did so, the *gacaca* system became embedded in a tight-knit community with its existing conflicts, reigning hierarchies, established communication practices, and local histories. Although imposed from above, violence and reconciliation are steered by forces and constraints, which leave enough flexibility to enable local dynamics to emerge. Different historical trajectories and social hierarchies influenced the nature of participation in the *gacaca* activities on each of the Rwandan hills.

It is impossible to point to a single decisive factor to explain the differences from hill to hill, but a few elements that stand out in local stories enable us to interpret those differences. First, the plight of the Tutsi population in Rukoma has a significant historical dimension: they settled in the inhospitable environment of Rukoma in the context of the 1959–63 events, and their experience of injustice resonates in the *gacaca* activities taking place more than forty-five years later. Furthermore, the genocide was an extreme event in Rukoma in terms of its magnitude, intensity, and speed. After the genocide, the Hutu population became the target of revenge killings and systematic targeting either in Rukoma itself or as they fled to the Congo. In Ntabona, on the other hand, the genocide was less intense, and violence alternated with periods of resistance. Nobody fled when the RPA arrived, although some people were jailed afterward. A significant number of Tutsi inhabitants survived the genocide in Ntabona, often thanks to good family ties and friendly relations with local Hutu. This hardly happened at all in Rukoma.

In the aftermath of the genocide, people perpetuated in their everyday life interactions the character and dynamics of the violence they had experienced. In Rukoma, many factors ranging from the construction of housing to the activities of the *gacaca* courts contributed to increased segregation. The power of sheer numbers also played an important role. The Tutsi were a majority in Rukoma, which is exceptional in Rwandan hills, while the opposite was true in Ntabona. In Rukoma, conflicts and tensions are often of an interethnic nature and are, therefore, quite polarizing, whereas in Ntabona, they tend to be more intraethnic. Thus, the murder of a Tutsi on each hill led to a spontaneous outburst of ethnic violence in Rukoma; in Ntabona it triggered revenge killings at the behest of police or military forces from outside the area, causing equal fear and frustration among both Hutu and Tutsi. All of these issues played a role in the unfolding of *gacaca* in localized settings.[18]

8

Shades of Heart

Killing someone is not only slicing his throat.

Lay judge, Jali, gacaca session on 20 May 2009

In the highly pragmatic life of the Rwandan hills, tensions and conflicts are kept in the dark because neighbors and villagers depend upon each other in their daily activities, and they fight for survival in conditions of shared impoverishment. In the immediate wake of the genocide, the realities of shared living space were marked by mutual fear, which diminished progressively with the passing of time. Of necessity, though, life returned to a form of normality. An expression often used to describe alliances between victims and perpetrators was "someone hides that he hates you and you hide that you know" (*umuntu aguhisha ko akwanga ukamuhisha ko ubizi*). It means that people are aware that the social or interpersonal relationship between them is not good but, nevertheless, they pretend to get along. Such pragmatic, strategic behavior is tied to the notion of *ubwenge*. The social imaginary of which *ubwenge* is a tenet needs additional examination to make sense of the unfolding and outcomes of the *gacaca* process.

Social imaginary is the way "people imagine their social existence, how they fit together with others, how things go on between them and their fellows, the expectations that are normally met and the deeper normative notions and images that underlie these expectations" (C. Taylor 2004, 23).[1] To deepen our understanding of the *gacaca* dynamics, we need to ask what "social cohesion," "reconciliation," and "justice" mean from the perspective of those involved in *gacaca*. The answers illuminate the sociocultural construction of Rwandan personhood, and understanding the conception of the person highlights the importance of the "moral truth" that resocializes and rehumanizes people who have experienced dehumanizing situations. Such a transformation takes place mainly through ritualized social interactions and exchanges.[2]

This chapter examines whether and how the operation of the *gacaca* courts facilitated or hindered this resocializing, rehumanizing process by not only tracing life before and after the *gacaca* activities but also by looking closely at the impact of acts of pardoning and restitution of goods pillaged and destroyed.

Living-With

In the ten years between the genocide and the start of the *gacaca* trials, victims and those who were involved in the violence but had no leading role in it lived together again on their respective hills—not always as neighbors since survivors had often been grouped into resettlement sites (*imidugudu*) but still in the same vicinity. Because they had no choice but to live together, they had to develop a way of life and ways of interacting with each other. It is important to understand the strategies and tactics employed in daily life in the decade before the state-sanctioned installation of the *gacaca* courts to verify whether their arrival facilitated or disturbed a natural process of dealing with the past.

In order to establish a broader insight into the meaning and nature of living-with (*kubana*) at the local level, I asked the participants in the 2009 group discussions, "What is, in your own words, social cohesion [*imibanire*]?" and "What are the signs of good social cohesion in your community?" (*Ni ibihe bimenyetso byerekana imibanire myiza hagati y'abantu?*; the question inquiring about the quality of the relations between people would be *Imiterere y'umubano hagati y'abantu*).

They most often cited the sharing of food and drinks, ceremonies of conviviality, and the exchange of gifts as signs of good social cohesion (*umibanire myiza* or *ubwuvikane* or *kubana neza*).[3] Mutual help or general collaboration between people, as well as greeting each other on pathways or neighborly visits, are considered to be signs of good social cohesion as well. Danielle de Lame (2005, 306–458) emphasizes the importance of ritualized exchanges that characterize and constitute social relations, especially the sharing of beer, at times solid food, but also marriage ceremonies and festivities: "The social ties that structure lived time and space materialize in exchanges. . . . The meaning of these exchanges comes both from the gift itself and from the relationship within which the transaction takes place" (451–58).

Daily actions and interactions in the years after the genocide had indeed become a way of dealing with the past, whether people were acting toward each other in positive or negative ways. A greeting on the pathway to the fields, the offer and sharing of banana beer in the local *cabaret* (pub), an invitation to a wedding, or a helping hand transporting a sick person to the hospital could catalyze restructured emotions and relationships. On the other hand, accusations of witchcraft, threats or suspicions of poisoning, the (interpretation of the) blink of an eye, or the failure to invite someone to a ceremony were enough to increase distrust. These actions are not simply instances of (the lack of) politeness or (ignorance of) routines of conduct; they also manifest the nature of "living-with" (*kubana*).

Illustrating this notion is the story of Sévérine (see chap. 4). In the months after the trial, Stanislas, who had been convicted of killing Sévérine's children but was set free because he had spent several years in pretrial detention, claimed that his relationship with her was normalized again, albeit fragile. He said, "When I meet her, we talk, although I don't know what she has in her heart (*umutima*), but for me, my heart is genuine." He continued, "I don't have a particular problem with the genocide survivors; they greet me and I greet them. When Sévérine asks me for something to drink, I buy her a drink without a problem. She does not ask me too often; when I tell her I don't have any money, she leaves." Although Stanislas was eager to paint a normal picture regarding his relationship with Sévérine in our private conversations, field observations made clear that in reality they had a strained relationship. In January 2007, at the height of the *gacaca* proceedings, I wrote the following observation:

> At dawn I go with my translator to the sector office to follow the *gacaca* activities related to cases of pillaging and theft that are going to take place. We pass the church and walk down a small dirt road toward the sector building. Groups of people are starting to gather. The sun is burning. We spot Sévérine; she walks toward us. We greet her. Together we move to the side of the road to find shelter for the sun under a small tree. We talk. She mentions she is not feeling very secure with the functioning of *gacaca*. There are no problems with people who need to compensate the goods they destroyed or pillaged, but the relationship with the people involved in killings is not good. While talking, more people gather. As usual, and since we know many people, we greet passersby not only verbally but also with a handshake or by placing our hands on their shoulders, a common greeting practice. People greeting us also greet Sévérine. I notice, however, that some greetings are not hearty; they are short and formulaic, the gestures mechanical. In a distance I spot Stanislas walking on the road. He is wearing a hat, as usual, moving slowly. He is approaching from the opposite direction, going toward the church. The conversation we are having with Sévérine flags. I feel a tension while he is approaching. He passes

without saying anything: no word, no sign, no handshake. Sévérine remains silent until he is out of hearing distance. She grins.

Once Stanislas was out of hearing distance, Sévérine restarted our conversation. She said: "my heart is upright" (*mpagaritse umutima*), through which she evoked her uneasiness with the nature of the interaction I had just witnessed. Sévérine and the killer of her children live together in the same area because they have to. On another occasion, Sévérine interacted with a neighboring couple in a totally different manner:

> I am walking with my translator on one of the very narrow pathways crossing the hill and demarcating the plots of land in Ntabona. We have just visited one of the women whose husband was recently killed in a conflict that arose from the *gacaca* proceedings.[4] The pathway leads to the main dirt road that connects Ntabona with the commercial center several kilometers farther away. While approaching this road, we notice Sévérine walking by. She stops and pauses until we reach her. We greet each other and chat a bit. We are standing in the middle of the road. On both sides there are rows with houses surrounded by banana groves. I notice a woman peering through the window of the house closest to us. A bit later she appears from the back of the house. She comes to greet us and Sévérine. Sévérine and the woman grab each other's shoulders. They smile. A conversation unfolds. Sévérine turns to me and my translator. She mentions this woman has been a good friend of hers for a long time. She explains she used to live in this area before and during the genocide before moving to the resettlement site for survivors. The husband of the woman also walks toward us. The greetings are as warm as with his wife. He invites us to enter his house. They have just prepared some sorghum beer and they want to share with us. The woman disappears to the back of the house to turn up again at the front after unlocking the main entrance to the house. We and Sévérine enter the house and take places on the wooden benches in the living room. The man goes into a backroom and returns with a gourd. He takes a sip through the straw and passes the drink on to Sévérine. Sévérine gently sips the beer. She talks and laughs while sipping. The container is passed on to my translator and later also on to me. Although I know my stomach is not up to these local brews, I also drink, a bit, in order not to offend the hosts. We stay in the house for about forty-five minutes. Sévérine explains that these people are very good friends of her. She mentions that the woman even tried to defend her house during the genocide when people came to pillage her belongings. Also later she has always been warmly welcomed in her house to share food and drinks as we are doing now.

When I asked Sévérine a few days later to comment on the interaction I had witnessed, she used the words "*umutima mwiza*," which literally mean

Shades of Heart

"good-hearted," to describe the personality of the woman who had helped her during the genocide. It is obvious that the generous and spontaneous sharing of drinks gives a specific meaning to the interaction described. Not just Sévérine but all Rwandans have been engaging the past in these daily practices and encounters over the years, and they continued to do so in the margins of the *gacaca* process. What one labels truth-telling, rendering justice, fostering reconciliation, or providing compensation takes root in the ambiguities of local life. Engaging the past is entangled in the web of a tightly knit face-to-face community, which is difficult for an outsider who is used to different preconceived categories to understand.[5] The notion of *umutima*—generally translated as "heart"—plays a pivotal role in this local epistemology.[6]

The Heart of the Matter—
A Matter of the Heart

As the case of Sévérine and other life-story narratives demonstrate, Rwandans and especially genocide survivors often refer to *umutima* when talking about the events of the past, and expressing the nature and level of trust and confidence they have in their neighbors, fellow villagers, or members of the other ethnic category. Due to the violence experienced in their midst, "the hearts have changed." In 2006, having had an initial experience with the *gacaca* process, two female Tutsi survivors spoke about their expectations for the future of *gacaca* by invoking the notion of *umutima*:

> A: People have lost good manners and habits due to the war. The education given to children has changed. I don't know what one ought to do to restore trust between people. Even on the radio they talk of unity and reconciliation, but I don't see anything changing; the *imitima* of people have become like those of animals.[7]
>
> Q: How do you see the *gacaca* process?
>
> A: The *gacaca* is equally a road to achieve reconciliation. You have to keep in mind that it is hard to relieve the sorrow of the *umutima* but on the level of cohesion, *gacaca* might be able to do something. The wounded *umutima* can be cured when people tell the "truth" to each other. When one knows well what happened there is a bit of an ease of mind (heart).[8]

Human beings changed because of the crimes committed, the violence experienced, or the dehumanizing acts observed. Especially since 2000 living conditions, the social universe, and daily interactions have returned to a form of normality (see chap. 4). But this outward appearance of normality reveals little about someone's state of mind, their interior attitudes and feelings. Outward appearances are deceptive, as popular expressions acknowledge: "the mouth does not always say what resides in the heart," or "the rancorous stomach, you give it milk and it vomits blood."[9] Conversely, the overall connotation of the deepest interior (or what is and remains invisible and inaccessible) can be seen as *nda* or interior. It is important to keep this in mind since speaking or not speaking the truth is a way of accessing the "invisible" side of the human person, his or her *umutima*.

In the Rwandan context, *umutima* is the force unifying the human being. Although the Western notion of "heart" is already rich in meaning (hence the reason *umutima* is generally translated as "the heart"), it does not fully capture the various connotations *umutima* has. *Umutima* is the center of reception of outward impulses and the locus of interior movement. Emotions, thoughts, and will are all interconnected and unified in this word. Man and animals both have *ubuzima*, meaning breath or health, but what distinguishes man from other animals is *umutima*. Therefore, the word has the broader connotation of "humanness": it is what defines us as human beings. Moreover, it defines what kind of human being one is, the nature of one's moral character.

Overall, *umutima* is the key to understanding the nature of Rwandan personhood.[10] As Rwandans say: "the heart is man's little king" (*kami ka muntu ni umutima we*) and "the heart of a person is his oracle" (*umutima w'umuntu ni yo ndagu*). At times during interviews, my Rwandan interlocutor would say, "[I need] to consult my *umutima*" (*kughisha umutima inama*), meaning that he or she needed to reflect on the issue we were talking about. During the *gacaca* sessions one could also hear: "the *umutima* is judging me" (*umutima urancira urubanza*), which evokes the existence of individual conscience in the realm of *umutima*. Apart from intelligence and conscience, will is also situated in *umutima*: "what makes the *umutima* suffer makes the legs travel from dawn onward" (*akababaje umutima kazindura amaguru*). "My *umutima* is always turned toward 'that'" (*agatima gahora kabirarikiye*) evokes the insight that desire and affection are also part of the notion of *umutima*. Finally, the proverbs, metaphors, and expressions that make use of the notion of *umutima* to describe an emotional state are abundant. People use them frequently to describe how they dealt with (violent) changes in their lives, as the collages derived from life-story interviews showed (chap. 4). The narratives collected during the *gacaca* sessions and the more specific discussions on participation in and experience of *gacaca* also contain numerous metaphors that use the movement of *umutima* to express one's feeling, situation, or state of mind during the *gacaca* sessions. To list some examples (with *umutima* translated as heart here):

Guhagalika umutima: to put the heart upright—fear, worries, uneasiness

Gukuka umutima: to have a "breakable" heart—to be terrified

Gusimbwa n'umutima: the heart leaps suddenly—to have a presage, to sense a bad omen

Kugira imitima myinshi: to have multiple hearts—to be undecided

Kubunza umutima: to make the heart wander—to be very worried

Kugira umutima mu mutwe: to have the heart in the head—to be terrified to the level of "insanity"

Kuburanya imitima: to put the hearts on trial—to be undecided

Umutima umvuyemo: the heart left me—a "mental" breakdown

Intimba iryana ku mutima kuruta igisebe cyo ku murundi: Grief causes stinging pain to the heart, more than a wound does to the leg—moral suffering is worse than physical pain

Both the opposite movement—a return of the heart to its original place—and the combining of two or more hearts into one evoke a calming, soothing effect:[11]

Kugarura umutima: to restore the heart in its place—to calm down, soothe tempers

Gushyitsa umutima hamwe: to have one's heart positioned in one place, to calm down—be at ease

Gusubiza umutima mu nda: to replace one's heart in the stomach (interior), to calm down, to soothe oneself

Gusubiza umutima mu gitereko: to situate the heart in its place again

The *umutima* someone possesses can also be qualified. It is sometimes said that "the 'heart-maker' did not make all hearts according to the same measurements" (*umubaji w'imitima ntiyayiringanije*). This expression evokes the wisdom that people differ both according to their personal characteristics (personality) and in a moral sense. Having or not having *umutima* can thus also be a moral judgment instead of a mere ontological distinction. Qualifying someone as "having no heart" in the Rwandan universe is the gravest insult. It deprives someone of his or her "humanness" and situates that person, first, in the realm of animals and, second, outside the moral realm. In interviews probing the experience of the *gacaca* activities, I heard the following:

Ameze nk'igisimba kitagira umutima: he resembles an animal without heart—he is animal-like, savage, occupied with personal survival only

Igipfamutima: man with a dead heart—a brute, someone without reason

Umugabo-Mbwa: a man-dog—untrustworthy person, without ideals and courage

Imburamutima: to go without a heart—to be inattentive, careless, immoral

Kutagira umutima: not to have a heart—to be unreflective, not open for
  advice

Kugira umutima muke: to have little heart—to have little reflective capacity, being hardly caring

Nta mutima agira: he has no heart—he is insensible, inattentive, careless,
  immoral

Umutima w'urutare mubi: a heart of stone; a "bad" heart—insensible person

Some people have referred to the *gacaca* period by stating that people's
"hearts were hardened." They meant there was not much "humanness" during
these years. On the other hand, people used other expressions to describe someone they considered to be living up to a high moral standard:

Kugira umutima mwiza: to have a good heart—someone who is attentive
  to others, has good morals

Kugira umutima utuza/utuje: to have a calm heart—someone who is calm,
  not brutal, and reflective

Kugira umutima utunganye: to have a clean heart—someone with a clean
  conscience

Kugira umutima woroshya: to have a humble heart—someone who is
  attentive, conciliatory, pardoning

Gushyika ku mutima: to "arrive" on the heart—something or someone is
  moving the senses in a positive manner

The use of these expressions signifies the experience or perception of "true
humanity" (*umuntu nyamuntu*). Women in particular might say that another
woman was "a person with a heart" (*umunyamutima*), an expression that means
that a particular woman "knows how to behave." In general, one could say
that "to have *umutima*" (*kugira umutima*) connotes the wide variety of meanings linked to "humanness": wisdom, righteousness, deliberation, prudence,
respect, courage and bravery, firmness, energy and forcefulness, and the like.
Especially when the adjective *mwiza* (good) is used as well, one intends to
express that someone "has good morals" (*afite imico myiza*).

Pardon and Restitution Reexamined

Given this local understanding of personhood, participation in
gacaca was a way of assessing people's *umutima*, thus humanity. Dealing with
the violence of the past in the Rwandan hills, either in the everyday context or
during participation in the *gacaca* practice, is ultimately a question of moralization: it is an exploration of the nature of the *umutima*—the "humanness"

and moral character—of oneself and others.[12] In the modern *gacaca*, by design the *forensic truth* had to be spoken, and the process could be a way to explore the *umutima* of the other. But because many participants experienced a problematic quest for the truth, the *gacaca* proceedings brought about only a particular type of moralization. Truth-telling or not, lying or the experience of lying, reveals something about someone's moral character. People aligned themselves with the truth that the center of society propagated, and they navigated the social terrain with an eye to beneficial outcomes.

But conviviality—even though it is key to the localized way of dealing with a violent past and living well together—is not about "speaking the truth," let alone the *forensic truth*. It is not about being strategic. Conviviality is about "acting true"; it is about practicing "moral truth." Conviviality is a practice that cannot be decreed or obliged and, if forced, loses its significance. It can, at best, be facilitated. And indeed, the modern *gacaca* system had—by design— a number of characteristics that aimed at facilitating such conviviality or ways of acting true. These characteristics include the confession procedure, which required the perpetrator to ask for pardon, and the cell-level *gacaca* proceedings that dealt with property looted and destroyed during the genocide, both of which lead to a closer reexamination of these features.

The *gacaca* law specified that the defendant should "apologize for the offenses that he or she had committed" (Republic of Rwanda 2004a, art. 54). These apologies "shall be made publicly to the victims in case they are still alive and to the Rwandan Society." But because accusations, not confessions, drove the *gacaca*, pardon was less important in actual practice. In 33 percent of the cases we observed at the sector level, the person standing trial actually did ask for pardon.[13] The law did not require victims to grant pardon to the defendants, but certain indirect means, such as speeches by dignitaries and local authority figures, often suggested that they do so. In the trials under observation, the victim(s) pardoned 4 percent of the defendants.[14]

Most defendants asking for pardon did so in a formulaic way, simply adding to their confession, "and I ask for pardon." A typical example of a formulaic request for pardon is the one Muhire, a resident of Rukoma, made on 10 February 2001 while he was in prison.[15] As usual, a judge read aloud his confession and his request for pardon at the beginning of his trial:

> In the attack against Mushoza's, I stole two goats and Mudaheranwa (Madonori) took a bicycle and unknown people were killed in the coffee plantation and Sezibera, Mudaheranwa (Madonori), and many others were involved in this attack. It was led by Sezibera; we killed two men, and Rima and Sezibera clubbed them to death, and I apologize to the victims and the state of Rwanda.

During his trial, he made no further physical or verbal indications of remorse, he did not again request pardon, and the victims did not announce that they had granted pardon. In general, victims did not consider these requests for pardon genuine and did not consider them to relate to the conception of personhood discussed earlier. In order to understand this, we need to make a distinction between formulaic and genuine acts of pardon, as Jennie Burnet (2008, 181) does. She states that a difference exists between *gusaba imbabazi* (to confess), an act that occurs mainly in the legal arena, and *kwicuza* (to accept moral responsibility and show remorse), an act that Roman Catholics refer to when asking pardon during confession.

Was there more room for genuine acts of pardon and reconciliation in the cell-level courts that handled cases of theft and destruction of property? Because the logic of cell-level trials was different, it could have been designed to facilitate a more restorative type of justice-seeking. The act of exchanging goods in the Rwandan sociocultural universe carries with it a number of connotations, including restoring harmony and the (re-)creation of a social bond in line with the conception of personhood. The concept of pardon is not typically implied in these actions, but it is closely associated with them.

We did observe acts of pardon and reconciliation during proceedings dealing with cases of looting and destruction of property. For example, in a cell-level court, the son of one of the victims pardoned twenty-four defendants who were supposed to compensate his family for pillaged and destroyed goods. The man announced: "Whether you recognize your fault or not, I pardon you anyway."[16] In another case in Runyoni, a male genocide survivor absolved two men obliged to compensate him with RWF 82,000 (USD 148), and his act provoked a lively discussion in the audience, among both Tutsi and Hutu.[17] The Hutu said that reconciliation required more such gestures, while the Tutsi survivors said that it was not useful to punish people with large fines when those people had no money. A participant in a trial in Jali that also dealt with property offenses made a similar reflection:[18]

> PRESIDENT (NDIKUBANDI): We now turn to the case of Gatama and Bigirimana. At the time of the genocide, Bigirimana was among the group who looted at Gatama's; Bigirimana looted corrugated iron sheets worth RWF 60,000 [USD 108].
>
> GATAMA PAUL: Bigirimana, who is in prison now, came with the group who destroyed my house but personally, he stole corrugated iron I estimate to be worth RWF 60,000. After Bigirimana went to prison, his wife Mukamusoni gave me RWF 36,000 [USD 65]. I told Mukamusoni that she wouldn't be able to find the remaining RWF 24,000 [USD 43], so I voluntarily gave up on those RWF 24,000.

MUKAMUSONI: I thank Gatama Paul in front of you all, and I declare that
this is a path to reconciliation.

In Rukoma too, a genocide survivor reduced the amounts of restitution money
in light of the precarious economic situation of the two men sentenced for
pillaging her belongings.[19] She did reduce the amount but only after the two
men had accepted the verdict of the court. A third man, represented by his
wife during the trial proceedings, was not granted such a favor because his
wife had denied the claims that her husband had been involved in the pillaging. She thus had to reimburse the full amount the judges decided upon.

In Runyoni, the mother of an absent defendant was obliged to pay the
sum of RWF 200,000 (USD 360) for two cows her son had pillaged.[20] The
woman did not contest the punishment and promised to do everything necessary to honor the agreement. In response, the victim reduced the amount to
a total of RWF 150,000 (USD 270) as a sign of goodwill. That amount is,
nevertheless, approximately half of the average yearly income in rural Rwanda.
But he added that this exchange would mean that their families would be
connected "with a pact." The man referred to a so-called *kunywana* or blood
pact, which historically would formalize a friendship, as opposed to a client
relationship. The exchange of gifts, especially cows, was central to such pacts,
and it carried a serious moral commitment; breaking the pact would cause
harm.[21] Because the man evoked the significance of a blood pact in the context
of the amicable settlement, I considered his words to be an important token
of some sort of "symbolic closure" (Hamber and Wilson 2002) for the people
involved.

Acts like those mentioned did not, however, dominate the nature of the
proceedings. More than half of the cases needed a criminal trial and thus functioned according to the prosecutorial and adversarial logic of sector-level trials
(see chap. 3). In addition, cases of looting and destruction of property were
often used to increase the number of people found guilty of genocide crimes.
To understand this trend, it is important to reiterate that restitution was not
individualized: it was a family affair. Thus, if a defendant on trial at the cell level
was deceased or abroad, a family member would represent that person. If the
absent defendant was convicted, his family had to execute the judgment. This
had no statutory basis but was a matter of custom. Especially near the end
of the *gacaca* process, the judges resorted to imposing collective punishments
on innocent people. Considering how suddenly they adopted the policy, they
probably acted on instructions from the SNJG. In a similar case in Jali, the
court found twenty-two people living in the vicinity of a genocide survivor
whose house had been pillaged collectively guilty of that crime because these

"people were unable to identify the person that had pillaged their neighbor."[22] In sum, they needed to repay the amount of RWF 1,200,000 (USD 2,162), or roughly five and a half times the average annual rural income at the time. We observed similar cases in the former province of Butare.[23] It is questionable whether this measure helped to reestablish the social bonds that genocide had broken.

Conclusion

Grappling with the multifarious meanings of *umutima* allows us to better understand the construction of Rwandan personhood and the epistemological framework that animates the Rwandan sociocultural universe. Recognizing the various aspects of *umutima* also illuminates the process of transformation that the *gacaca* process supposedly initiated. The genocide and the decade of violence in the 1990s still resonates today in a dialectic of humanity and inhumanity. Dealing with the violence of the past at the interpersonal level entails, first, rehumanizing and resocializing oneself and others by establishing that each person has "a heart" and thus *is* a "human being." And second, it is a process of moralization that explores the nature of the heart or one's moral character. In that way, dealing with the genocide is a "remaking of the moral world" (Richters, Rutayisire, and Dekker 2010). Because the notion of *umutima* is closely connected to the concept of *nda*—the stomach or deepest interior—it signals awareness that the heart is inaccessible to others but is where a person's *moral truth* lies: "magnanimity resides in the stomach (the interior)" (*ubupfura buba mu nda*).

Because (re)humanization or (re)socialization do not occur if an action or interaction is not perceived as genuine—and in fact actions and interactions that are perceived as nongenuine result in the opposite dynamic—the act of pardoning during the *gacaca* proceedings did not often result in any change in the social relationships between victims and perpetrators. Most of the confessed perpetrators, and at times also the victims, gave most such pardons in a formulaic, state-sanctioned manner. In addition, the *gacaca* proceedings that took place at the cell level and were organized as mediation—not as a trial—had the most conciliatory potential. On the one hand, cases where both parties attempted to give something appeared to have the most conciliatory potential. In such cases, the perpetrator restituted material objects or money according to his abilities, and the victim reduced the value of the stolen property. It was not the monetary value that mattered in these cases: it was the restoration of the social relationship through the act of giving. These acts allowed for a new or renewed conviviality, the sharing of drinks, invitations to festivities, and other forms of socializing.

On the other hand, whenever the restitution of property followed a judicial logic—when mediation was not an option—it created conflictual situations, an "us versus them" dynamic.[24] A high number of property cases needed such a trial proceeding. Mediated cases had more conciliatory potential because the nature of the settlement and the process of settling the dispute could tacitly imply an act of pardon. But most of these mediated cases happened under considerable pressure, and consequently people often perceived them as not genuine. This judicial and prosecutorial logic marks a break with the (evolving) *gacaca* institution as it existed previously. The logic of the modern *gacaca* disrupted what had existed among the population in the years between the genocide and the arrival of the "modern" court system.

Epilogue

The black box of Rwanda's grassroots transitional justice process has been opened. I began this study with the observation that one needs to distinguish the *gacaca* model as it emerged in the wake of the Rwandan genocide from its actual practice. We have now seen that the *gacaca* courts were, at one and the same time, a centralized and a decentralized justice system: they embodied the installation and completion of a process at the local level, but they were controlled and guided from above. They were also both a formal and an informal way of dispensing justice, and their core was retributive and adversarial. Their designers claimed the courts were homegrown, inspired by customary justice but in accordance with international human rights standards. Based on numerous observations of their practical functioning, one can conclude that the *gacaca* courts were something never seen before, a truly new form of justice. They mimicked a "traditional" conflict resolution mechanism but offered less potential for conciliation, but at the same time they imitated the modern legal system but with fewer safeguards for due process.

Ultimately, the incorporation of outside influences, especially the ideas that animate the global transitional justice paradigm, gave the court system its distinctive characteristics. These ideas and the policy choices that the RPF government made following the genocide changed the *gacaca* courts into a hybrid institution by fully incorporating elements of the original, informal conflict-resolution mechanism into the formal judicial system. These heterogeneous sources of inspiration and intended outcomes made the court system innovative, and its different traditions and objectives could reinforce each other. But the mixed influences could also be irreconcilable, neutralizing them and making the system fragile. The final assessment is mixed: all of these results actually occurred. Overall, we can say that the outcome of the *gacaca* experiment underscores the claim that "hybrid institutions will not result in predictable experiences and may even result in negative and conflict-promoting experiences" (Millar 2014, 1).

The primary message should be that initiating grassroots processes by altering and upgrading the tradition-based justice-and-reconciliation mechanism does not necessarily mean that the processes automatically become a better version of the original. Such upgrading can also be contradictory due to its design, and it does not necessarily bring together the "best" of all possible worlds: it is important not to go against the grain of existing logics. The *gacaca* experience also suggests it is important to devise complementary mechanisms and strategies. A compromise depends on the ability to achieve all objectives at once, and consequently it will inevitably lead to short-circuits—as was the case with Rwanda's *gacaca* courts. Transitional justice can learn from the "one objective, one instrument" thesis that Tinbergen (1952) formulated in a totally different context. Complementary approaches generally work better than an overall compromise. For example, a complementary approach could encompass a justice system with all the procedural safeguards to hold accountable those with high responsibility for crimes as well as grassroots mechanisms in line with the sociocultural habitat to restore harmony and reintegrate people into society.

Getting down into the Rwandan grass roots helps us to better articulate what is at play and what is at stake when dealing with the legacy of mass violence around the globe. Our voyage to the heart of the *gacaca* practice invites us to reconsider and rethink key concepts and received ideas in transitional justice. This kind of experience challenges dominant approaches in and discourse on transitional justice that suffer from "a sort of neo-imperialism" (Hinton 2010, 7), tend to promote a "transcendent, universal and unitary concept of justice" (Shaw and Waldorf 2010, 2), and aim to produce "certain forms of knowledge, persons and practices" (Riano Alcala and Baines 2012, 386). Instead, the *gacaca* experience teaches us to think about pragmatic ways of truth-seeking, to juxtapose state justice with the quotidian by taking into account contextual understandings of personhood, and, finally, to develop the awareness that transitional justice processes will be influenced not only by political actors but equally by the stable and recurring patterns of behavior that characterize societies.

Truth and its aspects is a repeated theme throughout all the chapters of this book, but truth has not proven to be only a positive or liberating force. Examining the *gacaca* courts shows that truth is indeed important and complex as well, and it raises the question: What is the truth and for whom?

The South African Truth and Reconciliation Commission identifies four notions of truth in its report (TRC-SA 1998, 110–17): forensic, narrative, social, and restorative. The *forensic* truth entails answers to the basic questions of who, where, when, how, and against whom, and it may include the context, causes, and patterns of violations. We have seen clearly that the forensic truth was dominant in the *gacaca* design. Hayner (2002, 100–101) is quite skeptical about truth coming from trials: "The purpose of criminal trials is not to expose the 'truth,' however, but to find whether the criminal standard of proof has been satisfied on specific charges."

That is exactly how the *gacaca* functioned. Or better, should have functioned: the anatomy of the *gacaca* practice also revealed that the standard of proof was often minimal, and at times judges convicted defendants even though the evidence had not proven guilt beyond a reasonable doubt. Hence the reasons why several respondents—especially those of Hutu ethnicity—insisted they were victims of injustice and partiality when they assessed the negative outcomes of the *gacaca* practice. More importantly, the forensic truth was often not reached, because different styles/interpretations of truth-telling circumvented the trial proceedings.

In the TRC report, other dimensions of the truth—narrative, social, and restorative—go beyond this factual delineation of "actions." *Narrative* truth (or *personal* truth) is related to the subjective experiences of people. Truth refers in this case to perceptions, stories, myths, and experiences. The objective is to record the lived reality by incorporating the "meaning" that victim and perpetrator, bystanders and witnesses attached to these facts. *Social* truth is a third dimension and refers to the interaction taking place through discussion and debate. And when justice systems not only collect factual knowledge but acknowledge events and restore the dignity of victims and survivors, one can speak of healing or *restorative* truth. Such truth connects facts and meaning, and situates them within human relationships.

Overall, the experience with *gacaca* was frictional because other expressive forms—namely *moral* truth, *effectual* truth, and what I refer to as the *Truth-with-a-Capital-T*—interacted with the dominating forensic truth. The first of these forms derives from the sociocultural context (chap. 8), the second is a consequence of the decentralized milieu in which the *gacaca* courts were inserted (chaps. 6 and 7), and the third results from the overall political context in which the *gacaca* activities took place (chap. 5). Friction did indeed operate at the heart of the *gacaca* process; friction does not need to be negative because it is a token of the introduction of new norms, as Shaw (2007) observed in the case of Sierra Leone. And it is to be expected because it reflects what Doughty (2015) calls the "inherent violence of social repair." To that extent, any transitional justice process will be frictional and painful, but the friction must be kept from creating a short circuit.

An analysis of the modern *gacaca*'s principles and a closer examination of its basic operational procedures reveal that the design of the court system rested on a correspondence theory of truth. This means that the courts were supposed to function according to a foundationalist epistemology: we can discover an objective reality if we adopt the correct approach and techniques. The objective truth is out there, and relevant evidence guides us in its direction.

The *gacaca* process was, by design, based on such an understanding of what constitutes the truth, and this fact should not surprise us. Beyond Rwanda, most transitional justice mechanisms operate, often tacitly, with such a theory of truth. This understanding of the truth also dominates the academic literature in the field of transitional justice. What the *gacaca* practice reveals is the need to take into account different theories of truth as well. The Rwandan experience shows the importance of thinking with a pragmatic theory of truth if we want to make sense of the nature and outcome of transitional justice processes.

A pragmatic conception of truth drove the *gacaca* process in practice. Two types or styles of truth-telling at play in the *gacaca* process—*effectual* truth and the *Truth-with-a-Capital-T*—reveal this. They epitomize the consequentialist ethics that characterized the *gacaca* in practice: a pragmatic theory of truth is based on the idea that what is true is that which is useful. In other words, what is true is that which gets things done and produces favorable outcomes in a particular space and time. Those in the field of transitional justice generally do not adhere to such an understanding of the truth. Pragmatic truth-telling activities do not reflect the inherent violence of social repair but point toward important flaws in the *gacaca* process that the courts' designers could have foreseen. We need to take these dimensions of the truth into account in any transitional justice process.

The state, or "authority" in the broadest sense of the word, weighed heavily on the nature of participation in *gacaca* and defined what was to be considered as true or false. The pragmatics of daily life and contextualized understandings of what counts as true also rerouted the *gacaca* process. At times, the composition of the collective, the power of sheer numbers, shaped the *gacaca* process on Rwanda's hills. The notion of *ubwenge* captures this complex process of truth-speaking as lying and lying as truth-speaking in the Rwandan case.

Foregrounding this insight does not imply an essentialization—that people cannot change their behaviors due to cultural or social background—of the Rwandan people. Such an argument is often evoked against analyses that take into account cultural dimensions of a process. Clearly, culture is not a cage in which people are trapped but is, instead, a web of meanings in which people are suspended, as Geertz (1973) eloquently put it. Not taking culture into account, especially with respect to grassroots transitional justice, cannot do otherwise but result in limited understanding. In his study of the cultural dimensions at work in the Special Court for Sierra Leone, Tim Kelsall (2013) states: "Many Sierra Leoneans have different ideas of social space and time, of causation, agency, responsibility, evidence, truth and truth-telling from those employed by international criminal courts" (17). He therefore advocates "a dialogical approach to legal institution building. This implies a genuine engagement with the worldview of the Other" (259).

The actual *gacaca* practice shows that the designers of the court system paid hardly any attention to such appropriate sociocultural engagement. This seems like a paradox, considering that many observers consider *gacaca* a homegrown solution derived from the Rwandan sociocultural fabric. Some representations of *gacaca* continue to hail the system for its sociocultural embeddedness, and its restorative and conciliatory potential. In my view, the *gacaca* design went against the grain of Rwandan sociocultural practices.

"Living together again" is a practice forged locally, and the state can either facilitate or hinder the processes that promote it (Theidon 2006, 456). What the modern *gacaca*, with its prosecutorial logic, did not easily facilitate was a process of "acting true," "showing ways of being," or demonstrating "good-heartedness" (chap. 8). Such actions qualify the nature of "being" and "human-ness" that the Rwandan social and cultural universe deems important. People explore these issues through particular expressive forms, such as sharing, conviviality, mutual help, and daily salutations. These are the acts and events of reconciliation at the interpersonal level.

In Rwanda, the real, nonstate administration of justice and facilitation of reconciliation is taking place outside the *gacaca* activities, in line with the importance of the heart (*umutima*) in the local epistemology; *gacaca* was only to a minor extent capable of engaging with these sociocultural understandings of the dynamics of violence and reconciliation. Beyond the Rwandan case, ethnographic or anthropological studies with a transitional justice focus often evoke the notion of "heart." Especially Kimberly Theidon's and Rosalind Shaw's ethnographic material on Peru and Sierra Leone points at such a local epistemology that might be part of a framework resembling the one I explored in Rwanda. Theidon refers to the process of "becoming human" (2000, 551) and "the change of heart" as "moral conversion" (2006, 451). Shaw depicts the importance of "cooling warm hearts" to "re-establish moral relationships" (2005, 129) and stresses the importance of the remaking of "moral subjectivi-ties" through "embodied performances of the truth" that "display a change in the speakers' hearts" (2007, 129).

My findings also contest whether the forensic truth heals, as the field of transitional justice often claims it does. Dialogue and even silence, which occurred before, after, and in the margins of the *gacaca* process, also had a healing function. The initial phase of the process disturbed this very informal way of dealing with the past precisely because *gacaca* required speaking "the truth," that is, the truth based on a correspondence theory. Numerous empirically informed studies undertaken in a wide variety of contexts, such as South Africa (Ross 2003), Burundi (Nee and Uvin 2010), or Bosnia and Herzegovina (Eastmond and Mannergren Selimovic 2012), confirm that the forensic truth is not necessarily the primary driver of reconciliation with past violence.

In the aftermath of violence in India, Veena Das (2007, 7) observed that "life was recovered not through some grand gestures in the realm of the transcendent but through a descent into the ordinary." A thorough assessment and understanding of the social practices of the population in question is necessary to verify whether an adaptation or implementation of a traditional justice-and-reconciliation mechanism or any other transitional justice mechanism will be productive. The strength of these so-called traditional justice mechanisms, including grassroots or place-based approaches in general, probably lies in the fact that they function in line with the sociocultural habitat of the population in their daily activities. A human rights body or the transitional justice industry may not see a localized approach as an effective way of dealing with the past, but it is *the way of the local population*, partly out of necessity, partly out of choice. Paradoxically, the activities of the *gacaca* were embedded in but also went against the local social imaginary and the practices already developed over time to deal with the past. They did and did not fit into the pragmatism of the peasants' lifestyle, and they were not fully adapted to the realpolitik of the microcosmos: in fact, a localized mechanism needs an approach that is sensitive to context.

Therefore, effective transitional justice systems do not go against the grain and do not change the logic of tradition-based justice-and-reconciliation mechanisms. Careful understanding of contextual knowledge and situational ethics avoids short circuits between local realities and imposed transitional justice models with universal design principles based on quasi-transcendent ideas of justice as well as monolithic conceptions of personhood. Legal systems, as Engle Merry (1988, 871) highlights, are "embedded in very different ways of thinking about the fact/law dichotomy, the nature of evidence, and the meaning of judging." The turn in the global transitional justice paradigm toward decentralized, localized, or place-based initiatives or processes should be accompanied by more attention to something that has been a blind spot until now. Very few studies that stress the importance of localizing transitional justice by focusing on spontaneous and informal initiatives or "indigenous" mechanisms have also attempted to map their underlying principles systematically. Writing on Guatemala, for example, Lieselotte Viaene (2010a) emphasizes the need to take into account the "internal logic of the cosmos," meaning the indigenous epistemology or belief systems among the Maya Q'eqchi' Indians to understand their way of dealing with a violent past. What matters, therefore, is a process of localization based on an understanding of the fundamental local principles of social existence and justice.

(Legal) anthropologists have repeatedly emphasized the importance of such foundations for the understanding of the living law of a given society. Law is "part of a distinctive manner of imagining the real" (Geertz 1983, 173), and it is embedded in locally specific systems of meaning. In his writings about an intercultural legal theory, Etienne Le Roy (1999, 189–203) underlines the importance of identifying the elements that make up legality, or rather, "juridicity": every society has its own unique ways of imagining the phenomenon of law. Foblets and Truffin (2004, 265) state that "foundational representations fashion, in a manner that is different in every society, the boundaries of humanity." An emerging interest in grassroots approaches in the broader field of transitional justice therefore needs a conceptual or even paradigmatic shift from mechanisms, institutions, or people (localized or not, tradition-based or not) to something more encompassing: that being the foundations of the living law in a society. Such an exercise will not necessarily result in more restorative conceptions of justice. Writing about Uganda and South Africa, respectively, both Allen (2006) and Wilson (2001) warn against misguided romantic notions of African cultures as antiretribution.

The *gacaca* experience also reveals something about the nature of transition. When stripping the phenomenon of transition—the process underlying transitional justice initiatives—to its basics and its nonnormative core, one arrives at a "liminal" period with respect to a society's norms and moral values (Teitel 2000, 220; Wilson 2001, 19). The findings presented in this study underscore Teitel's (2000) and Carothers's (2002) arguments that we should let go of a normative understanding of the transition paradigm. Such a framework almost automatically equated transition with a shift to liberal democracy and a radical change vis-à-vis a previous regime and order. Villia Jefremovas (2002, 126–27) observed that "little has changed [regarding the] patterns of power" in Rwandan society, and I have demonstrated this in the present book. It is here that the customary claim so often associated with the *gacaca* courts needs to be located.

Long-standing popular practices, the micropolitics of social navigation, and *how* power operates in society do not necessarily change through a transitional justice process. Quite the contrary: such a process can enhance and consolidate these practices. The *gacaca* experience demonstrated a continuation and even consolidation of patterns that have long characterized Rwandan society: self-limiting behavior, distrust and suspicion, strategic behavior and communication, patron-client dynamics, obedience to authority, and the like. Existing conflicts often informed the proceedings as well. Whether an irritating neighbor, an avaricious parent, a long-standing feud over land, or simple envy provoked the conflict, an accusation of participation in the genocide could be used to settle a score (chap. 6). In addition, the experiences of being falsely accused were widespread (chap. 4). In this book the "play of power" between individuals, neighbors, families, lineages, the rich and the poor, the rulers and the ruled at the local level is brought to mind and illustrated, and these patterns shaped the trajectory of the *gacaca* process as well. Nonetheless, *gacaca* was only to a limited extent able to recast or redirect these patterns. Patterns of power—not just the political actors, as Jelena Subotic (2009) stresses in her work on the Balkans—can "hijack" a transitional justice process.

Despite these insights, or even because of them, it is paramount to continue asking the questions Ariel Dorfman (1994, 49) raised in the afterword to *Death and the Maiden*:

> How to heal a country that has been traumatized by repression if the fear to speak out is still omnipresent everywhere? And how do you reach the "truth" if lying has become a habit? How do we keep the past alive without becoming its prisoner? How do we forget it without risking its repetition in the future? Is it legitimate to sacrifice the truth to ensure peace? And what are the consequences of suppressing that past and the truth it is whispering or howling to us? Are people free to search for justice and equality if the threat of a military intervention haunts them? And given these circumstances, can violence be avoided? And how guilty are we all of what happened to those who suffered most? And perhaps the greatest dilemma of them all: how to confront these issues without destroying the national consensus, which creates democratic stability?

Appendix I: Important Dates

I use and slightly adapt the overview provided in Republic of Rwanda (2012).

30 August 1996: Organic Law No. 08/96 of 30/8/1996, which organized the prosecution of genocide crimes and other crimes against humanity committed since 1 October 1990, established special benches in ordinary and military courts, and charged these courts with trying cases involving genocide crimes

1 May 2000: Organic Law No. 9/2000 of 1/5/2000, which amended the structure of the Supreme Court and established six departments, including one to initiate the *gacaca* courts program

26 January 2001: Organic Law No. 40/2000 of 26/1/2001, which governed the creation of *gacaca* courts, organized the prosecution of genocide crimes and other crimes against humanity committed in Rwanda between 1 October 1990 and 31 December 1994, and provided for the setting up of a *gacaca* court at every administrative level of local government (cell, sector, district, municipality, and province)

4–7 October 2001: Countrywide election of *inyangamugayo* judges for the *gacaca* courts

18 June 2002: Public inauguration of the pilot phase of the *gacaca* courts by the president of the Republic

19 June 2002: Start of information collection in seventy-nine cells and in twelve pilot-phase sectors selected from the districts and Kigali City

25 November 2002: Increase of pilot-phase sectors with information collection in 672 cell *gacaca* courts in 106 sectors selected from every district and municipality

4 June 2003: Article 152 of the Constitution of the Republic of Rwanda, which provided for the establishment of the National Service of Gacaca Courts (SNJG)

28 April 2004: Law No. 08/2004 of 28/4/2004, which established the National Service of Gacaca Courts (SNJG), set forth its organization, duties, and functioning, replacing the Supreme Court's Department of Gacaca Courts

19 June 2004: Organic Law No. 16/2004 of 19/6/2004, which established the organization, jurisdiction, and functioning of *gacaca* courts charged with prosecuting and trying the perpetrators of the crime of genocide and other crimes against humanity, and which replaced Organic Law No. 40/2000 of 26/1/2001

20 June 2004: Reorganization of *gacaca* courts so that they would work only at cell and sector levels

24 June 2004: Public inauguration of the activities of *gacaca* courts at all levels throughout the country by the president of the Republic

15 January 2005: Start of information collection throughout the country

10 March 2005: Start of trials before *gacaca* courts in pilot sectors

30 June 2006: Official end of information collection phase at the national level

12 July 2006: Publication of Organic Law No. 28/2006 of 27/6/2006, which modified and complemented Organic Law No. 16/2004 of 19/6/2004

15 July 2006: Start of genocide trials in *gacaca* courts throughout the country

1 March 2007: Publication of Organic Law No. 10/2007 of 1/3/2007, which amended Organic Law No. 16/2004 of 19/6/2004, as modified and complemented to that date

1 June 2008: Publication of Organic Law No. 13/2008 of 19/5/2008, which modified and complemented Organic Law No. 16/2004 of 19/6/2004, as modified and complemented to that date

23 June 2008: Start of trials of Category 1 cases in *gacaca* courts

23 October 2009: First official closing ceremony of *gacaca* court activities at sector level (Juru sector, Bugesera district, Eastern province), although activities at sector level had ended earlier in many locations

5 August 2010: Final official closing ceremony of *gacaca* court activities at sector level (Kagano Sector, Nyamasheke district, Western province)

18 June 2012: Official closure of *gacaca* court activities at the national level by the president of the Republic

Appendix II: Supplementary Tables

Table 6. Defendant categorization, June 2004–March 2007

	Cat. 1	Cat. 2 1st & 2nd	Cat. 2 3rd	Cat. 3
	1	2A	2B	3
	1. planners, organizers, supervisors & ringleaders 2. persons in leadership positions[a] 3. well-known murderers 4. torturers 5. rapists 6. persons dehumanizing dead bodies	1. "ordinary killers" in serious attacks 2. attackers wanting to kill but failing	3. those who committed attacks against others, without the intention to kill	those who committed property offenses
	Ordinary court	Sector gacaca	Sector gacaca	Cell gacaca
Without confession	Death penalty or life	25–30 years	5–7 years	Civil reparation
Confession before listing suspects	25–30 years	7–12 years[b]	1–3 years[b]	Civil reparation
Confession after listing suspects	25–30 years	12–15 years[b]	3–5 years[b]	Civil reparation
Accessory sentence	Perpetual and total loss of civil rights	Permanent loss of a listed number of civil rights[c]	—	—

Source: Republic of Rwanda (2004a)—Organic Law No. 16/2004 of 19/6/2004.
Note: Mitigating circumstances for people who had been between 14 and 18 years at the time of events. Reeducation for those younger than 14 years at the time of events.
[a] Leadership positions at prefecture, subprefecture, and commune level as well as in political parties, army, gendarmerie, communal police, religious denominations, or in militia. Persons in a position of authority at the sector and cell level are classified in the category corresponding to the alleged offense committed but will receive the most severe penalty within that category if found guilty.
[b] Commutation of half of sentence to community service on probation.
[c] Listed civil rights: voting; expert witnessing; carrying firearms; serving in the armed forces, police, and public service; serving as teacher or medical staff in public or private service.

Table 7. Defendant categorization, March 2007–May 2008

	Cat. 1	Cat. 2 1st, 2nd & 3rd	Cat. 2 4th & 5th	Cat. 2 6th	Cat. 3
	1	2A	2B	2C	3
	1. persons in leadership positions[a] 2. rapists	1. well-known murderers 2. torturers 3. persons dehumanizing dead bodies	1. "ordinary killers" in serious attacks 2. attackers wanting to kill but failing	those who committed attacks against others without the intention to kill	those who committed property offenses
	Ordinary court	Sector gacaca	Sector gacaca	Sector gacaca	Cell gacaca
Without confession	Death penalty or life imprisonment	30 years or life	15–19 years	5–7 years[b]	Civil reparation
Confession before listing suspects	20–24 years	20–24 years[b]	8–11 years[b]	1–2 years[b]	Civil reparation
Confession after listing suspects	25–30 years	25–29 years[b]	12–14 years[b]	3–4 years[b]	Civil reparation
Accessory sentence	Permanent loss of a listed number of civil rights[c]	No confession: permanent loss— Confession: temporal loss— of a listed number of civil rights[c]	No confession: permanent loss— Confession: temporal loss— of a listed number of civil rights[c]	—	—

Source: Republic of Rwanda (2007a)—Organic Law No. 10/2007 of 01/03/2007.
Note: Mitigating circumstances for people who had been between 14 and 18 years at the time of events. Reeducation for those younger than 14 years at the time of events.
[a] Leadership positions at prefecture, subprefecture, and commune level as well as in political parties, army, gendarmerie, communal police, religious denominations, or in militia. Persons in a position of authority at the sector and cell level are classified in the category corresponding to the alleged offense committed but will receive the most severe penalty within that category if convicted.
[b] Commutation of half of sentence to community service on probation; 1/6 of sentence is suspended and ⅓ of the sentence is served in custody.
[c] Listed civil rights: to be elected; to become leaders; to serve in the armed forces, police, and other security organs; to be a teacher, medical staff member, magistrate, public prosecutor, or judicial counsel.

Table 8. Defendant categorization, June 2008 onward

	Cat. 1 1st	Cat. 1 2nd	Cat. 2 1st, 2nd & 3rd	Cat. 2 4th & 5th	Cat. 2 6th	Cat. 3
	1A	1B	2A	2B	2C	3
	1. planners and organizers 2. persons who occupied positions of national or prefectural leadership and authority	1. inciters, supervisors, and ringleaders 2. persons in leadership positions[a] 3. persons who committed rape or sexual torture	1. well-known murderers 2. torturers 3. persons dehumanizing dead bodies	1. "ordinary killers" 2. attackers wanting to kill but failing	those who committed attacks against others without the intention to kill	those who committed property offenses
	Ordinary court	Sector gacaca	Sector gacaca	Sector gacaca	Sector gacaca	Cell gacaca
Without confession	Life imprisonment with special provisions	Life imprisonment with special provisions	30 years or life imprisonment	15–19 years	5–7 years[b]	Civil reparation
Confession before listing suspects	20–24 years	20–24 years	20–24 years[b]	8–11 years[b]	1–2 years[b]	Civil reparation
Confession after listing suspects	25–30 years	25–30 years	25–29 years[b]	12–14 years[b]	3–4 years[b]	Civil reparation

| Accessory sentence | Permanent loss of a listed number of civil rights[c] | Permanent loss of a listed number of civil rights[c] | No confession: permanent loss—Confession: temporal loss—of a listed number of civil rights[c] | No confession: permanent loss—Confession: temporal loss—of a listed number of civil rights[c] | — | — |

Source: Republic of Rwanda (2008b)—Organic Law No. 13/2008 of 1/6/2008.
Note: Mitigating circumstances for people who had been between 14 and 18 years at the time of events. Reeducation for those younger than 14 years at the time of events.
[a] Leadership positions at prefecture, subprefecture, and commune level as well as in political parties, army, gendarmerie, communal police, religious denominations, or militia. Persons in a position of authority at the sector and cell level are classified in the category corresponding to the alleged offense committed but will receive the most severe penalty within that category if convicted.
[b] Commutation of half of sentence to community service on probation; ⅙ of sentence is suspended and ⅓ of the sentence is served in custody.
[c] Listed civil rights: to be elected; to become leaders; to serve in the armed forces, police, and other security organs; to be a teacher, member of a medical staff, magistrate, public prosecutor, or judicial counsel.

Table 9. *Gacaca* data—Systematic observation by location

		Ntabona		Runyoni		Rukoma		Jali		All	
		N	%	*N*	%	*N*	%	*N*	%	*N*	%
Total		307	100%	686	100%	226	100%	508	100%	1727	100%
Nature of observation 1	Complete	141	45.9%	115	16.8%	106	46.9%	56	11.0%	418	24.2%
	Extensive summary	132	43.0%	65	9.5%	0	0.0%	438	86.2%	635	36.8%
	Verdict	34	11.1%	506	73.8%	120	53.1%	14	2.8%	674	39.0%
Nature of observation 2	Almost all data	273	88.9%	180	26.2%	106	46.9%	494	97.2%	1,053	61.0%
	Limited data	34	11.1%	506	73.8%	120	53.1%	14	2.8%	674	39.0%
Level of observation	Sector	282	91.9%	575	83.8%	160	70.8%	279	54.9%	1,296	75.0%
	Sector—Appeal	24	7.8%	102	14.9%	60	26.5%	175	34.4%	361	20.9%
	Sector—Revision	1	0.3%	9	1.3%	6	2.7%	54	10.6%	70	4.1%

Table 10. *Gacaca* data—Systematic observation by year

		2006		2007		2008		2009		2010		Total	
		N	%	N	%	N	%	N	%	N	%	N	%
	Total	45	2.6%	1,241	71.9%	67	3.9%	272	15.7%	102	5.9%	1,727	100.0%
Nature of observation 1	Complete	0	0.0%	349	83.5%	16	3.8%	53	12.7%	0	0.0%	418	100.0%
	Extensive summary	44	6.9%	233	36.7%	43	6.8%	215	33.9%	100	15.7%	635	100.0%
	Verdict	1	0.1%	659	97.8%	8	1.2%	4	0.6%	2	0.3%	674	100.0%
Nature of observation 2	Almost all data	44	4.2%	582	55.3%	59	5.6%	268	25.5%	100	9.5%	1,053	100.0%
	Limited data	1	0.1%	659	97.8%	8	1.2%	4	0.6%	2	0.3%	674	100.0%
Level of observation	Sector	45	.5%	1,009	77,9%	32	2.5%	131	10,1%	79	6,1%	1,296	100,0%
	Sector—Appeal	0	0.0%	220	60.9%	11	3.0%	115	31.9%	15	4.2%	361	100.0%
	Sector—Revision	0	0.0%	12	17.1%	24	34.3%	26	37.1%	8	11.4%	70	100.0%

Table 11. Interventions by trial category

	Ntabona N trials = 139 N interventions = 5,231			Runyoni N trials = 124 N interventions = 8,617			Rukoma N trials = 105 N interventions = 4,938			Jali[a] N trials = 53 N interventions = 8,126			All N trials = 421 N interventions = 26,912		
	Mean	Median	%Tot	Mean	Median	%Tot	Mean	Median	%Tot	Mean	Median	%Tot	Mean	Median	%Tot
Accused	8	7	21.7%	15	11	21.9%	15	13	31.8%	8	5	5.4%	12	8	18.7%
À charge	4	3	10.3%	7	4	9.5%	5	2	10.7%	7	4	4.7%	5	3	8.4%
À décharge	3	3	9.2%	4	2	5.2%	2	0	3.7%	3	2	1.8%	3	2	4.7%
Total décharge[b]	0	0	1.1%	0	0	0.5%	1	0	1.1%	0	0	0.3%	0	0	0.7%
Neutral	4	2	9.8%	17	7	24.0%	6	4	13.2%	36	3	23.8%	12	3	19.2%
Inyangamugayo	18	15	47.5%	27	22	38.4%	18	13	38.3%	98	10	64.0%	31	16	47.9%
Inyangamugayo other courts[c]	0	0	0.4%	0	0	0.3%	0	0	0.2%	0	0	0.0%	0	0	0.2%
Authorities	0	0	0.1%	0	0	0.2%	0	0	0.9%	0	0	0.1%	0	0	0.3%
Security personnel	0	0	0.1%	0	0	0.0%	0	0	0.0%	0	0	0.0%	0	0	0.0%
Total	37.63	29.00	100%	69.49	55.50	100%	47.03	34.00	100%	153.32	27.00	100%	63.92	35.00	100%

Note: The interventions presented in this table cover all the possible interventions during a trial. The sum of these interventions is the total of all interventions during a trial. Interventions are defined as all-verbal utterances made by a trial participant. An intervention begins when someone starts speaking and ends when another person starts speaking. The subsequent person's speech is then considered a new intervention. An intervention can thus be short or long but is in both cases considered as a single intervention. If a person who already intervened speaks again after one or more individuals have made interventions in the meantime, this is considered a new intervention. Only trials where all the verbal interventions were recorded verbatim have been considered for this analysis.

[a] The number of interventions for Jali (8,126) is exceptionally high compared to the number of trials (53). This is because the trials observed verbatim in Jali were (by coincidence) exceptionally lengthy trials.

[b] Indicates the accused was not present during the event he or she is accused of.

[c] Refers to *inyangamugayo* belonging to courts at other administrative levels (cell, sector, or sector appeal) or in other areas who were summoned to the trial in order to provide additional information they had obtained at their level or in their area regarding the case/accused.

Table 12. Interventions by ethnicity, genocide relation, and gender

	Ntabona N trials = 139 N interventions = 1,403			*Runyoni* N trials = 124 N interventions = 3,294			*Rukoma* N trials = 105 N interventions = 1,307			*Jali* N trials = 53 N interventions = 2,440			*All* N trials = 421 N interventions = 8,444		
	Mean	*Median*	*%Tot*	*Mean*	*Median*	*%Tot*	*Mean*	*Median*	*%Tot*	*Mean*	*Median*	*%Tot*	*Mean*	*Median*	*%Tot*
Ethnicity															
Hutu	6	4	57.7%	15	11	58.1%	4	2	33.1%	28	3	60.9%	11	4	55.0%
Tutsi	4	2	42.3%	11	5	41.9%	8	5	66.9%	18	6	39.1%	9	4	45.0%
Genocide Relation															
No prison	3	1	26.6%	8	3	18.5%	1	0	10.0%	24	3	51.6%	6	1	28.1%
Liberated from prison	3	2	28.6%	7	4	27.7%	2	0	18.8%	3	0	6.5%	4	2	20.4%
Prisoner	0	0	2.1%	3	0	11.9%	1	0	4.3%	1	0	2.7%	1	0	6.4%
Survivor	4	2	42.8%	11	5	40.4%	8	5	66.8%	18	6	39.1%	9	4	44.5%
Old-caseload returnee	0	0	0.0%	0	0	0.0%	0	0	0.0%	0	0	0.0%	0	0	0.0%
Gender															
Male	6	4	59.4%	19	13	69.5%	9	5	73.1%	36	8	77.2%	14	5	70.4%
Female	4	2	40.6%	8	3	30.5%	3	1	26.9%	11	2	22.8%	6	3	29.6%
Total	10	6	100%	26	17	100%	12	7	100%	46	9	100%	20	8	100%

Note: Interventions by the accused, the *inyangamugayo*, security personnel, and authorities (state agents) are not considered here. This table focuses on the local inhabitants (including victims) involved in the trial.

Table 13. Indictments

	Ntabona N defendants = 305 N charges = 446		Runyoni N defendants = 502 N charges = 775		Rukoma N defendants = 210 N charges = 303		Jali N defendants = 507 N charges = 813		All N defendants = 1,524 N charges = 2,337	
	All charges	Per defendant	All charges	Per defendant	All charges	Per defendant	All charges	Per defendant	All charges	Per defendant
Organizer—planner	0.0%	0.0%	0,9%	1.4%	0.3%	0.5%	0.2%	0.4%	0.4%	0.7%
Supervisor—inciting people	1.6%	2.3%	1.8%	2.8%	2.0%	2.9%	1.4%	2.2%	1.6%	2.5%
Well-known murderer	2.9%	4.3%	2.2%	3.4%	0.3%	0.5%	0.0%	0.0%	1.3%	2.0%
Leadership position (general)	0.0%	0.0%	0.1%	0.2%	0.0%	0.0%	0.0%	0.0%	0.0%	0.1%
Leadership position (national—prefecture)	0.0%	0.0%	0.0%	0.0%	0.0%	0.0%	0.1%	0.2%	0.0%	0.1%
Leadership position (sous-préfécture/commune)	0.0%	0.0%	0.3%	0.4%	0.0%	0.0%	0.0%	0.0%	0.1%	0.1%
Torturer	3.1%	4.6%	1.3%	2.0%	4.0%	5.7%	1.5%	2.4%	2.1%	3.1%
Rapist	0.0%	0.0%	0.3%	0.4%	0.7%	1.0%	4.1%	6.5%	1.6%	2.4%
Dehumanizing acts on a dead body	0.2%	0.3%	1.2%	1.8%	0.7%	1.0%	0.6%	1.0%	0.7%	1.1%
Ordinary killer in serious attacks	11.4%	16.7%	12.3%	18.9%	12.9%	18.6%	18.6%	29.8%	14.4%	22.0%
Participation in attacks in order to kill without killing	43.5%	63.6%	48.3%	74.5%	61.4%	88.6%	32.7%	52.5%	43.6%	66.9%
Participation in attack without intention to kill	11.7%	17.0%	0.5%	0.8%	0.0%	0.0%	1.5%	2.4%	2.9%	4.5%

Property offense (pillaging/destruction)	21.5%	31.5%	9.4%	14.5%	7.6%	11.0%	6.3%	10.1%	10.4%	15.9%
Manning roadblock	0.4%	0.7%	6.2%	9.6%	0.3%	0.5%	1.0%	1.6%	2.5%	3.9%
Erecting roadblock	0.0%	0.0%	1.4%	2.2%	0.0%	0.0%	0.9%	1.4%	0.8%	1.2%
Organization of meetings (to coordinate attacks)	0.7%	1.0%	1.7%	2.6%	0.0%	0.0%	0.0%	0.0%	0.7%	1.0%
Illegal possession of firearm	0.2%	0.3%	5.7%	8.8%	2.6%	3.8%	2.5%	3.9%	3.1%	4.8%
Distribution of firearms	0.0%	0.0%	0.4%	0.6%	0.0%	0.0%	0.2%	0.4%	0.2%	0.3%
Denunciation/guiding killers	2.2%	3.3%	3.4%	5.2%	2.3%	3.3%	1.8%	3.0%	2.5%	3.8%
Violation of *gacaca* procedures	0.0%	0.0%	1.8%	2.8%	1.3%	1.9%	24.6%	39.4%	9.3%	14.3%
Member of militia	0.4%	0.7%	1.0%	1.6%	1.7%	2.4%	1.4%	2.2%	1.1%	1.7%
Other	0.0%	0.0%	0.0%	0.0%	2.0%	2.9%	0.7%	1.2%	0.5%	0.8%

Note: Percentages are based on combined charges against 1,524 defendants (multiple charges possible). Total percentages are >100%. Indictments are compiled based on actual charges observed during trials. They therefore include charges not stipulated in the *gacaca* law. Notably, at certain times and in some localities, courts charged defendants with crimes the *gacaca* law did not cover, for example, the distribution of firearms, the erection and manning of roadblocks, or the guidance and support of killers. Normally, the *inyangamugayo* read out the charges against the accused at the start of the trial. These charges were sometimes not explicitly mentioned at that time. Sometimes additional (alleged) crimes committed by the accused also surfaced during the unfolding of the trial. The accused would then also be judged for these additional charges at the end of the trial. In those cases where one of these phenomena occurred, we coded the charges based on information on the charges available through the actual trial proceedings.

Table 14. Categorization of *gacaca* laws, 2004, 2007, and 2008

	Ntabona *N defendants = 305* *N charges = 446*		*Runyoni* *N defendants = 502* *N charges = 775*		*Rukoma* *N defendants = 210* *N charges = 303*		*Jali* *N defendants = 507* *N charges = 813*		*All* *N defendants = 1,524* *N charges = 2,337*	
	All charges	*Per defendant*	*All charges*	*Per defendant*	*All charges*	*Per defendant*	*All charges*	*Per defendant*	*All charges*	*Per defendant*
2004 Law										
Category 1	6.3%	8.9%	8.5%	11.4%	7.1%	9.0%	9.0%	13.0%	8.1%	11.1%
Category 2A	56.3%	79.0%	67.9%	91.0%	77.5%	98.6%	51.0%	73.6%	60.9%	83.9%
Category 2B	15.0%	21.0%	10.7%	14.3%	3.0%	3.8%	4.8%	6.9%	8.5%	11.7%
Category 3[a]	22.4%	31.5%	10.8%	14.5%	8.6%	11.0%	7.0%	10.1%	11.6%	15.9%
Gacaca procedure(s)	0.0%	0.0%	2.1%	2.8%	1.5%	1.9%	27.4%	39.4%	10.4%	14.3%
Other	0.0%	0.0%	0.0%	0.0%	2.2%	2.9%	0.8%	1.2%	0.6%	0.8%
2007 Law										
Category 1	2.1%	3.0%	4.7%	6.6%	2.5%	3.3%	6.6%	9.9%	4.6%	6.5%
Category 2A	5.1%	7.2%	10.2%	14.1%	8.6%	11.4%	5.4%	8.1%	7.3%	10.4%
Category 2B	55.7%	78.7%	62.3%	86.5%	74.1%	98.1%	49.2%	73.2%	57.9%	82.1%
Category 2C	14.8%	21.0%	10.3%	14.3%	2.9%	3.8%	4.6%	6.9%	8.3%	11.7%
Category 3[a]	22.3%	31.5%	10.5%	14.5%	8.3%	11.0%	6.8%	10.1%	11.2%	15.9%
Gacaca procedure(s)	0.0%	0.0%	2.0%	2.8%	1.4%	1.9%	26.5%	39.4%	10.1%	14.3%
Other	0.0%	0.0%	0.0%	0.0%	2.2%	2.9%	0.8%	1.2%	0.6%	0.8%

2008 Law

Category 1A	0.0%	0.0%	1.0%	1.4%	0.4%	0.5%	0.3%	0.4%	0.5%	0.7%
Category 1B	2.1%	3.0%	4.6%	6.4%	2.5%	3.3%	6.6%	9.9%	4.5%	6.4%
Category 2A	5.1%	7.2%	10.1%	14.1%	8.6%	11.4%	5.4%	8.1%	7.3%	10.4%
Category 2B	55.7%	78.7%	61.7%	86.5%	73.8%	98.1%	49.1%	73.2%	57.7%	82.1%
Category 2C	14.8%	21.0%	10.2%	14.3%	2.9%	3.8%	4.6%	6.9%	8.3%	11.7%
Category 3[a]	22.3%	31.5%	10.4%	14.5%	8.2%	11.0%	6.7%	10.1%	11.2%	15.9%
Gacaca procedure(s)	0.0%	0.0%	2.0%	2.8%	1.4%	1.9%	26.5%	39.4%	10.1%	14.3%
Other	0.0%	0.0%	0.0%	0.0%	2.2%	2.9%	0.8%	1.2%	0.6%	0.8%

Note: Percentages are based on combined charges against 1,524 defendants (multiple charges possible). Total percentages are >100%. For an overview of the categories, see tables 6, 7, and 8 in this appendix.

[a] Category 3 crimes are listed only if a property crime is mentioned on the charges against the accused during the sector-level trial. The percentages are thus incomplete since the sector-level trials do not deal with property crimes. Property-related offenses were therefore not always mentioned at sector-level trials. Percentages of people only accused at the cell level (property crimes) are not included here.

# Glossary

Kinyarwanda

abacengezi (pl., sing.: *umucengezi*): Literally, infiltrators. Refers to the members of security forces and militia of the defeated Hutu government that fled Rwanda. Following the genocide, they attacked Rwanda from camps in Zaïre (currently DR Congo).

abakada (pl., sing.: *umukada*): Refers to RPF collaborators or "intermediaries," used mostly after the genocide.

abiru (pl., sing.: *umwiru*): Keepers of the royal secrets, members of the court nobility.

akazu (sing., pl.: *utuzu*): Literally, little house. Refers to the inner circle of power surrounding President Habyarimana.

ceceka: To keep quiet; to stop talking, crying, weeping, conversing, and the like. From the verb *guceceka*.

gacaca: (1) Literally, species of grass that makes a natural lawn and is highly appreciated by domestic animals, family of the *cynodon dactylon*; (2) place where people meet to reconcile neighbors; (3) (semi-)informal conflict-resolution mechanism; (4) jurisdiction: court system installed to prosecute genocide crimes.

ibyitso (pl., sing.: *icyitso*): Accomplice. Term used by the Habyarimana government to refer to alleged RPA/RPF collaborators during the 1990–94 civil war.

igihango: Blood pact.

igitero (sing., pl.: *ibitero*): Attacking party. Refers to a group of attackers—militia, army, or ordinary citizens—chasing targeted individuals.

imibanire: The nature of living together (social cohesion).

imidugudu (pl., sing.: *umudugudu*): Literally, agglomeration. Refers to the grouped settlements introduced in the context of a villagization policy following the genocide. Term for an official administrative level since the 2006 territorial reform.

imihigo (pl., sing.: *umuhigo*): Literally, a vow. Refers to performance contracts in postgenocide Rwanda.

inda (sing. and pl.): Belly.

ingando (sing. and pl.): Literally, camp. Refers to so-called solidarity or reeducation camps in the postgenocide period.

ingengabitekerezo ya jenoside: Genocide ideology.

Inkotanyi (sing. and pl.): Literally, the invincible. Popular name of the Rwandan Patriotic Army (RPA) and, by extension, the RPF.

inshuti (sing. and pl.): Friend.

Interahamwe (sing. and pl.): Literally, those working together. Refers to the youth wing of the MRND political party in the years preceding the genocide and the militia that played a major role in the killing of Tutsi during the genocide. After the genocide, the term is often used to refer to anyone who committed crimes during the genocide and/or anyone who adheres to the so-called genocide ideology.

inyangamugayo (sing. and pl.): Literally, a person of integrity. Refers to lay judges presiding over the *gacaca* courts installed to deal with genocide crimes.

inzu (sing., pl.: *amazu*): (1) Literally, house; (2) sublineage.

itorero (sing., pl.: *amatorero*): Literally, club. Refers to decentralized reeducation activities taking place at the lowest administrative levels of Rwandan postgenocide society.

itsembasemba (sing. and pl.): Massacre.

kanyanga (sing. and pl.): Strong artisanal alcoholic liquor.

Kinyarwanda: The language of Rwanda.

kubana: To live together.

kunywana: To make a blood pact.

kwibwiriza: Norm-abiding behavior; self-censorship.

Leta: Kinyarwandanized French for "L'état" or the state.

maneko (sing. and pl.): Intelligence agent; informant.

nyumbakumi (Swahili): Ten houses. Refers to the local official responsible for the lowest administrative level (officially abolished in 2011).

ubumuntu: Sense of humanity.

ubushera (sing. and pl.): Nonalcoholic sorghum beer.

ubuzima (sing. and pl.): (1) Life; (2) health.

ubwenge (sing. and pl.): Literally, intelligence. Also refers to trickery, lying, and deceit.

ubwiyunge: Reconciliation.

Uganda Waragi: Ugandan-made gin.

umuganda (sing. and pl.): Community works.

umuntu (sing., pl.: *abantu*): Man.

umuryango (sing., pl.: *imiryango*): Literally, family. Also refers to the RPF in the postgenocide period. The RPF presents itself as a family.

umutima (sing., pl.: *imitima*): (1) Literally, heart, central organ of blood circulation; (2) seat of human life: sensations, emotions, sentiments, consciousness, will, and the like; (3) moral character.

umwami (sing., pl.: *abami*): King. Traditional authority in Rwandan history.

Other

À charge: Against the defendant.

À décharge: In support of the defendant.

bourgmestre: Mayor.

cabaret (sing., pl.: *cabarets*): Bar.
cachot: (Small) detainment facility, often in a communal setting.
colline (sing., pl.: *collines*): Hill.
mutuelle (de santé): (Health) insurance plan.
rescapé(e) (sing., pl.: *rescapé[e]s*): Genocide survivor.
virtù: Virtue.

    Notes

Introduction

1. Studies advocate the need to localize transitional justice processes or to study these processes at the grassroots or from below (Oomen 2007; Arriaza and Roht-Arriaza 2008; Lundy and McGovern 2008; McEvoy and McGregor 2008). Recent studies are also bringing into focus the cultural context of transitional justice processes or customary approaches to deal with the violence of the past (Wilson 2001; Pouligny, Chesterman, and Schnabel 2007; Huyse 2008; Huyse and Salter 2008; Shaw and Waldorf 2010; Viaene 2010b; Viaene and Brems 2010).

2. These objectives can be found on almost all official documents about the modern *gacaca*, in a number of the *gacaca* laws, in speeches by Rwandan dignitaries before, during, and after the process, and on government websites.

3. See, for example, the majority of the documents on the website of the National Service of the Gacaca Courts (SNJG), http://www.inkiko-gacaca.gov.rw/En/EnIntroduction.htm. The actual communications of these state agents have similar characteristics. See, for example, the presentation made by the executive secretary of the National Service of Gacaca Courts, Domitilla Mukantaganzwa, during a conference on judicial reforms in Kigali (Mukantaganzwa 2008).

4. And the numeric does not necessarily have to be correct. For example, with respect to the *gacaca* courts proceedings, many state actors refer to numbers ranging from 860,000 to almost two million "individuals" accused and processed through the *gacaca* system, while these numbers actually refer to "cases." One "individual" can be linked to multiple "cases" (see chap. 3).

5. His opinion on *gacaca* is available in Rusagara 2005.

6. A British newspaper referred to the issue earlier (Booth 2010).

7. See also the remarks by Susan Thomson (2014) following a mistaken use of Twitter accounts belonging to Rwandan president Kagame. See also Rhodes 2014.

8. It seems the Rwandan government paid an additional London-based PR firm to, among other things, denounce accusations of genocide crimes by Rwanda in the

Democratic Republic of Congo (DRC), as an interview with a representative of the PR firm, recorded with a hidden camera, reveals (Newman and Wright 2011).

9. See Vandeginste 1999, 2000; Drumbl 2000a, 2000b, 2005; Sarkin 2000, 2001; Gaparayi 2001; Reyntjens and Vandeginste 2001; Daly 2002; Digneffe and Fierens 2003; Harrell 2003; Ntampaka 2003; Uvin and Mironko 2003; Uvin 2003; Corey and Joireman 2004; Goldstein Bolocan 2004; Staub 2004; Tiemessen 2004; Wierzynska 2004; Betts 2005; Fierens 2005; Lin 2005; Raper 2005; Schabas 2005; Wells 2005; Kirkby 2006; Longman 2006; McKenna 2006; Venter 2007; Uvin n.d. Publications from a later date incorporate secondary insights from primary observations in their analysis (e.g., Nagy 2009).

10. See Human Rights Watch 2001, 2002a, 2002b, 2004; Amnesty International 2000, 2002a, 2002b.

11. See Oomen 2005; Chakravarty 2006; Meyerstein 2007.

12. See African Rights 2000; Liprodhor 2000; Gasibirege and Babalola 2001; Republic of Rwanda 2003; Longman et al. 2004; Morril 2004; Babalola et al. n.d.

13. Penal Reform International (PRI) focused mainly on the social dimension of the *gacaca* practice; Lawyers Without Borders (Avocats Sans Frontières [ASF]) adopted a purely legal perspective. See the reports on the website of Penal Reform International at http://www.penalreform.org/publications/gacaca-research-reports and the reports by Avocats Sans Frontières (2005, 2006, 2007a, 2007b, 2010) at http://www.asf.be/fr/publications.

14. Honeyman et al. 2002, 2004; Karekezi et al. 2004; Buckley-Zistel 2005, 2006; Molenaar 2005; Waldorf 2006, 2010; Clark 2007, 2008, 2010; Ingelaere 2007a, 2008, 2009a, 2009b, 2011a; Brounéus 2008, 2010; Burnet 2008; Rettig 2008, 2011; Van Billoen 2008; Megwalu and Loizides 2010; Thomson and Nagy 2010; Doughty 2011; Rimé et al. 2011; Takeuchi 2011; Thomson 2011a. I leave aside a multitude of master's theses written on the topic. Many of them provide interesting insights and, at times, adopt a perspective "from below" based on a period of fieldwork in rural Rwanda. See, for example, Leegwater 2005.

15. Republic of Rwanda 2007a, 2008b, 2010; African Rights 2008.

16. Moreover, the empirical basis of Clark's analysis is much more limited than this study's. Clark's analysis is based on the observation of approximately eighty *gacaca* trials, and he does not provide a systematic analysis of the trial proceedings. In addition, Clark's book does not cover the entire period *gacaca* was operational in Rwandan society.

17. Morse (2003, 190) defines a theoretical drive as "the overall direction of the project as determined from the original questions or purpose. . . . [It] is primarily inductive or deductive." In contrast, working deductively is more suited to test a hypothesis. An inductive stance solicits a qualitative approach while the use of quantitative methods is best suited for testing. An inductive theoretical drive and the use of primarily qualitative methods and data assured that the research remained open to unexpected findings.

Chapter 1. From Genocide to *Gacaca*

1. Only a tiny segment of the population is Twa. The literature on Rwanda often uses the following approximations, based on censuses conducted during the colonial period: Hutu (84 percent), Tutsi (14 percent), and Twa (1 percent). The contemporary ethnic composition of the population is unknown.

2. For a comprehensive insight into the dynamics of the genocide, see Des Forges 1999 and Straus 2006.

3. See also Guichaoua 2005; Straus 2006; and Fujii 2009.

4. Apart from the *gacaca* courts, although in the background and at a much slower rate, other transitional justice strategies have been adopted and different mechanisms installed. The main responsibility for achieving accountability had originally been placed on the ordinary Rwandan justice system, but the tribunals of first instance simply could not handle the vast number of cases. In November 1994, UN Security Council Resolution 995 established the International Criminal Tribunal for Rwanda (ICTR) to prosecute individuals responsible for crimes of genocide and other violations of international law in order to make sure that such gross violations of human rights would not go unpunished. In addition to the ICTR proceedings held in Arusha in neighboring Tanzania, there have been other trials held in third countries based on universal jurisdiction law. Alongside this dominant "punitive" approach, a more restorative component has been added by the establishment of the fund for the assistance of the survivors of the genocide (Fonds d'Assistance aux Rescapés du Génocide, FARG). A fund reserved for the compensation of victims (Fonds d'Indemnisation, FIND) was also conceived but never became operational (Rombouts 2004). A National Unity and Reconciliation Commission (NURC) was set up in 1999 with a mandate that can be summarized as promoting unity and reconciliation, most visibly through the organization of the *ingando* solidarity camps for reintegration and reeducation. A discourse of reconciliation started to surface in 2000. Now every sociopolitical initiative, from poverty alleviation programs to resettlement plans to (political) decentralization, is framed in the language of "reconciliation," "strengthening unity," "empowerment," and the "rebuilding of social relations."

5. I am relying on the few sources available on the pregenocide *gacaca* (Van Houtte et al. 1981; Reyntjens 1990; Ntampaka 1995, 2003; UNHCHR 1996), works on the history of Rwanda (e.g., Vansina 2004), and interviews with older informants during fieldwork.

6. *Umucaca* refers to the plant, the species of grass; *agacaca* refers to the physical space covered with this type of grass.

7. Urugwiro is the name of the presidential premises where the meetings took place. This name was adopted to refer to the meetings.

8. See especially the document Peter Uvin (n.d.) prepared for the Belgian government. It is an interesting overview of the issues at stake for donors at the time.

9. For an early depiction of the proposed modernized court system, see Vandeginste 1999.

10. This meant that many convicts returned to prison or went to prison for the
first time. One of the objectives of the installation of the *gacaca* process was, however,
to alleviate the pressure on the prison system. Therefore, in a first modification in
2007, more differentiation was introduced with respect to Category 2 crimes. In addition, this modification also brought with it the "slicing" of sanctions when a convict
had confessed and the court had accepted his confession: the court commuted half the
sentence to community service on probation, suspended a sixth of the sentence, and
required a third of the sentence to be served in custody. Moreover, convicts had to do
community service first and, only later, serve time in prison. I discuss the rationale
behind this procedure in the following paragraphs.

11. The new organic laws that came into effect in March 2007 and June 2008 and
modified the 2004 law cannot be applied retroactively. This fact made the *gacaca* process rather arbitrary. One could receive a sentence but a couple of months later receive
a less-severe punishment for the same crimes. However, the 2004 law stipulated that
people convicted based on the 2000 law had to serve their sentences based on the
modifications in the 2004 law (Republic of Rwanda 2004a, art. 41). Very few persons
had been tried based on the 2000 *gacaca* law.

12. The ordinary justice system would not be up to the task of dealing with the
number of Category 1 cases it was going to receive. Therefore, the main modification
introduced in the 2007 and 2008 laws was the introduction of a differentiation in
Category 1 crimes. Some of these crimes, including rape and sexual torture, were chan-
neled toward the *gacaca* courts.

13. In January 2006 these administrative structures were fundamentally changed
through an extensive administrative reform, but the *gacaca* courts and their jurisdictions continued functioning according to the initial administrative structure.

14. A sector is not a village in the common sense of the word. By long-standing
practice, Rwandan households have been dispersed on hills, and "sector" refers to the
households on one hill. Only in recent years have people been increasingly grouped
together in what is referred to as *imidugugu* or agglomerations. Throughout the book,
I refer to sectors as villages because people living on Rwanda's hills relate to their sectors since those living elsewhere relate to a village.

15. A modification of the *gacaca* law in 2007 adjusted this situation by adding the
provision that an alleged perpetrator could also be prosecuted in the *gacaca* court of
that person's residence if it was impossible to prosecute him or her "by the *gacaca* court
where the crime was committed or when it was committed beyond the borders of
Rwanda." In none of the cases we observed did this actually happen.

16. Some observers consider this categorization a separate, additional phase in the
gacaca process. Because only the *inyangamugayo* were involved in this categorization,
and because categorization continued during the trial phase, I do not consider this to
be a separate phase.

17. Based on my field observations of almost two thousand trials. I discuss the nature of these observations in detail in chap. 2.

18. Between December 2007 and July 2008, there were no or few *gacaca* meetings. This "unofficial" interruption of the proceedings was due to the SNJG's instruction that the courts halt operation until a new *gacaca* law came into effect in June 2008.

19. Field observation, Bugesera region, March–April 2007. In the sectors systematically observed, this resulted in the installation of one to seven additional courts of first instance.

20. Field observation, Ntabona, 17 July 2007, sess. 55.

21. The Rwandan government has issued confusing communications about these numbers. Officials of the SNJG and members of the Rwandan government and administration generally referred to "individuals" when communicating about these statistics throughout the period that *gacaca* was operational. I asked a number of officials several times whether they were referring to cases or individuals, and I never received a clear answer. An understanding of the number of individuals tried, convicted, or acquitted is important to understanding not only the dynamics of the genocide but also the collectivization or individualization of guilt.

22. The concluding report states that funds used since 2001 totaled 29,665,828,082 Rwandan francs (RWF) (SNJG 2012). Conversion throughout this study is based on the average exchange rates between 1 July 2006 and 1 January 2012: 1 Euro = RWF 766.499 and 1 USD = RWF 555.056.

23. One of these thousands was a Belgian priest, Guy Theunis. For an inside perspective on life in a Rwandan prison and personal reflections on participating in the *gacaca* process as a defendant, see Theunis 2012.

Chapter 2. Learning "to Be Kinyarwanda"

1. See also many reports prepared by the Human Rights Center, University of California, Berkeley, summarizing findings of population-based surveys conducted in several countries. Available at http://www.law.berkeley.edu/11937.htm (accessed 13 September 2012).

2. One could make a distinction between *kumenya Kinyarwanda* and *kumenya Ikinyarwanda* to capture these two meanings. The latter refers to knowing the language, the former to knowing Rwandan practices. For example, one says *kurya Kinyarwanda* (eating à la Rwandaise) or *kubyina Kinyarwanda* (dancing in a Rwandan way).

3. Informal interview, central Rwanda, June 2006. On surveillance in postgenocide Rwanda, see also Purdekova 2011a.

4. At this time, I had been working on a series of separate research projects, each of limited duration and with no guarantees of future funding, and I was aware that learning a new language can take years.

5. Pierre Bourdieu is the most prominent advocate of a research stance that solicits the continuous reflection on the "field" and the process of doing research. (See, e.g., Bourdieu and Wacquant 1992.)

6. In order to guarantee anonymity and to protect research participants, I have changed all names of locations and individuals. I can provide actual names upon request.

7. Appendix II provides an overview of the trials monitored in each of the research sites as well as the distribution of the observations over the years.

8. The logic of trials at the cell level was different from sector-level trials, as I will explain in chapter 8. Multiple defendants were tried jointly during trials at the cell level. Sector-level trials primarily dealt with defendants sequentially. Hence the reason the number of trials observed at the cell level involved many more defendants.

9. A limited number of trials were translated in situ during the observation process.

10. Approximately fifty of these variables focus on specific information on the genocide. These data have less to do with the actual *gacaca* process and are, therefore, not considered in the current analysis.

11. In all interview formats, interviewees had the option of participating anonymously. If they chose that option, we recorded only demographic information. In addition, I conducted numerous informal conversations that I did not officially record.

12. I modeled this procedure on the work of, for example, Varshney 2002 and Gibson and Woolcock 2005.

13. For information on the situation of Twa in relation to the policy of unity and reconciliation in Rwanda, see Thomson 2009 and Adamczyk 2011.

14. See Eltringham 2004 for a discussion of these new identities. See also Hintjens (2001, 2008) for an insightful discussion of identity politics in Rwanda.

15. I did not use the category of "new-caseload returnees" (people returning to Rwanda after fleeing the country in the wake of the genocide in 1994) because this category is no longer salient in social life in the Rwandan hills.

16. Some communities did not have old-case returnees; others did not have released prisoners.

17. McLean-Hilker 2009 and Sommers 2012 have focused on youth in postgenocide Rwanda.

18. Due to practical circumstances, life-story interviewing in one location took place in December 2007–January 2008. I integrated the findings from this location into the present book, but I did not use them in previous publications that made use of the life-story data (Ingelaere 2007b, 2009b, 2010b).

19. The lists identifying people according to these categories were initially compiled in 2007. By 2011, the *gacaca* process had continued. More people were accused in *gacaca*. A person was recategorized if he or she was accused in *gacaca* after 2007. The 2011 life-story survey focused on the period from 2000 to 2011 in order to complete and complement the 2007 survey results.

20. I recorded the reasons people were not available in order to assess what influence attrition might have in the follow-up survey. The reasons were diverse, without a clear pattern that might skew the comparison between the two waves. On the other hand, a number of people were not included in the second wave because they were

imprisoned or performing community service. Most of these people had finished their prison sentences or had completed their community service by 2015, and I managed to retrace them that year even though I do not consider their interviews in this study.

21. I discuss other methodological aspects in chap. 4, which systematically presents the quantified/structured findings of the life-history approach.

22. I refer to that information regarding six research locations in Ingelaere 2007b, 56–57.

23. During one phase of the research, two of my Rwandan field assistants organized group discussions without my presence. In such cases, one researcher facilitated the group discussion and the second recorded it. These group discussions were organized in 2009.

24. Bent Flyvbjerg (2001) elaborated on the Aristotelian concept of *phronesis* in a broader argument on the characteristics of the social sciences and in an attempt to make social science matter (again). I prefer to use the phrase "*phronesis*-like research" (Flyvbjerg 2001, 129, 162), because I cannot claim to have fully taken into consideration all dimensions of a "phronetic social science." However, if I understand Flyvbjerg correctly, a phronetic social science is neither paradigm nor method, and "*phronesis*-like" research is practiced in many ways.

25. See Flyvbjerg 2001. This is also related to the mixing of methods as discussed in Creswell and Clark 2007, 21–27.

Chapter 3. *Gacaca* Mechanics

1. Field observation, Runyoni, 31 July 2007, trial 370.

2. I define the gathering of a *gacaca* court as a "*gacaca* session" (see chap. 2). A *gacaca* session is not defined by law or regulations, and one could thus deal with multiple accused persons. If there were more accused, the court dealt with them either together in a joint subsession or, as usually happened, sequentially.

3. "Survivor" refers to genocide survivors; "prisoners" are individuals who were incarcerated at the time of the trial proceedings; "released prisoners" had been in prison for alleged participation in the genocide but had been released before trial; those "accused in *gacaca*" are individuals accused of genocide crimes who had not been imprisoned at the time of the proceeding; people referred as "no-survivor/no prison" are those who were not genocide survivors and had been neither imprisoned nor accused of genocide crimes when the trial was taking place.

4. Particular observations made by the field assistant (observer) or me during the trial are enclosed in brackets.

5. Field observation, Runyoni, 15 November 2007, trial 800.

6. Field observation, Rukoma, cell R, 24 May 2007, trial 40.

7. *Umudugudu* means "agglomeration." Since the 2006 territorial reform, the administrative entity *umudugudu* is similar to what a cell used to be before this reform. More information on administrative levels can be found in chap. 5.

8. Field observation, Runyoni, cell-level meeting with authorities, cell N, 7 June 2007.

9. Field observation, Ntabona, cell M, 30 October 2007, trial 96.

10. Field observation, Rukoma, cell R, trial 52, 7 June 2007.

11. As mentioned, I did not systematically observe the cell level but base this information on an analysis of 124 cell-level *gacaca* gatherings. (In twenty-four cases, the information was not available because the sessions were adjourned.) In September 2007 the National Service of the Gacaca Courts (SNJG) provided me with an overview of the total number of cases in each research site (SNJG, Status Report 7/09/2007, on file with the author). Taking the four research areas together, we see slightly more trials (53.4 percent) organized compared to amicable settlements (46.6 percent). These SNJG data do not reflect the final outcomes, because most of the proceedings at cell level were organized after 2007.

12. Field observation, Runyoni, cell N, trial 789, 1, 3, and 6 November 2007.

13. During a cell-level *gacaca* trial in Runyoni, one of the accused, a former prisoner, explained that "in prison, we did not collect information regarding property." Field observation, Runyoni, cell RG, 3 August 2007, trial 377.

14. Field observation, Jali, 15 September 2009, trial 471.

15. Field observation, Runyoni, 21 July 2009, sess. 280.

16. Field observation, Kibuye region, western Rwanda, May–June 2009.

17. Officially, the *nyumbakumi* have not been part of the state structures since the territorial and administrative reform that came into effect in January 2006. But in 2005, during the official period of information collection, they were part of that structure. After 2006 and in practice, the *nyumbakumi* continue to be appointed and solicited by authorities higher up in the administration, although this may vary depending on the locality (see administrative structures and authority figures in chap. 5).

18. Confessing and pleading guilty also required the defendant to ask for pardon. Pardon will be examined in detail in chap. 8.

19. SNJG, monthly progress reports (on file with author).

20. Field observation, Ntabona, 10 July 2007, sess. 51.

21. Field observation, Ntabona, 3 August 2007, sess. 65.

22. Field observation, Rukoma, 26 July 2007, sess. 42.

23. Field observation, Rukoma, 10 May 2007, trial 18.

24. Field observation, Rukoma, 9 August 2007, trial 113.

25. I return to the issue of pardon in chap. 8.

26. Field observation, Jali, 9 September 2008, sess. 84.

27. In addition, we established an average attendance rate of ninety individuals during fifty-one gatherings of the *gacaca* courts at the cell level, a level that was not systematically observed.

28. The attendance rate was much higher during the information-collection phase since everyone was obliged to attend these proceedings. Compulsion to attend diminished with the start of the trial phase.

29. Field observation, Runyoni, 15 July 2006, sess. 1.

30. Field observation, Runyoni, 24 August 2006, sess. 8.

31. Field observation, Runyoni, July–August 2007, multiple sess.

32. Field observation, Jali, 26 August 2008, trial 132.

33. Field observation, Runyoni, 14 August 2008, trial 842.

34. I use the median interventions in order to exclude the skewing influence of a very limited number of exceptionally long trials. See appendix II, table 11, for an overview.

35. NGOs that monitored the *gacaca* process over time underscore this observation. PRI (2008, 33) came to the conclusion that "a tendency to reject witnesses for the defense [existed]." ASF reports repeatedly note the absence of a "contradictory debate" that should mark a criminal procedure (ASF 2005, 2006, 2007a, 2007b, 2010).

36. It remains unclear whether the courts needed to establish the specific intent to commit genocide. In practice, as an analysis of almost two thousand *gacaca* trials shows, the *gacaca* courts hardly ever established this intent but rather simply took it for granted. According to Haveman (2011, 400–401), the courts were not required to establish this intent, and the crimes they dealt with were "ordinary crimes" from a legal position. But the 2001 *gacaca* law (and subsequent amendments) stipulate that the *gacaca* courts try people prosecuted for offenses "committed with the intention of perpetrating genocide or crimes against humanity" (Republic of Rwanda 2001b, art. 1).

37. Field observation, Runyoni, 17 July 2007, trial 286.

38. The total number of trials where all necessary information was available is 1,053. See chap. 2 for an explanation of the coding of *gacaca* observations.

39. These 176 violent "events" are the total number of criminal events that were dealt with in the sector. An "event" is every genocidal act that is punishable under the *gacaca* law.

40. Remarkably, 14.3 percent of the defendants were (also) charged with a violation of the *gacaca* procedures. According to articles 29 and 30 of the 2004 *gacaca* law (Republic of Rwanda 2004a), the court judges could decide to impose punishments for people making "slanderous denunciations" or "refusing to testify." The latter is defined by law as "avoiding to speak or deliberately evading the question put to him or her" and not appearing after being summoned. In addition, punishments could be imposed for "anyone who exercises pressures, attempts to exercise pressures, or threatens the witnesses or the Seat members of the *gacaca* court." Article 30 stipulates that these punishments could also be used regarding "offenses committed outside the Court." Article 71 gave the judges the ability to deal with "troublemakers" by putting them in detention for a maximum of forty-eight hours. In most cases, procedural punishments related to perjury. Two strategies were observed: (1) the person accused of these offenses was given a punishment when the verdict of the trial in question was pronounced, or (2) applying procedures, the *inyangamugayo* organized a separate trial to deal with the issue. As stipulated in article 32 of the *gacaca* legislation, the latter strategy should have been followed except for people defined as "troublemakers." Article 31 allowed a defendant to appeal the decision taken in a case in which there were procedural violations.

41. Field observation, Jali, 4 September 2009, trials 437 and 438.

42. Field observation, Rukoma, 27 September 2007, trial 154.

43. If there were more trials during that session, all trials would have the same deliberation time. Because these deliberations happened in private, it was impossible to establish the deliberation time per individual.

44. At the cell level, 90.1 percent of the people who had opted for a trial (thus, no amicable settlement) were convicted. The acquittal rate at the cell level was thus approximately 10 percent. However, we did not systematically observe trials at cell level. The information is based on a total of ninety-seven trials conducted at the cell level that dealt with a total of 1,001 defendants.

45. According to this report, at the sector level the acquittal rate would have been 36 percent.

46. Community service, an important part of the sentencing in *gacaca*, generally took place in work camps.

47. Field observation, Ntabona, 5 June 2007, trial 108.

48. Field observation, Runyoni, cell N, 1, 3, and 6 November 2007, trials 781, 785, and 788 (considered as one trial).

49. Field observation, Jali, 6 October 2009, trial 146. In the former province of Butare, we observed other instances where entire neighborhoods were instructed to compensate genocide victims. Field observation, Butare area, southern Rwanda, April 2009.

50. Based on 1,475 cases where this information was available. A life sentence was coded as 999 months or 83.25 years.

51. "Community service" sounds lenient, but it generally took place in camps where convicts were forced to do hard labor, such as mining and cutting stones (PRI 2007; 2010, 29–32). See chap. 4 for more on this issue.

52. Based on 1,656 cases where this information was available. The final report on the *gacaca* process (Republic of Rwanda 2012) suggests that 9 percent of the total cases tried resulted in appeal: 24 percent at the sector level (the level analyzed here) and 4 percent at the cell level.

53. Defendants could appeal judgments at the sector level. The *gacaca* court of appeal located in the same sector also dealt with the appeal. This appeal court was composed of (an)other group(s) of elected judges, residents of the same locality. Opposition could be made against judgments in absentia, and the court that had dealt with the case in the first instance would handle such appeals. The party absent during the initial trial had fifteen days to oppose the judgment if there were "legitimate reasons" that impeded participation during the initial trial. In review-of-judgment cases, the parties involved could ask for such a review although "parties against the defendant" was broadened to include "their descendants" as well. The 2004 *gacaca* law stipulated that judgments could be subject to review when there was a difference in the judgments of defendants tried by both the ordinary justice system and the *gacaca* courts as well as judgments rendered in violation of the legal provisions (Republic of Rwanda 2004a, art. 93). In 2008 this was modified by incorporating the possibility to review cases where "new evidence contradicting what [the judgment] was based on is discovered." This modification also made it possible for "any person in the interest

of justice [who] may request for review of a case" (Republic of Rwanda 2008a, art. 2). A modification of the *gacaca* law in 2007 had already introduced the possibility for an unlimited number of appeals, stating that "cases tried by the *gacaca* court of appeal at the first resort are appealed against in the nearest *gacaca* court of appeal" (Republic of Rwanda 2007b, art. 6). It is difficult to speculate what motivated the legislature to introduce these provisions; one of the consequences, though, was that it introduced the possibility of eternal litigation either in the *gacaca* system or in the ordinary justice system.

Chapter 4. Experiencing *Gacaca*

1. Names of individuals and localities have been changed to ensure confidentiality.

2. Community service is referred to as TIG, the acronym of the French term for community service, *travaux d'intérêt général*.

3. See Newbury and Newbury 2000 on this type of research approach that focuses on the micro-level dynamics in the peasantry.

4. For a comparison of these results over time and a survey conducted before the nationwide implementation of *gacaca*, see Ingelaere 2009a, 510–13.

5. This expression signifies that even when one does the impossible, one will never restore confidence in the population. An expression with an identical significance is "*niyo wateka ibuye rigashya*" (when you cook a stone until it becomes edible).

6. This expression means that one cannot do anything against a person who feels strongly because that person is very well represented by the government. It gives the one who feels represented in this way the right to do whatever he or she wants, and those who undergo injustice as a result cannot do anything about it.

7. This expression refers to the era of the monarchy, when the Hutu worked as servants for the Tutsi.

8. Power is symbolized by the drum in Rwandan custom. This expression signifies that no matter how many people try to shout, make noise, and do other things to circumvent the will of power, power will always prevail. The one who has power—the one who has the drum in his hands—will always reach his goal, despite the popular will.

9. Old-caseload returnee.

10. See the introduction and chap. 2 for an explanation of my fieldwork and method regarding the use of this survey instrument.

Chapter 5. The Weight of the State

1. Life-story interview, 12 March 2011, Rwezamenyo, southeast Rwanda, female, Hutu, accused in *gacaca*, peasant, married, six children, born in 1954.

2. Such a dynamic is not entirely new in postgenocide Rwanda. Helen Codere (1962, 53), writing on precolonial Rwanda, noticed that further "proof of his loyalty and worthwhileness as a vassal was his ability and willingness to furnish useful information to his overlord, including information about the conduct of other vassals."

3. Interview, Runyoni, central Rwanda, March 2006, anonymous.

4. Vansina (2004, 95) also uses this expression in his discussion of the centralization of power of the Nyinginya kingdom in the eighteenth and nineteenth centuries.

5. Field observation, Jali, cell G, 13 February 2007.

6. Field observation, Bugesera region, southeast Rwanda, 24 March 2006.

7. Based on 1,086 observations of sector-level trials. At the cell level—a level we did not systematically observe—we recorded a presence of local authority figures in 28 percent of the cases where this information was available (N=57).

8. This approach had been adopted in a systematic way since 2007, based on an analysis of the overall research environment, the need to overcome obstacles such as self-censorship, widespread secrecy, and constraint in public display (Ingelaere 2010a). In 2007 I chose to resort to systematic life-story interviewing as the result of insights into the strengths and weaknesses of the research techniques I had used from 2004 to 2006. The research process was divided into several phases, of which some were more open-ended and exploratory. An extensive discussion and documentation of the research process can be found in chap. 2.

9. Method and fieldwork activities are discussed in chap. 2.

10. Life-story survey, 2011 (N words=574,081). Conducted with Nvivo 9.2. This list considers only nouns. Words without meaning (e.g., the, it, he, she, as) were omitted. The life-story interviews were open-ended, and I avoided leading or suggestive terms as much as possible. However, I facilitated responses by structuring the respondent's narrative according to five themes (migration, economy, security, confidence, and [political] representation) and by referring to years. Although additional nouns (confidence, security, representation, economic, situation, and year) were often used, I did not consider them in the ranking, nor did I include the words "level" (since we used a ranking exercise on a scale not considered here during the interviews) and "person" (the French word [*personne*], which can mean both an individual and no one). I combined tallies for singular and plural and for nouns with similar meanings, for example: authority, state, and government (although the word "authority" had the highest frequency). I also tallied together references to health and sickness.

11. Interview, Runyoni, central Rwanda, Tutsi, genocide survivor, age unknown, male.

12. He is referring to killings happening in the margins of the *gacaca* activities.

13. He is referring to a *gacaca* session I had observed the previous day, where it was mentioned that intimidation takes place in the community. The expression "taking to their hoe" evokes this experience of intimidation.

14. Compare this interview with Albert with what Sebarenzi writes about his own experience with interpretations of Rwandan history: "What's more, the massacres of 1973 had come after a period of peace. Everyone thought civilians would be safe. No one believed Tutsi would be targeted again. When my father realized how wrong they were, I don't think he ever trusted periods of peace in Rwanda to last. I think he knew that a cosmetic peace hiding the blemishes of discrimination could not last. He was right. Violence did come again, and this time it was far worse than anyone could ever have imagined" (Sebarenzi 2009, 44).

15. Some observers (Waldorf 2006, 61; HRW 2011, 119) suggest that the change in the *gacaca* law in 2004 excluded "war crimes" from *gacaca*'s competence. But it remains open for interpretation whether this is actually the case legally (compare Republic of Rwanda 2001c, preamble and art.1, with Republic of Rwanda 2004a, preamble and art. 1). In practice, however, there was indeed a trend toward excluding these issues from *gacaca*'s competence.

16. See Phil Clark's statements on *gacaca* and RPF crimes, for example: "It's not talked about a lot in the literature on *gacaca*, but the population discusses RPF crimes explicitly during many *gacaca* trials" (quoted in Stefanowicz 2011). Moreover, the fact that, in the *gacaca* hearings we observed, RPF crimes were *never* discussed cannot be due to proximity to Kigali, as Phil Clark suggests in the same interview. Except for Runyoni, all my research locations are situated in very remote rural areas, and all sites except for Ntabona experienced killings by or supervised by RPA/RPF troops.

17. Field observation, Byumba area, northern Rwanda, March 2005.

18. Field observation, Ruhengeri area, northern Rwanda, June 2006.

19. Song recorded in the diary of a student attending an *ingando* in the second half of 2009.

20. For specific information on reconciliation and healing in northern Rwanda, a region that experienced multiple forms of violence, see Richters 2010.

21. Focus group discussion, northern Rwanda, May 2006: (1) peasant, male, Hutu, age sixty; (2) peasant, male, Hutu, age seventy-seven.

22. Focus group discussion, southeast Rwanda, March 2006: (1) peasant, female, Hutu, age forty-six; (2) peasant, female, Hutu, age forty-one; (3) peasant, female, Hutu, age forty-two.

23. Life-story interview, round 2, 21 March 2011, Rukoma, eastern Rwanda, female, Hutu, no prison/not accused in *gacaca*, peasant, married, five children, born in 1964.

24. Life-story interview, round 2, 20 May 2011, Jali, northern Rwanda, male, Hutu, accused in *gacaca*, peasant, married, four children, born in 1975.

25. Field observation, Ntabona, central Rwanda, March 2006.

26. This observation also has consequences with respect to memory, public or private, in Rwanda. I do not explicitly focus on memory and memory practices in this study. Other studies do so (Vidal 2001; de Lame 2003; Rosoux 2005; Burnet 2009; Lemarchand 2009, 99–108; Meierhenrich 2009; Brandstetter 2010; King 2010).

Chapter 6. Navigating the Social

1. I borrow the concept of effectual truth from Machiavelli, who coined it in *The Prince*, although I give it my own interpretation here. Machiavelli's effectual truth resonates with the Rwandan cultural concept of *ubwenge* (lit., intelligence) as discussed in this chapter. Also, I interpret Machiavelli's notion of effectual truth as a suggestion that truth is equated with utility in the ethics he describes. Mansfield (1998, xi) writes in his introduction to *The Prince*: "When Machiavelli denies that imagined republics and principalities 'exist in truth,' and declares that the truth in these or all matters is the effectual truth, he says that no moral rules exist, not made by men, which men must

abide by. The rules or laws that exist are those made by governments or other powers acting under necessity, and they must be obeyed out of the same necessity. Whatever is necessary may be called just and reasonable, but justice is no more reasonable than what a person's prudence tells him he must acquire for himself, or must submit to, because men cannot afford justice in any sense that transcends their own preservation."

2. Field observation, Runyoni, 21 August 2007, trial 462.

3. On secrecy in Rwanda, see also de Lame 2004. Insights regarding cultural dimensions of communication in Rwanda are available in Rukebesha 1985, Overdulve 1997, and Ntampaka 1999.

4. Interview, prison, central Rwanda, April 2007, peasant, male, Hutu, prisoner, age thirty-five.

5. Field observation, Jali, 22 May 2007 and 24 July 2007, general meeting and trial 62.

6. Based on the average exchange rates between 1 July 2006 and 1 January 2012: 1 Euro = RWF 766.499 and 1 USD = RWF 555.056. In order to understand these monetary aspects related to the *gacaca* process, it is important to keep in mind that the yearly average income in 2010–11 was RWF 289,337 (USD 521) for all of Rwanda and RWF 218,521 (USD 394) for residents outside of Kigali, the majority of the population and the locus of this study (Republic of Rwanda n.d.).

7. Field observation, Ntabona, 5 June 2007, trial 109.

8. Field observation, Runyoni, cell NY, 3 November 2007, trial 785.

9. Field observation, Runyoni, 15 June 2008, trial 849.

10. Field observation, Runyoni, cell NY, 1 November 2007, trial 781.

11. Field observation, Runyoni, cell NY, 3 November 2007, trial 785.

12. Field observation, Jali, 9 September 2008, trial 136.

13. Field observation, Ntabona, 5 June 2007, trial 110.

14. Field observation, Rukoma, 6 December 2007, trial 242.

15. Field observation, Jali, 23 June 2008, trial 116.

16. "Wrap" refers to what in Africa is called a "pagne" in French (printed cloth for a skirt or turban).

17. Field observation, Jali, 5 May 2009, trial 312.

18. Field observation, Jali, 24 November 2009, trial 594.

19. Field observation, Runyoni, cell NY, 1 November 2007, trial 780.

20. *Abakada* were people working for the RPF/RPA in the period immediately following the genocide. Often they were local inhabitants whom RPF members and RPA soldiers (who lacked insight into local dynamics when they took power) considered to be trustworthy. The RPF/RPA used these so-called *abakada* not only for awareness activities but also as sources of information regarding the involvement of local inhabitants during the genocide and their particular activities and opinions at that time. Sometimes, as in this case, the *abakada* were also tasked with supervising restitution to genocide survivors.

21. Field observation, Runyoni, cell NY, 16 October 2007, trial 741, and several informal interviews in private with trial participants.

22. Field observation, Runyoni, 11 September 2007, trial 550.

23. Field observation, Jali, 14 September 2009, trial 465.

24. Field observations, Jali, April–May 2011.

25. Field observation, Jali, 21 April 2009, sess. 109.

26. I disagree here with Phil Clark (2010) and Kristin Doughty (2015), although I do agree with their emphasis on the ways people were using *gacaca* sessions within the structural constraints of the court system design and on the influence of the state and political situation in the postgenocide era.

27. Peter Uvin (n.d.) made this observation in his preliminary reflection on the possible use of *gacaca* to deal with the legacy of the genocide.

Chapter 7. A Thousand Hills, a Thousand *Gacacas*

1. Analyses emphasizing the reactive nature of agency as resistance to power often make use of James Scott's (1990) analytical apparatus of public and hidden transcripts. I do follow Scott with respect to his analytical distinction between public and private transcripts, but I do not consider the private transcript (all of those private conversations and behaviors) automatically reactive to a situation of dominance. In other words, the private transcript does not need to be automatically qualified as resistance. I consider behavior resistance only when there is a clear consciousness of resisting or a collective effort to resist.

2. On 20 October 1993 Tutsi soldiers killed President Melchior Ndadaye, a Hutu and the first democratically elected president of Burundi. His assassination caused large-scale killings, which the Hutu organized against the Tutsi as an ethnic group. The armed forces, dominated by Tutsi soldiers and officers, responded in kind, mass-killing the Hutu population. Many Hutu peasants sought to flee Burundi and enter refugee camps in Rwanda. See Lemarchand 1994 and Reyntjens 1995b.

3. Rwandan collaborators and I collected the figures from the *gacaca* courts in the Ntabona and Rukoma cells. This was the only time that we consulted *gacaca* records in situ, and we did so with the permission of the chair of the courts and in the presence of at least two *inyangamugayo*, (see chap. 2). We collected data at the information-gathering stage of the *gacaca* process. Later, the cell presidents of the courts filled in questionnaires on (1) past and present population levels in villages and towns and (2) data they had collected about the period of violence and genocide in 1994 (deaths, survivors, prisoners, destruction, and the like). These two items were gathered together in May and June 2006, after the information-gathering phase of the *gacaca* courts. Because the survey used a recall method and more data could be added in the subsequent trial phase (see chaps. 1 and 3), the figures are approximations.

4. On villagization in Rwanda, see Hilhorst and Van Leeuwen 2000, Van Leeuwen 2001, C. Newbury 2011, and Leegwater 2015.

5. See appendix II, table 12.

6. See chap. 3, table 2.

7. Field observation, Rukoma, 26 July 2007, trial 96.

8. Field observation, Rukoma, 30 October 2008 and 6 November 2008, trial 251.

9. Field observation, Rukoma, 4 and 11 October 2007 and 27 November 2008, trial 252.

10. Field observation, Rukoma, 27 January 2009 and 3 February 2009, trial 254 (revision 1), and 28 September 2009 and 8, 15, and 16 October 2009, trial 264 (revision 2).

11. See also his monograph on life and "the play of power" on a rural hill (Gravel 1968b).

12. These "death lists" should not be interpreted literally but as plans or intentions to execute a selected number of individuals.

13. Field observation, Ntabona, 5 June 2007, trial 108.

14. See appendix II, table 12.

15. See appendix II, table 11.

16. See chap. 3 for a comparison of the cases of appeal by sector.

17. See also Vidal 1998 for reflections on this article and the social dynamics at work in the Rwandan peasantry. A sample comprising several loci would be needed to thoroughly examine similarities and differences between the dynamic processes at play at the local level. For the sake of brevity, I have compared only two hills.

18. Human Rights Watch (2007) documented killings in the margins of the *gacaca* activities.

Chapter 8. Shades of Heart

1. The notion of social imaginary is closely related to what Pierre Bourdieu (1990) calls *habitus*, and Charles Taylor (2001, 172–96) explicitly makes this link. Social imaginary also resembles the notions of background or *Lebenswelt* that a wide range of philosophers use. However, I make use of social imaginary and Taylor's precise definition because he clearly situates the concept in the sphere of ethics, the guiding principles of behavior.

2. On the importance of ritual in transitional justice, see Kelsall 2005.

3. *Umibanire myiza* means "good living together with one another"; *ubwumvikane* means "social *entente*"; *kubana neza* means "good living-with."

4. See the discussion on the Ntabona killings in chap. 7.

5. See Uvin 2009, Nee and Uvin 2010, and Ingelaere and Kohlhagen 2012 for similar observations regarding the Burundian case.

6. The notion of "heart" is central to the anthropological studies by Theidon (2000, 2006) and Shaw (2005, 2007) on transitional justice processes (see chap. 9). A discussion of *umutima* in the Rwandan context can be found in Nothomb 1965 and Crepeau 1985. I have borrowed some of the expressions and proverbs that make use of *umutima* from these works if they had not already surfaced in the fieldwork data. These works—as well as those by Kagame (1956, 1976) and Tempels (1959)—also informed me as I interpreted fieldwork data and constructed the epistemological framework discussed in the following sections. However, apart from Crepeau (1985), these authors were clergymen in search of "stones of arrival" in the local culture in order to "better" evangelize and Christianize local customs, worldviews, and people.

This issue needs to be taken into account in order to separate genuine ethnographic/anthropological insights from Christian distortions (although most of the authors attempt to do so themselves).

7. Interview, southeastern Rwanda, February 2006: peasant, female, Tutsi, genocide survivor, age fifty.

8. Interview, southeastern Rwanda, February 2006: peasant, female, Tutsi, genocide survivor, age thirty-four.

9. In the Rwandan context, you give milk to someone you like or appreciate, but that person can suddenly "turn your milk into blood," an image that corresponds to putting a knife in your back.

10. I analyze Rwandan personhood or "the social construction of the moral person" somewhat differently than Christopher C. Taylor does (1990, 1023). He emphasizes the dialectic of "flow" and "anomic flow" in the construction of the self (1988, 1990, 1992). I agree with him that "flow"/"anomic flow" was an important metaphor in Rwandan social life and cosmology, and still is, even now: "In order for there to be peace on the hillside, neighbors must occasionally give beer to one another" (1988, 1348). Based on my own fieldwork, though, I believe that while the importance attached to conviviality resonates with the idea of flow, the construction of the moral person (self) centers around the notion of "heart."

11. One often hears "the reconstruction of the hearts" (*gusana imitima*) in official discourses on dealing with the psychological consequences of the genocide. The expression refers to the popular transitional justice notion of "healing."

12. Theidon's (2000, 2006) and Shaw's (2005, 2007) anthropological studies, respectively in Peru and Sierra Leone, stress the importance of reestablishing moral relationships in the aftermath of intimate communal violence.

13. This information is based on 1,350 observed trials.

14. I also considered testimony *à décharge* by victims (thus in defense of the accused) as an act of pardon because the local population generally considered it as such. Such testimony occurred in 18 percent of the (limited) cases of pardon by victims we observed.

15. Field observation, Rukoma, 10 May 2007, trial 19.

16. Field observation, Runyoni, cell N, 10 October 2007, trial 733.

17. Field observation, Runyoni, cell R, 30 October 2007, trial 778.

18. Field observation, Jali, cell G, 13 February 2007, trial 4.

19. Field observation, Rukoma, cell R, 7 June 2007, trial 53.

20. Field observation, Runyoni, cell RG, 3 August 2007, trial 377.

21. Such a blood pact was sometimes also called *gihango*. I would like to thank Gillian Matthys for explaining the historical meaning of a blood pact in the Rwandan sociocultural universe.

22. Field observation, Jali, 20 October 2009, trial 150.

23. Field observation, Butare area, southern Rwanda, April 2009.

24. See Ingelaere 2011a.

References

Books and Articles

Adamczyk, Christiane. 2011. "'Today, I Am No Mutwa Anymore': Facets of National Unity Discourse in Present-Day Rwanda." *Social Anthropology* 19 (2): 175–88.

African Rights. 2000. *Confessing to Genocide: Responses to Rwanda's Genocide Law.* Kigali: African Rights.

———. 2008. *Survivors and Post-genocide Justice in Rwanda: Their Experiences, Perspectives, and Hopes.* Kigali: African Rights.

Allen, Tim. 2006. *Trial Justice: The International Criminal Court and the Lord's Resistance Army.* London: Zed Books.

Amnesty International. 2000. *Rwanda: The Troubled Course of Justice.* London: Amnesty International.

———. 2002a. *Rwanda: Gacaca—A Question of Justice.* London: Amnesty International.

———. 2002b. *Rwanda: Gacaca—Gambling with Justice.* London: Amnesty International.

Ansoms, An. 2009. "Faces of Rural Poverty in Contemporary Rwanda: Linking Livelihoods, Profiles, and Institutional Processes." PhD diss., University of Antwerp.

Apuuli, Kasaija Phillip. 2009. "Procedural Due Process and the Prosecution of Genocide Suspects in Rwanda." *Journal of Genocide Research* 11 (1): 11–30.

Arriaza, Laura, and Naomi Roht-Arriaza. 2008. "Social Reconstruction as a Local Process." *International Journal of Transitional Justice* 2 (2): 152–72.

Arthur, Paige, ed. 2011. *Identities in Transition: Challenges for Transitional Justice in Divided Societies.* Cambridge: Cambridge University Press.

Atkinson, Robert. 1998. *The Life Story Interview.* London: Sage.

Avocats sans frontières (ASF). 2005. *Monitoring des juridictions gacaca: Phase de jugement. Rapport analytique No. 1.* Brussels: ASF.

———. 2006. *Monitoring des juridictions gacaca: Phase de jugement. Rapport analytique No. 2.* Brussels: ASF.

————. 2007a. *Monitoring des jurisdictions gacaca: Phase de jugement. Rapport analytique No. 3*. Brussels: ASF.

————. 2007b. *Monitoring des jurisdictions gacaca: Phase de jugement. Rapport analytique No. 4*. Brussels: ASF.

————. 2010. *Monitoring des jurisdictions gacaca: Phase de jugement. Rapport analytique No. 5*. Brussels: ASF.

Babalola, Stella, Jean Karimbizi, Sow Boubacar, and John Bosco Ruzibuka. n.d. *Evaluation of the Gacaca Promotional Campaign in Rwanda*. Kigali: Ministry of Justice.

Baines, Erin K. 2007. "The Haunting of Alice: Local Approaches to Justice and Reconciliation in Northern Uganda." *International Journal of Transitional Justice* 1 (1): 91–114.

Baker, Bruce. 2007. "'He Must Buy What He Stole and Then We Forgive': Restorative Justice in Rwanda and Sierra Leone." *Acta Juridica* 1:171–92.

Barron, Patrick, Claire Smith, and Michael Woolcock. 2004. "Understanding Local Level Conflict in Developing Countries: Theory, Evidence, and Implications from Indonesia." *Social Development Papers: Conflict Prevention and Reconstruction* 19. Washington, DC: World Bank.

Baxter, Victoria. 2002. *Empirical Research Methodologies of Transitional Justice Mechanism*. Conference Report, Stellenbosch, South Africa: Centre for the Study of Violence and Reconciliation, 18–20 November.

Begley, Larissa. 2009. "The Other Side of Fieldwork: Experiences and Challenges of Conducting Research in the Border Area of Rwanda/Eastern Congo." *Anthropology Matters* 11 (2): 1–11.

Betts, Alexander. 2005. "Should Approaches to Post-Conflict Justice and Reconciliation Be Determined Globally, Nationally or Locally?" *European Journal of Development Research* 17 (4): 735–52.

Booth, Robert. 2010. "Does This Picture Make You Think of Rwanda? . . . If So, a British PR Firm Has Done Its Job, and Many States Want a Similar Makeover." *Guardian*, 3 August.

Bornkamm, Paul Christoph. 2012. *Rwanda's Gacaca Courts: Between Retribution and Reparation*. Oxford: Oxford University Press.

Bourdieu, Pierre. 1990. *The Logic of Practice*. Cambridge, MA: Polity Press.

Bourdieu, Pierre, and Loïc J. D. Wacquant. 1992. *An Invitation to Reflexive Sociology*. Chicago: University of Chicago Press.

Brandstetter, Anna-Maria. 2010. *Contested Pasts: The Politics of Remembrance in Post-Genocide Rwanda*. Wassenaar, Netherlands: NIAS.

Brounéus, Karin. 2008. "Truth-Telling as Talking Cure? Insecurity and Retraumatization in the Rwandan *Gacaca* Courts." *Security Dialogue* 39 (1): 55–76.

————. 2010. "The Trauma of Truth Telling: Effects of Witnessing in the Rwandan *Gacaca* Courts on Psychological Health." *Journal of Conflict Resolution* 54 (3): 408–37.

Brubaker, Rogers. 2004. *Ethnicity without Groups*. Cambridge, MA: Harvard University Press.

Buckley-Zistel, Susanne. 2005. "'The Truth Heals?': *Gacaca* Jurisdictions and the Consolidation of Peace in Rwanda." *Die Friedens-Warte* 80 (1–2): 113–30.

———. 2006. "Remembering to Forget: Chosen Amnesia as a Strategy for Local Coexistence in Post-Genocide Rwanda." *Africa* 76 (2): 131–50.

Burnet, Jennie. 2008. "The Injustice of Local Justice: Truth, Reconciliation, and Revenge in Rwanda." *Genocide Studies and Prevention* 3 (2): 173–93.

———. 2009. "Whose Genocide? Whose Truth? Representations of Victim and Perpetrator in Rwanda." In *Genocide: Truth, Memory, and Representation*, edited by Alexander L. Hinton and Kevin L. O'Neill, 80–110. Durham, NC: Duke University Press.

Carothers, Thomas. 2002. "The End of the Transition Paradigm." *Journal of Democracy* 13 (1): 5–21.

Centre de Lutte Contre l'Impunité et l'Injustice au Rwanda. 2005. *Mémorandum sur l'impossibilité d'une justice équitable et l'instauration d'une nouvelle forme d'apartheid et d'esclavage au Rwanda*. Brussels: Centre de Lutte Contre l'Impunité et l'Injustice au Rwanda.

Chakravarty, Anuradhna. 2006. "*Gacaca* Courts in Rwanda: Explaining Divisions within the Human Rights Community." *Yale Journal of International Affairs* 1 (2): 132–45.

———. 2012. "'Partially Trusting' Field Relationships: Opportunities and Constraints of Fieldwork in Rwanda's Postconflict Setting." *Field Methods* 24 (3): 251–71.

Chrétien, Jean-Pierre. 2006. *The Great Lakes of Africa: Two Thousand Years of History*. Translated by Scott Straus. New York: Zone Books.

Clark, Phil. 2007. "Hybridity, Holism, and 'Traditional' Justice: The Case of the *Gacaca* Courts in Post-Genocide Rwanda." *George Washington International Law Review* 39 (4): 765–837.

———. 2008. "The Rules (and Politics) of Engagement: The *Gacaca* Courts and Post-Genocide Justice, Healing, and Reconciliation in Rwanda." In *After Genocide: Transitional Justice, Post-Conflict Reconstruction, and Reconciliation in Rwanda and Beyond*, edited by Phil Clark and Zachary D. Kaufman, 297–319. London: Hurst.

———. 2010. *The Gacaca Courts, Post-Genocide Justice and Reconciliation in Rwanda: Justice without Lawyers*. Cambridge: Cambridge University Press.

———. 2014. "Bringing the Peasants Back in, Again: State Power and Local Agency in Rwanda's *Gacaca* Courts." *Journal of Eastern African Studies* 8 (2): 193–213.

Codere, Helen. 1962. "Power in Ruanda." *Anthropologica* 4 (1): 45–84.

Cohen, Stanley. 2002. *States of Denial: Knowing about Atrocities and Suffering*. Cambridge, MA: Polity Press.

Corey, Allison, and Sandra F. Joireman. 2004. "Retributive Justice: The *Gacaca* Courts in Rwanda." *African Affairs* 103 (410): 73–79.

Crepeau, Pierre. 1985. *Paroles et sagesse: Valeurs sociales dans les proverbes du Rwanda*. Tervuren, Belgium: Musée Royal de l'Afrique Centrale.

Creswell, John W., and Vicki L. Plano Clark. 2007. *Designing and Conducting Mixed Methods Research*. Thousand Oaks, CA: Sage.

Daly, Erin. 2002. "Between Punitive and Reconstructive Justice: The *Gacaca* Courts in Rwanda." *New York University Journal of International Law and Politics* 34: 355–96.

Das, Veena. 2007. *Life and Words: Violence and the Descent into the Ordinary.* Berkeley: University of California Press.

de Lame, Danielle. 2003. "Deuil, commémoration, justice dans les contextes Rwandais et Belge: Otages existentiels et enjeux politiques." *Politique Africaine* 92:39–55.

———. 2004. "Mighty Secrets, Public Commensality, and the Crisis of Transparency: Rwanda through the Looking Glass." *Canadian Journal of African Studies* 38 (2): 279–317.

———. 2005. *A Hill among a Thousand: Transformations and Ruptures in Rural Rwanda.* Madison: University of Wisconsin Press.

De Ycaza, Carla. 2010. "Performative Functions of Genocide Trials in Rwanda: Reconciliation through Restorative Justice? An Examination of the Convergence of Trauma, Memory, and Performance through Legal Responses to Genocide in Rwanda." *African Journal of Conflict Resolution* 10 (3): 9–28.

Des Forges, Alison. 1999. *Leave None to Tell the Story: Genocide in Rwanda.* New York: Human Rights Watch.

Digneffe, Françoise, and Jacques Fierens, eds. 2003. *Justice et gacaca: L'expérience Rwandaise et le génocide.* Namur, Belgium: Presses Universitaires de Namur.

Dorfman, Ariel. 1994. *Death and the Maiden.* London: Nick Hern Books.

Doughty, Kristin. 2011. "Contesting Community: Legalized Reconciliation Efforts in the Aftermath of Genocide in Rwanda." PhD diss., University of Pennsylvania.

———. 2015. "Law and the Architecture of Social Repair: *Gacaca* Days in Post-Genocide Rwanda." *Journal of the Royal Anthropological Institute* 21 (2): 419–37.

Drumbl, Mark A. 2000a. "Punishment Postgenocide: From Guilt to Shame to 'Civis' in Rwanda." *New York University Law Review* 75 (5): 1221–326.

———. 2000b. "Sclerosis: Retributive Justice and the Rwandan Genocide." *Punishment and Society* 2 (3): 287–307.

———. 2005. "Law and Atrocity: Settling Accounts in Rwanda." *Ohio Northern University Law Review* 31:41–72.

———. 2007. *Atrocity, Punishment, and International Law.* Cambridge: Cambridge University Press.

Eastmond, Marita, and Johanna Mannergren Selimovic. 2012. "Silence as Possibility in Postwar Everyday Life." *International Journal of Transitional Justice* 6 (3): 502–24.

Eltringham, Nigel. 2004. *Accounting for Horror: Post-Genocide Debates in Rwanda.* London: Pluto Press.

Emerson, Robert M., Rachel I. Fretz, and Linda L. Shaw. 1995. *Writing Ethnographic Fieldnotes.* Chicago: University of Chicago Press.

Engle Merry, Sally. 1988. "Legal Pluralism." *Law and Society Review* 22 (5): 869–96.

Engle Merry, Sally, and N. Milner. 1995. *The Possibility of Popular Justice: A Case Study of Community Mediation in the United States.* Ann Arbor: University of Michigan Press.

Fenrich, Jeanmarie, Paolo Galizzi, and Tracy E. Higgins, eds. 2011. *The Future of African Customary Law*. Cambridge: Cambridge University Press.

Ferme, Marianne. 2001. *The Underneath of Things: Violence, History, and the Everyday in Sierra Leone*. Berkeley: University of California Press.

Fierens, Jacques. 2005. "Gacaca Courts: Between Fantasy and Reality." *Journal of International Criminal Justice* 3:896–919.

Finnström, Svensker. 2003. *Living with Bad Surroundings: War and Existential Uncertainty in Acholiland, Northern Uganda*. Uppsala, Sweden: Uppsala University Library.

Fletcher, Laurel E., and Harvey M. Weinstein. 2015. "Writing Transitional Justice: An Empirical Evaluation of Transitional Justice Scholarship in Academic Journals." *Journal of Human Rights Practice* 7 (2): 177–98.

Flyvbjerg, Bent. 2001. *Making Social Science Matter: Why Social Inquiry Fails and How It Can Succeed Again*. Cambridge: Cambridge University Press.

Foblets, Marie-Claire, and Barbara Truffin. 2004. "At the Heart of Legal Anthropology: Analyses of Peace Processes." In *Healing the Wounds: Essays on the Reconstruction of Societies After War*, edited by Marie-Claire Foblets and Trutz von Trotha, 259–71. Oxford: Hart Publishing.

Foucault, Michel. 1980. *Power/Knowledge: Selected Interviews and Other Writings, 1972–1977*. Brighton, UK: Harvester.

Fujii, Lee-Ann. 2009. *Killing Neighbors: Webs of Violence in Rwanda*. Ithaca, NY: Cornell University Press.

———. 2010. "Shades of Truth and Lies: Interpreting Testimonies of War and Violence." *Journal of Peace Research* 47 (2): 231–41.

Fukuyama, Francis. 1992. *The End of History and the Last Man*. New York: Free Press.

Gahima, Gerald. 2013. *Transitional Justice in Rwanda: Accountability for Atrocity*. New York: Routledge.

Gaparayi, Idi Tuzinde. 2001. "Justice and Social Reconstruction in the Aftermath of Genocide in Rwanda: An Evaluation of the Possible Role of the *Gacaca* Tribunals." *African Human Rights Law Journal* 1:78–106.

Gasibirege, Simon, and Stella Babalola. 2001. *Perceptions about the Gacaca Law in Rwanda: Evidence from a Multi-Method Study*. Special Publication No. 19. Baltimore, MD: Johns Hopkins University School of Public Health, Center for Communication Programs.

Geertz, Clifford. 1973. *The Interpretation of Cultures*. New York: Basic Books.

———. 1983. *Local Knowledge: Further Essays in Interpretive Anthropology*. London: Fontana Press.

Gibson, Christopher L., and Michael Woolcock. 2005. *Empowerment and Local Level Conflict Mediation in Indonesia: A Comparative Analysis of Concepts, Measures, and Project Efficacy*. World Bank Policy Research Working Paper 3713. Washington, DC: World Bank.

Gibson, James L. 2006. *Overcoming Apartheid: Can Truth Reconcile a Divided Nation?* New York: Russell Sage Foundation.

Goldstein Bolocan, Maya. 2004. "Rwandan *Gacaca*: An Experiment in Transitional Justice." *Journal of Dispute Resolution* 2:355–400.

Golooba-Mutebi, Frederick, and David Booth. 2013. *Bilateral Cooperation and Local Power Dynamics: The Case of Rwanda*. London: Overseas Development Institute.

Gravel, Pierre B. 1968a. "Diffuse Power as a Commodity: A Case Study from Gisaka (Eastern Rwanda)." *International Journal of Comparative Sociology* 9 (3–4): 163–76.

———. 1968b. *Remera: A Community in Eastern Ruanda*. The Hague: Mouton.

Gready, Paul. 2003. "Introduction." In *Political Transition: Politics and Culture*, edited by P. Gready, 1–26. London: Pluto Press.

———. 2010. "'You're Either with Us or against Us': Civil Society and Policy Making in Post-Genocide Rwanda." *African Affairs* 109 (437): 637–57.

Guichaoua, André. 2005. *Rwanda 1994: Les politiques du génocide à Butare*. Paris: Editions Karthala.

Haile, Dadimos. 2008. "Rwanda's Experiment in People's Courts (*Gacaca*) and the Tragedy of Unexamined Humanitarianism: A Normative/Ethical Perspective." Discussion Paper, 1 January 2008. Antwerp: Institute of Development Policy and Management.

Hamber, Brandon, and Grainne Kelly. 2005. *A Place for Reconciliation? Conflict and Locality in Northern Ireland*. Democratic Dialogue Report 18. Belfast: Democratic Dialogue.

Hamber, Brandon, and Richard Wilson. 2002. "Symbolic Closure through Memory, Reparation, and Revenge in Post-Conflict Societies." *Journal of Human Rights* 1 (1): 35–53.

Harrell, Peter E. 2003. *Rwanda's Gamble: Gacaca and the New Model of Transitional Justice*. New York: Writers Club Press.

Haveman, Roelof H. 2011. "*Gacaca* in Rwanda: Customary Law in Case of Genocide." In *The Future of African Customary Law*, edited by Jeanmarie Fenrich, Paolo Galizzi, and Tracy E. Higgins, 387–420. Cambridge: Cambridge University Press.

Hayner, Patricia B. 2002. *Unspeakable Truths: Facing the Challenge of "Truth" Commissions*. London: Routledge.

Hilhorst, Thea, and Matthijs Van Leeuwen. 2000. "Emergency and Development: The Case of *Imidugudu*, Villagization in Rwanda." *Journal of Refugee Studies* 13 (3): 264–80.

Hintjens, Helen M. 2001. "When Identity Becomes a Knife: Reflecting on Genocide in Rwanda." *Ethnicities* 1 (1): 25–55.

———. 2008. "Post-Genocide Identity Politics in Rwanda." *Ethnicities* 8 (1): 5–41.

Hinton, Alexander Laban. 2010. *Transitional Justice: Global Mechanisms, Local Realities after Genocide and Mass Violence*. New Brunswick, NJ: Rutgers University Press.

Hirondelle News Agency. 2007. "Approximately a Million People Have Appeared before the *Gacaca* Courts." 12 December.

———. 2009. "1994 Genocide: *Gacaca* Courts Discharge One Million Cases So Far." 3 April.

————. 2011. "Official Closing Session for *Gacaca* Courts to Be Held May 4." 23 December.

Hobsbawn, Eric, and Terence Ranger, eds. 1983. *The Invention of Tradition*. Cambridge: Cambridge University Press.

Honeyman, Catherine, Shakirah Hudani, Alfa Tiruneh, Justina Hierta, Leila Chirayath, Andrew Iliff, and Jens Meierhenrich. 2004. "Establishing Collective Norms: Potentials for Participatory Justice in Rwanda." *Peace and Conflict: Journal of Peace Psychology* 10 (1): 1–24.

Honeyman, Catherine, and Jens Meierhenrich. 2002. *Gacaca Jurisdictions: Transnational Justice in Rwanda; Observations from June 10–August 8, 2002*. Cambridge, MA: Harvard University.

Hughes, Caroline, Joakom Öjendal, and Isabell Schierenbeck. 2015. "The Struggle versus the Song—The Local Turn in Peacebuilding: An Introduction." *Third World Quarterly* 36 (5): 817–24.

Human Rights Watch (HRW). 2001. "Rwanda: Elections May Speed Genocide Trials." 4 October.

————. 2002a. "Justice or Therapy." 31 July.

————. 2002b. "Rwanda: Deliver Justice for Victims of Both Sides." 12 August.

————. 2004. *Struggling to Survive: Barriers to Justice for Rape Victims in Rwanda*. New York: Human Rights Watch.

————. 2007. *"There Will Be No Trial": Police Killings of Detainees and the Imposition of Collective Punishments*. New York: Human Rights Watch.

————. 2008. *Law and Reality: Progress in Judicial Reform in Rwanda*. New York: Human Rights Watch.

————. 2011. *Justice Compromised: The Legacy of Rwanda's Community-Based Gacaca Courts*. New York: Human Rights Watch.

Huntington, Samuel P. 2006. *Political Order in Changing Societies*. New Haven, CT: Yale University Press.

Huyse, Luc. 2003. "The Process of Reconciliation." In *Reconciliation after Violent Conflict*, edited by David Bloomfield, Teresa Barnes, and Luc Huyse, 19–33. Stockholm: International Idea.

————. 2008. "Introduction: Tradition-Based Approaches in Peacemaking, Transitional Justice, and Reconciliation Policies." In *Traditional Justice and Reconciliation Mechanisms after Violent Conflict: Learning from African Experiences*, edited by Luc Huyse and Mark Salter, 1–22. Stockholm: International Idea.

Huyse, Luc, and Mark Salter, eds. 2008. *Traditional Justice and Reconciliation Mechanisms after Violent Conflict: Learning from African Experiences*. Stockholm: International Idea.

Hyden, Goran. 1980. *Ujaama in Tanzania: Underdevelopment and an Uncaptured Peasantry*. Berkeley: University of California Press.

Ingelaere, Bert. 2006. "Changing Lenses and Contextualizing the Rwandan (Post-) Genocide." In *L'Afrique des Grands Lacs: Dix ans de transitions conflictuelles, Annuaire*

2005–2006, edited by Filip Reyntjens and Stefaan Marysse, 389–414. Paris: L'Harmattan.

————. 2007a. "A la recherche de la vérité dans les juridictions *gacaca* au Rwanda." In *L'Afrique des Grands Lacs, Annuaire 2006–2007*, edited by Filip Reyntjens and Stefaan Marysse, 41–74. Paris: L'Harmattan.

————. 2007b. *Living the Transition: A Bottom-Up Perspective on Rwanda's Political Transition*. Discussion Paper 2007.06. Antwerp: Institute of Development Policy and Management.

————. 2008. "The *Gacaca* Courts in Rwanda." In *Traditional Justice and Reconciliation Mechanisms after Violent Conflict: Learning from African Experiences*, edited by Luc Huyse and Mark Salter, 25–59. Stockholm: International Idea.

————. 2009a. "'Does the Truth Pass across the Fire without Burning?': Locating the Short Circuit in Rwanda's *Gacaca* Courts." *Journal of Modern African Studies* 47 (4): 507–28.

————. 2009b. "Living the Transition: Inside Rwanda's Conflict Cycle at the Grassroots." *Journal of Eastern African Studies* 3 (3): 438–63.

————. 2010a. "Do We Understand Life after Genocide? Center and Periphery in the Construction of Knowledge in Post-Genocide Rwanda." *African Studies Review* 53 (1): 41–59.

————. 2010b. "Peasants, Power, and Ethnicity: A Bottom-Up Perspective on Rwanda's Political Transition." *African Affairs* 109 (435): 273–92.

————. 2011a. "The Rise of Meta-Conflicts during Rwanda's *Gacaca* Process." In *L'Afrique des Grands Lacs, Annuaire 2010–2011*, edited by S. Marysse, F. Reyntjens, and S. Vandeginste, 303–18. Paris: L'Harmattan.

————. 2011b. "The Ruler's Drum and the People's Shout: Accountability and Representation on Rwanda's Hills." In *Remaking Rwanda: State Building and Human Rights after Mass Violence*, edited by Scott Straus and Lars Waldorf, 67–78. Madison: University of Wisconsin Press.

————. 2012. "From Model to Practice: Researching and Representing Rwanda's 'Modernized' *Gacaca* Courts." *Critique of Anthropology* 32 (4): 388–414.

Ingelaere, Bert, J.-B. Havugimana, and S. Ndushabandi. 2009. "La Benevolencija Rwanda: Grassroots Project Evaluation." La Benevolencija, Amsterdam. http://www.ua.ac.be/main.aspx?c=bert.ingelaereandn=34219.

Ingelaere, Bert, and Dominik Kolhagen. 2012. "Situating Social Imaginaries in Transitional Justice: The *Bushingantahe* in Burundi." *International Journal of Transitional Justice* 6 (1): 40–59.

Jackson, Michael. 1998. *Minima Ethnographica: Intersubjectivity and the Anthropological Project*. Chicago: University of Chicago Press.

————. 2002. *The Politics of Storytelling: Violence, Transgression, and Intersubjectivity*. Copenhagen: Museum Tusculanum Press.

Jamar, Astrid. 2012. "Deterioration of Aid Coordination in *Gacaca* Implementation: Dealing with the Past for a Better Future?" In *Rwanda Fast Forward*, edited by Maddalena Campioni and Patrick Noack, 76–95. Hampshire, UK: Palgrave Macmillan.

Jefremovas, Villia. 2002. *Brickyards to Graveyards: From Production to Genocide in Rwanda*. Albany: State University of New York Press.

Jones, Nick A. 2010. *The Courts of Genocide: Politics and the Rule of Law in Rwanda and Arusha*. Oxfordshire, UK: Routledge.

Jones, Nick A., and Rob Nestor. 2011. "Sentencing Circles in Canada and the Gacaca in Rwanda: A Comparative Analysis." *International Criminal Justice Review* 21 (1): 39–66.

Kagame, Alexis. 1956. *La philosophie Bantu-Rwandaise de l'être*. Classe des sciences morales et politiques: Mémoires in 8. Nouvelle série, tome xii, fasc. 1. Brussels: Académie royale des sciences coloniales.

———. 1976. *La philosophie Bantu comparée*. Paris: Présence Africaine.

Karbo, Tony, and Martha Mutisi. 2008. "Psychological Aspects of Post-Conflict Reconstruction: Transforming Mindsets: The Case of the Gacaca in Rwanda." Paper presented at the Ad Hoc Expert Group Meeting on Lessons Learned in Post-Conflict State Capacity: Reconstructing Governance and Public Administration Capacities in Post-Conflict Societies, Accra, Ghana, 2–4 October.

Karekezi, Urusaro A., Alphonse Nshimiyimana, and Beth Mutamba. 2004. "Localizing Justice: *Gacaca* Courts in Post-Genocide Rwanda." In *My Neighbour, My Enemy: Justice and Community in the Aftermath of Mass Atrocity*, edited by Eric Stover and Harvey M. Weinstein, 69–84. Cambridge: Cambridge University Press.

Kelsall, Tim. 2005. "Truth, Lies, Ritual: Preliminary Reflections on the Truth and Reconciliation Commission in Sierra Leone." *Human Rights Quarterly* 27:361–91.

———. 2013. *Culture under Cross-Examination: International Justice and the Special Court for Sierra Leone*. Cambridge: Cambridge University Press.

King, Elisabeth. 2009. "From Data Problems to Data Points: Challenges and Opportunities of Research in Postgenocide Rwanda." *African Studies Review* 52 (3): 127–48.

———. 2010. "Memory Controversies in Post-Genocide Rwanda: Implications for Peacebuilding." *Genocide Studies and Prevention* 5 (3): 293–309.

Kirkby, Coel. 2006. "Rwanda's *Gacaca* Courts: A Preliminary Critique." *Journal of African Law* 50:94–117.

Lahiri, Karen. 2009. "Rwanda's Gacaca Courts: A Possible Model for Local Justice in International Crime." *International Criminal Law Review* 9:321–32.

Leegwater, Margot. 2005. "Revisting the Horrors: Gacaca Courts in Rwanda and Their Struggle for Justice after Genocide." Master's thesis, Free University, Amsterdam.

———. 2015. *Sharing Scarcity: Land Access and Social Relations in Southeast Rwanda*. Leiden: African Studies Centre.

Le Roy, Etienne. 1999. *Le jeu des lois: Une anthropologie "dynamique" du droit*. Paris: LGDJ.

Lemarchand, Rene. 1994. "Managing Transition Anarchies: Rwanda, Burundi, and South Africa in Comparative Perspective." *Journal of Modern African Studies* 32 (4): 581–604.

———. 2007. "Consociationalism and Power Sharing in Africa: Rwanda, Burundi, and the Democratic Republic of the Congo." *African Affairs* 106 (422): 1–20.

———. 2009. *The Dynamics of Violence in Central Africa*. Philadelphia: University of Pennsylvania Press.

Lin, Olivia. 2005. "Demythologizing Restorative Justice: South Africa's Truth and Reconciliation Commission and Rwanda's *Gacaca* Courts in Context." *Journal of International and Comparative Law* 21:41–85.

Liprodhor, 2000. *Juridictions gacaca au Rwanda: Résultats de la recherche sur les attitudes et les opinions de la population Rwandaise*. Kigali: Liprodhor.

Longman, Timothy. 1995. "Genocide and Socio-Political Change: Massacres in Two Rwandan Villages." *Issue: A Journal of Public Opinion* 13 (2): 18–21.

———. 2006. "Justice at the Grassroots? *Gacaca* Trials in Rwanda." In *Transitional Justice in the Twenty-First Century: Beyond Truth versus Justice*, edited by Naomi Roht-Arriaza and Javier Mariezcurrena, 206–28. Cambridge: Cambridge University Press.

Longman, Timothy, Phuong N. Pham, and Harvey M. Weinstein. 2004. "Connecting Justice to Human Experience: Attitudes toward Accountability and Reconciliation in Rwanda." In *My Neighbour, My Enemy: Justice and Community in the Aftermath of Mass Atrocity*, edited by Eric Stover and Harvey M. Weinstein, 206–25. Cambridge: Cambridge University Press.

Longman, Timothy, and Theoneste Rutagengwa. 2004. "Memory, Identity, and Community in Rwanda." In *My Neighbour, My Enemy: Justice and Community in the Aftermath of Mass Atrocity*, edited by Eric Stover and Harvey M. Weinstein. Cambridge: Cambridge University Press.

Lundy, Patricia, and Mike McGovern. 2008. "Whose Justice? Rethinking Transitional Justice from the Bottom Up." *Journal of Law and Society* 35 (2): 265–92.

Machiavelli, Niccola. 1998. *The Prince*. Translated by H. C. Mansfield. 2nd ed. Chicago: University of Chicago Press.

Malkki, Liisa H. 1995. *Purity and Exile: Violence, Memory, and National Cosmology among Hutu Refugees in Tanzania*. Chicago: University of Chicago Press.

Mamdani, Mahmood. 2001. *When Victims Become Killers: Colonialism, Nativism, and the Genocide in Rwanda*. Princeton, NJ: Princeton University Press.

Mansfield, Harvey C. 1998. "Introduction." In *The Prince*, by Niccola Machiavelli, translated by Harvey C. Mansfield, vii–xxiv. 2nd ed. Chicago: University of Chicago Press.

Margalit, Avishai. 1996. *The Decent Society*. Cambridge, MA: Harvard University Press.

Mazimpaka, Magnus. 2011. "Human Rights Watch under Scrutiny over Controversial *Gacaca* Report." *Independent*, 11 June.

McEvoy, Kieran. 2007. "Beyond Legalism: Towards a Thicker Understanding of Transitional Justice." *Journal of Law and Society* 34 (4): 411–40.

McEvoy, Kieran, and Lorna McGregor, eds. 2008. *Transitional Justice from Below: Grassroots Activism and the Struggle for Change*. Oxford: Hart Publishing.

McKenna, Kate. 2006. "*Gacaca*—A Paradigm for Restorative Justice in Rwanda." *Trinity College Law Review* 9:5–27.

McLean-Hilker, Lyndsay. 2009. "Everyday Ethnicities: Identity and Reconciliation among Rwandan Youth." *Journal of Genocide Research* 11 (1): 81–100.

Megwalu, Aamaka, and Neophytos Loizides. 2010. "Dilemmas of Justice and Reconciliation: Rwandans and the *Gacaca* Courts." *African Journal of International and Comparative Law* 18:1–23.

Meierhenrich, Jens. 2009. "The Transformation of *lieux de mémoire*: The Nyabarongo River in Rwanda, 1992–2009." *Anthropology Today* 25 (5): 13–19.

Meyerstein, Ariel. 2007. "Between Law and Culture: Rwanda's *Gacaca* and Postcolonial Legality." *Law and Social Inquiry* 32 (2): 467–508.

Mgbako, Chi. 2005. "*Ingando* Solidarity Camps: Reconciliation and Political Indoctrination in Post-Genocide Rwanda." *Harvard Human Rights Journal* 18:201–24.

Millar, Gearoid. 2014. "Disaggregating Hybridity: Why Hybrid Institutions Do Not Produce Predictable Experiences on Peace." *Journal of Peace Research* 51 (4): 501–14.

Molenaar, Arthur. 2005. *Gacaca: Grassroots Justice after Genocide; The Key to Reconciliation in Rwanda?* Research Report 77/2005. Leiden: African Studies Centre.

Moore, Sally Falk. 1992. "Treating Law as Knowledge: Telling Colonial Officers What to Say to Africans about Running 'Their Own' Native Courts." *Law and Society Review* 26 (1): 11–46.

Morril, Constance F. 2004. "Reconciliation and the *Gacaca*: The Perceptions and Peace-Building Potential of Rwandan Youth Detainees." *Online Journal of Peace and Conflict Resolution* 6 (1): 1–66.

Morse, J. M. 2003. "Principles of Mixed Methods and Multimethod Research Design." In *Handbook of Mixed Methods in Social and Behavioral Research*, edited by Abbas Tashakkori and Charles Teddlie, 189–208. Thousand Oaks, CA: Sage.

Mukantaganzwa, Domitilla. 2008. "Le processus des juridictions gacaca au Rwanda." Presentation at International Conference on Post Judicial [*sic*] Reforms in Rwanda, Kigali, Rwanda, 16–18 June. On file with the author.

Musoni, James. 2007. "75 Percent of Population Have Reconciled." *New Times* (Kigali), 12 April.

Musoni, Protais. 2003. "Building a Democratic Culture: Rwanda's Experience and Perspectives." Paper Presented at Conference on Elections and Accountability in Africa, Wilton Park, Sussex, UK, 21–25 July. On file with the author.

Nagy, Rosemary. 2009. "Traditional Justice and Legal Pluralism in Transitional Context: The Case of Rwanda's *Gacaca* Courts." In *Reconciliation(s): Transitional Justice in Postconflict Societies*, edited by Joanna R. Quinn, 86–115. Montreal: McGill-Queen's University Press.

National Service of the Gacaca Courts (SNJG). See websites below.

National Unity and Reconciliation Commission (NURC). See websites below.

Nee, Ann, and Uvin, Peter. 2010. "Silence and Dialogue: Burundians' Alternatives to Transitional Justice." In *Localizing Transitional Justice: Interventions and Priorities After Mass Violence*, edited by Rosalind Shaw and Lars Waldorf, 157–82. Stanford, CA: Stanford University Press.

New Times (Kigali). 2012. "Gacaca Closes Shop." 19 June.

———. 2013. "Imihigo: Do the Scores Reflect What's on the Ground?" 2 October.

Newbury, Catherine. 2011. "High Modernism at the Ground Level: The *Imidugudu* Policy in Rwanda." In *Remaking Rwanda: State Building and Human Rights after Mass Violence*, edited by Scott Straus and Lars Waldorf, 223–39. Madison: University of Wisconsin Press.

Newbury, Catherine, and David Newbury. 1999. "A Catholic Mass in Kigali: Contested Views of Genocide and Ethnicity in Rwanda." *Canadian Journal of African Studies* 33 (2/3): 292–328.

———. 2000. "Bringing the Peasants Back In: Agrarian Themes in the Construction and Corrosion of Statist Historiography in Rwanda." *American Historical Review* 105 (3): 832–77.

Newbury, David. 2009. *The Land beyond the Mists: Essays on Identity and Authority in Precolonial Congo and Rwanda*. Athens: Ohio University Press.

Newman, Melanie, and Oliver Wright. 2011. "Caught on Camera: Top Lobbyists Boasting How They Influence the PM." *Independent*, 6 December.

Nkusi, Laurent. 1987. "Dire et ne pas dire au Rwanda." In *Sagesse et vie quotidien en Afrique: Actes du symposium international de philosophie (Kigali, 31 Juillet–7 Août 1983); Suivi de Journée Alexis Kagame: Vie et œuvre; Kigali 8 Août 1983*. Kigali: Ministère de l'enseignement supérieur et de la recherche scientifique.

Nothomb, Dominique. 1965. *Un humanisme africain: Valeurs et pierres d'attente*. Brussels: Editions Lumen Vitae.

Ntampaka, Charles. 1995. "Le retour à la tradition dans le règlement des différends: Le *gacaca* du Rwanda." *Dialogue* 186: 95–104.

———. 1999. "Vérité et opinion dans la société rwandaise traditionelle." *Dialogue* 221: 3–24.

———. 2003. "Le *gacaca*: Une juridiction pénale populaire." In *Construire l'état de droit: Le Burundi et la région des grands lacs*, edited by Charles de Lespinay and Emile Mworoha, 219–36. Paris: L'Harmattan.

Olivier de Sardan, Jean-Pierre. 2008. *La rigueur du qualitatif: Les contraintes empiriques de l'interprétation socio-anthropologique*. Louvain-La-Neuve, Belgium: Bruylant-Academia.

Olsen, Tricia D., Leigh A. Payne, and Andrew G. Reiter. 2010. *Transitional Justice in Balance: Comparing Processes, Weighing Efficacy*. Washington, DC: USIP Press Books.

Olwine, Brittany A. 2011. "One Step forward, but Two Steps Back: Why Gacaca in Rwanda Is Jeopardizing the Good Effect of Akayesu on Women's Rights." *William and Mary Journal of Women and the Law* 17 (3): 639–63.

Oomen, Barbara. 2005. "Donor-Driven Justice and Its Discontents: The Case of Rwanda." *Development and Change* 36 (5): 887–910.

———. 2007. "Transitional Justice and Its Legitimacy: The Case for a Local Perspective." *Netherlands Quarterly of Human Rights* 25 (1): 141–48.

Organization for Social Science Research in Eastern and Southern Africa (OSSREA). 2007. *Rapid and Extensive Assessment of Performance Management Contracts—Imihigo*. Kigali: OSSREA—Rwanda Chapter.

Overdulve, Cornelis M. 1997. "Fonction de la langue et de la communication au Rwanda." *Neue Zeitschrift fur Missionswissenschaft* 53 (4): 271–83.

Penal Reform International (PRI). 2003. *The Guilty Plea Procedure, Cornerstone of the Rwandan Justice System.* Research Report on the *Gacaca* 4. Paris: PRI.

———. 2004. *From Camp to Hill: The Reintegration of Released Prisoners.* Research Report on the *Gacaca* 6. Paris: PRI.

———. 2005. *Integrated Report on the Pilot Phase, January 2002–December 2004.* Research Report on the *Gacaca* 7. Paris: PRI.

———. 2006. *Information Collection during the National Phase.* Research Report on the *Gacaca* 8. Paris: PRI.

———. 2007. *Judgements on Property Offence Cases.* Research Report on the *Gacaca* 10. Paris: PRI.

———. 2008. *Monitoring and Research Report on the Gacaca: Testimonies and Evidence in the Gacaca Courts.* Paris: PRI.

———. 2010. *Final Monitoring and Research Report on the Gacaca Process.* Paris: PRI.

Plummer, Ken. 2001. *Documents of Life 2.* London: Sage.

Pottier, Johan. 1989. "'Three's a Crowd': Knowledge, Ignorance, and Power in the Context of Urban Agriculture in Rwanda." *Africa* 59 (4): 461–77.

———. 2002. *Re-Imagining Rwanda: Conflict, Survival, and Disinformation in the Late Twentieth Century.* Cambridge: Cambridge University Press.

Pouligny, Beatrice, Simon Chesterman, and Alfred Schnabel, eds. 2007. *After Mass Crime: Rebuilding States and Communities.* Tokyo: United Nations University Press.

Pozen, Joanna, Richard Neugebauer, and Joseph Ntaganira. 2014. "Assessing the Rwanda Experiment: Popular Perceptions of *Gacaca* in Its Final Phase." *International Journal of Transitional Justice* 8 (1): 31–52.

Prunier, Gérard. 1998. *The Rwanda Crisis: History of a Genocide.* New York: Columbia University Press.

Purdekova, Andrea. 2008. *Repatriation and Reconciliation in Divided Societies: The Case of Rwanda's "Ingando."* RSC Working Paper No. 43. Oxford: Refugee Studies Centre.

———. 2011a. "'Even If I Am Not Here, There Are So Many Eyes': Surveillance and State Reach in Rwanda." *Journal of Modern African Studies* 49 (3): 475–97.

———. 2011b. *Rwanda's Ingando Camps: Liminality and the Reproduction of Power.* RSC Working Paper No. 80. Oxford: Refugee Studies Centre.

Quinn, Joanna R., ed. 2009. *Reconciliation(s): Transitional Justice in Postconflict Societies.* Montreal: McGill-Queen's University Press.

Rao, Vijayendra, and Michael Woolcock. 2003. "Integrating Qualitative and Quantitative Approaches in Program Evaluation." In *The Impact of Economic Policies on Poverty and Income Distribution: Evaluation Techniques and Tools,* edited by François Bourguignon and Luiz A. Pareira da Silva, 165–90. Oxford: Oxford University Press.

Raper, Jessica. 2005. "The *Gacaca* Experiment: Rwanda's Restorative Dispute Resolution Response to the 1994 Genocide." *Pepperdine Dispute Resolution Law Journal* 5 (1): 1–57.

Republic of Rwanda. 1996. "Loi Organique No. 8196 du 30/8/96 sur l'organisation des poursuites des infractions constitutives du crime de genocide ou de crimes contre l'humanité, commieses à partir du 1er octobre 1990." *Official Gazette of the Republic of Rwanda*, 1 September.

———. 1999. *Report on the Reflection Meetings Held in the Office of the President of the Republic from May 1998 to March 1999*. Kigali: Office of the President of the Republic.

———. 2001a. "National Decentralization Policy." May. http://www.kigalicity.gov.rw /IMG/pdf/National_Decentralization_Policy.pdf.

———. 2001b. "Organic Law No. 40/2000 of 26/1/2001 Setting Up Gacaca Jurisdictions and Organizing Prosecutions for Offenses Constituting the Crime of Genocide or Crimes against Humanity Committed between October 1, 1990 and December 31, 1994." *Official Gazette of the Republic of Rwanda*, 26 January.

———. 2001c. "Presidential Order No. 12/01 of 26/6/2001 Establishing Modalities for Organizing Elections of Members of *Gacaca* Jurisdictions' Organs." *Official Gazette of the Republic of Rwanda*, 26 June.

———. 2003. *Sondage d'opinion sur la participation à la gacaca et la réconciliation nationale*. Kigali: National Unity and Reconciliation Commission.

———. 2004a. "Organic Law No. 16/2004 of 19/6/2004 Establishing the Organization, Competence, and Functioning of Gacaca Courts Charged with Prosecuting and Trying the Perpetrators of the Crime of Genocide and Other Crimes against Humanity, Committed between October 1st, 1990 and December 31, 1994." *Official Gazette of the Republic of Rwanda*, 19 June.

———. 2004b. *Process of Collecting Information Required in Gacaca Courts*. Kigali: National Service of the Gacaca Courts.

———. 2005a. *Trial Procedure in Gacaca Courts*. Kigali: National Service of the Gacaca Courts.

———. 2006a. *Genocide and Strategies for Its Eradication*. Kigali: Republic of Rwanda.

———. 2006b. *Making Decentralized Service Delivery Work in Rwanda: Putting the People at the Center of Service Provision*. Kigali: Minaloc.

———. 2006c. "Manuel pour les camps de solidarité et autres formations: Service de l'éducation civique." Kigali: National Unity and Reconciliation Commission. Original manuscript in Kinyarwanda; the author's Rwandan field assistants created this unauthorized translation into French. On file with the author.

———. 2006d. "Organic Law No. 28/2006 of 27/6/2006 Modifying and Complementing Organic Law No. 16/2004 of 19/6/2004 Establishing the Organization, Competence and Functioning of Gacaca Courts Charged with Prosecuting and Trying the Perpetrators of the Crime of Genocide and Other Crimes Against Humanity, Committed Between October 1st, 1990 and December 31, 1994." *Official Gazette of the Republic of Rwanda*, 27 June.

———. 2007a. *Cohésion sociale 2005–2006: Sondage d'opinion*. Kigali: National Unity and Reconciliation Commission.

———. 2007b. "Organic Law No. 10/2007 of 01/03/2007 Modifying and Complementing Organic Law No. 16/2004 of 19/6/2004 Establishing the Organization,

Competence and Functioning of Gacaca Courts Charged with Prosecuting and Trying the Perpetrators of the Crime of Genocide and Other Crimes Against Humanity, Committed Between October 1st, 1990 and December 31, 1994 as Modified and Complemented to Date." *Official Gazette of the Republic of Rwanda*, 1 March.

———. 2008a. "Organic Law No. 13/2008 of 19/05/2008 Modifying and Complementing Organic Law No. 16/2004 of 19/6/2004 Establishing the Organization, Competence and Functioning of Gacaca Courts Charged with Prosecuting and Trying the Perpetrators of the Crime of Genocide and Other Crimes Against Humanity, Committed Between October 1st, 1990 and December 31, 1994 as Modified and Complemented to Date." *Official Gazette of the Republic of Rwanda*, 19 May.

———. 2008b. *Social Cohesion in Rwanda: An Opinion Survey: Results 2005–2007.* Kigali: National Unity and Reconciliation Commission.

———. 2010. *Reconciliation Barometer.* Kigali: National Unity and Reconciliation Commission.

———. 2012. *Summary of the Report Presented at the Closing Ceremony of the Gacaca Courts Activities.* Kigali: National Service of the Gacaca Courts. http://inkiko-gacaca.gov.rw/english/wp-content/uploads/2012/06/gacaca-report-summary.pdf.

———. n.d. *EICV 3 Thematic Report: Income.* Kigali: National Institute of Statistics of Rwanda.

Rettig, Max. 2008. "*Gacaca*: Truth, Justice, and Reconciliation in Postconflict Rwanda?" *African Studies Review* 51 (3): 25–50.

———. 2011. "The Sovu Trials: The Impact of Genocide Justice on One Community." In *Remaking Rwanda: State Building and Human Rights After Mass Violence*, edited by Scott Straus and Lars Waldorf, 194–209. Madison: University of Wisconsin Press.

Reyntjens, Filip. 1985. *Pouvoir et droit au Rwanda: Droit public et évolution politique, 1916–1973.* Tervuren, Belgium: Musée Royal de L'Afrique Centrale.

———. 1990. "Le *gacaca* ou la justice du gazon au Rwanda." *Politique Africaine* 40: 31–41.

———. 1995a. "*Akazu*, 'escadrons de la mort' et autres 'Réseau Zéro': Un historique des résistances au changement politiques depuis 1990." In *Les crises politiques au Burundi et au Rwanda (1993–1994)*, edited by André Guichaoua, 265–73. Paris: Editions Karthala.

———. 1995b. *L'Afrique des grands lacs en crise: Rwanda, Burundi, 1988–1994.* Paris: Editions Karthala.

———. 2004. "Rwanda: Ten Years On: From Genocide to Dictatorship." *African Affairs* 103 (411): 177–210.

———. 2011. "Constructing the Truth, Dealing with Dissent, Domesticating the World: Governance in Post-Genocide Rwanda." *African Affairs* 110 (438): 1–34.

———. 2013. *Political Governance in Post-Genocide Rwanda.* Cambridge: Cambridge University Press.

Reyntjens, Filip, and Stef Vandeginste. 2001. "Traditional Approaches to Negotiation and Mediation: Examples from Africa: Burundi, Rwanda, and Congo." In *Peacebuilding: A Field Guide*, edited by Luc Reychler and Thania Paffenholz, 128–38. London: Lynne Rienner.

Rhodes, Tom. 2014. "Twitter War Shines Light on How Rwanda Intimidates Press." *Committee to Protect Journalists* (blog), 24 March. https://cpj.org/blog/2014/03/twitter-war-shines-light-on-how-rwanda-intimidates.php.

Riano Alcala, Pilar, and Erin Baines. 2012. "Editorial Note." *International Journal of Transitional Justice* 6 (3): 385–93.

Richters, Annemiek. 2010. "Suffering and Healing in the Aftermath of War and Genocide in Rwanda: Mediations through Community-Based Sociotherapy." In *Mediations of Violence in Africa: Fashioning New Futures from Contested Pasts*, edited by Lidwien Kapteijns and Annemiek Richters, 173–210. Leiden: Brill.

Richters, Annemiek, Theoneste Rutayisire, and Cora Dekker, 2010. "Care as a Turning Point in Sociotherapy: Remaking the Moral World in Post-Genocide Rwanda." *Medische Antropologie* 22 (1): 93–108.

Richters, Annemiek, Theoneste Rutayisire, T. Sewimfura, and E. Ngendahayo. 2010. "Psychotrauma, Healing, and Reconciliation in Rwanda: The Contribution of Community-Based Sociotherapy." *African Journal of Traumatic Stress* 1 (2): 55–63.

Rimé, Bernard, Patrick Kanyangara, Vincent Yzerbyt, and Dario Paez. 2011. "The Impact of *Gacaca* Tribunals in Rwanda: Psychosocial Effects of Participation in a Truth and Reconciliation Process after a Genocide." *European Journal of Social Psychology* 41 (6): 695–706.

Rombouts, Heidy. 2004. *Victim Organisations and the Politics of Reparation: A Case Study on Rwanda*. Antwerp: Intersentia.

Rose, Laurel L. 1995. "Justice at the Local Level: Findings and Recommendations for Future Actions." In *USAID Rwanda Rule of Law Design: Four-Week Interim Report*, 83–163. Kigali: USAID, 4 May.

Ross, Fiona. 2003. *Bearing Witness: Women and the Truth and Reconciliation Commission in South Africa*. London: Pluto Press.

Rosoux, Valérie. 2005. "La gestion du passé au Rwanda: Ambivalence et poids du silence." *Genèses* 61:28–46.

Rukebesha, Aloys. 1985. *Esotérisme et communication sociale*. Kigali: Printer Set.

Rusagara, Frank. 2005. "*Gacaca* as a Reconciliation and Nation-Building Strategy in Post-Genocide Rwanda." *Conflict Trends* 2:20–25.

———. 2006. "The Continued Négationisme of the Rwandan Genocide." *New Times* (Kigali), 11 January.

Sanford, Victoria. 2003. *Buried Secrets: Truth and Human Rights in Guatemala*. New York: Palgrave Macmillan.

Sarkin, Jeremy. 2000. "Promoting Justice, Truth, and Reconciliation in Transitional Societies: Evaluating Rwanda's Approach in the New Millennium of Using Community Based *Gacaca* Tribunals to Deal with the Past." *International Law FORUM du droit international* 2:112–21.

———. 2001. "The Tension between Justice and Reconciliation in Rwanda: Politics, Human Rights, Due Process, and the Role of the *Gacaca* Courts in Dealing with the Genocide." *Journal of African Law* 45 (2): 143–72.

Sarkin, Jeremy, and Erin Daly. 2004. "Too Many Questions, Too Few Answers: Reconciliation in Transitional Societies." *Columbia Human Rights Law Review* 35:661–728.

Schabas, William. 2005. "Genocide Trials and *Gacaca* Courts." *Journal of International Criminal Justice* 3:879–95.

———. 2008. "Transfer and Extradition of Genocide Suspects to Rwanda." Paper presented at the Extradition of Rwandese Genocide Suspects to Rwanda: Issues and Challenges (conference hosted by REDRESS and African Rights), Brussels, Belgium, 1 July. On file with the author.

Schotsmans, Martien. 2011. "'But We Also Support Monitoring': INGO Monitoring and Donor Support to *Gacaca* Justice in Rwanda." *International Journal of Transitional Justice* 5 (3): 390–411.

Scott, James. 1990. *Domination and the Arts of Resistance: Hidden Transcripts*. New Haven, CT: Yale University Press.

———. 1998. *Seeing Like a State: How Certain Schemes to Improve the Human Condition Have Failed*. New Haven, CT: Yale University Press.

Sebarenzi, Joseph. 2009. *God Sleeps in Rwanda: A Personal Journey of Transformation*. Oxford: Oneworld Publications.

Shaw, Rosalind. 2005. *Rethinking Truth and Reconciliation Commissions: Lessons from Sierra Leone*. United States Institute of Peace Special Report No. 130. Washington, DC: U.S. Institute of Peace.

———. 2007. "Memory Frictions: Localizing the Truth and Reconciliation Commission in Sierra Leone." *International Journal of Transitional Justice* 1 (2): 183–207.

Shaw, Rosalind, and Lars Waldorf, eds. 2010. *Localizing Transitional Justice: Interventions and Priorities after Mass Violence*. Stanford, CA: Stanford University Press.

Sommers, Marc. 2012. *Stuck: Rwandan Youth and the Struggle for Adulthood*. Athens: University of Georgia Press.

Sosnov, Maya. 2008. "The Adjudication of Genocide: *Gacaca* and the Road to Reconciliation in Rwanda." *Denver Journal of International Law and Policy* 36 (2): 125–53.

Staub, Ervin. 2004. "Justice, Healing, and Reconciliation: How the People's Courts in Rwanda Can Promote Them." *Peace and Conflict: Journal of Peace Psychology* 10 (1): 25–32.

———. 2011. *Overcoming Evil: Genocide, Violent Conflict, and Terrorism*. Oxford: Oxford University Press.

Stefanowicz, C. 2011. "*Gacaca* Highlights Failure to Deal with RPF Crimes." *Think Africa Press*, 8 March.

Straus, Scott. 2006. *The Order of Genocide: Race, Power, and War in Rwanda*. Ithaca, NY: Cornell University Press.

Straus, Scott, and Lars Waldorf. 2011. "Seeing Like a Post-Conflict State." In *Remaking Rwanda: State Building and Human Rights after Mass Violence*, edited by Scott Straus and Lars Waldorf, 3–21. Madison: University of Wisconsin Press.

Subotic, Jelena. 2009. *Hijacked Justice: Dealing with the Past in the Balkans*. Ithaca, NY: Cornell University Press.

Takeuchi, Shinichi. 2011. *Gacaca and DDR: The Disputable Record of State-Building in Rwanda*. Jica-Ri Working Paper No. 32. Tokyo: JICA Research Institute.

Taylor, Charles. 2001. "Two Theories of Modernity." In *Alternative Modernities*, edited by Dilip Parameshwar Gaonkar, 172–96. Durham, NC: Duke University Press.

———. 2004. *Modern Social Imaginaries*. Durham, NC: Duke University Press.

Taylor, Christopher C. 1988. "The Concept of Flow in Rwandan Popular Medicine." *Social Science and Medicine* 27 (12): 1343–48.

———. 1990. "Condoms and Cosmology: The 'Fractal' Person and Sexual Risk in Rwanda." *Social Science and Medicine* 31 (9): 1023–28.

———. 1992. *Milk, Honey, and Money: Changing Concepts in Rwandan Healing*. Washington, DC: Smithsonian Institution Press.

Teddlie, Charles, and Abbas Tashakorri. 2003. "Major Issues and Controversies in the Use of Mixed Methods in the Social and Behavioral Sciences." In *Handbook of Mixed Methods in Social and Behavioral Research*, edited by Charles Teddlie and Abbas Tashakorri, 3–49. Thousand Oaks, CA: Sage.

Tempels, Placide. 1959. *Bantu Philosophy*. Paris: Présence Africaine.

Teitel, Ruti G. 2000. *Transitional Justice*. Oxford: Oxford University Press.

Tertsakian, Carina. 2008. *Le Château: The Lives of Prisoners in Rwanda*. London: Arves Books.

Theidon, Kimberly. 2000. "'How We Learned to Kill Our Brother: Memory, Morality, and Reconciliation in Peru." *Bulletin of the French Institute of Andean Studies* 29 (3): 539–54.

———. 2006. "Justice in Transition: The Micropolitics of Reconciliation in Postwar Peru." *Journal of Conflict Resolution* 50 (3): 433–57.

Theunis, Guy. 2012. *Mes soixante-quinze jours de prison à Kigali*. Paris: Karthala.

Thomson, Susan M. 2009. "Ethnic Twa and Rwandan National Unity and Reconciliation Policy." *Peace Review: A Journal of Social Justice* 21 (3): 313–20.

———. 2010. "Getting Close to Rwandans since the Genocide: Studying Everyday Life in Highly Politicized Research Settings." *African Studies Review* 53 (3): 19–34.

———. 2011a. "The Darker Side of Transitional Justice: The Power Dynamics behind Rwanda's *Gacaca* Courts." *Africa* 81 (3): 373–90.

———. 2011b. "Re-Education for Reconciliation: Participant Observations on *Ingando*." In *Remaking Rwanda: State Building and Human Rights after Mass Violence*, edited by Scott Straus and Lars Waldorf, 331–39. Madison: University of Wisconsin Press.

———. 2013. *Whispering Truth to Power: Everyday Resistance to Reconciliation in Postgenocide Rwanda*. Madison: University of Wisconsin Press.

———. 2014. "Rwanda's Twitter-Gate: The Disinformation Campaign of Africa's Digital President." *African Arguments*, March 17. http://africanarguments.org/2014/03/17/rwandas-twitter-gate-the-disinformation-campaign-of-africas-digital-president-by-susan-thomson.

Thomson, Susan M., and Rosemary Nagy. 2010. "Law, Power, and Justice: What Legalism Fails to Address in the Functioning of Rwanda's *Gacaca* Courts." *International Journal of Transitional Justice* 5 (1): 11–30.

Tiemessen, Alana. 2004. "After Arusha: *Gacaca* Justice in Post-Genocide Rwanda." *African Studies Quarterly* 8 (1): 57–76.

Tinbergen, Jan. 1952. *On the Theory of Economic Policy*. Amsterdam: North Holland.

Truth and Reconciliation Commission of South Africa (TRC-SA). 1998. *Report*. Vol. 1. London: Macmillan.

Tsing, Anna L. 2005. *Friction: An Ethnography of Global Connection*. Princeton, NJ: Princeton University Press.

Turner, Victor. (1969) 1977. *The Ritual Process: Structure and Anti-Structure*. Ithaca, NY: Cornell University Press.

United Nations High Commissioner for Human Rights (UNHCHR). 1996. *Gacaca: Le droit coutumier au Rwanda*. Kigali: UNHCHR.

U.S. Department of Justice. 2011a. *Communications Program Supporting the 30th Anniversary of the Announcement of the People's Authority of Libya*. Exhibit A to registration statement pursuant to the Foreign Agents Registration Act of 1938, as amended. Registration No. 6055. Washington, DC: U.S. Department of Justice, 8 December.

———. 2011b. *Master Service Agreement by and between Government of Rwanda and W2 Group, Inc.* Exhibit A to registration statement pursuant to the Foreign Agents Registration Act of 1938, as amended. Registration No. 6055. Washington, DC: U.S. Department of Justice, 8 December.

Uvin, Peter. 2003. "The *Gacaca* Tribunals in Rwanda." In *Reconciliation after Violent Conflict*, edited by David Bloomfield, Teresa Barnes, and Luc Huyse, 116–21. Stockholm: International Idea.

———. 2009. *Life after Violence: A People's Story of Burundi*. London: Zed Books.

———. n.d. "The Introduction of a Modernized *Gacaca* for Judging Suspects of Participation in the Genocide and the Massacres of 1994 in Rwanda." A discussion paper prepared for the Belgian Secretary of State for Development Cooperation. On file with the author.

Uvin, Peter, and Charles Mironko. 2003. "Western and Local Approaches to Justice in Rwanda." *Global Governance* 9:219–31.

Van Billoen, Salomé. 2008. *Les juridictions gacaca au Rwanda: Une analyse de la complexité des représentations*. Brussels: Bruylant.

Vandeginste, Stef. 1999. "Justice, Reconciliation, and Reparation after Genocide and Crimes against Humanity: The Proposed Establishment of Popular Gacaca Tribunals in Rwanda." Paper presented at The All-Africa Conference on African Principles of Conflict Resolution and Reconciliation, Addis Ababa, Ethiopia, 8–12 November.

———. 2000. "Les juridictions gacaca et la poursuite des suspects auteurs du génocide et des crimes contre l'humanité au Rwanda." In *L'Afrique des Grands Lacs, Annuaire 1999–2000*, edited by Filip Reyntjens and Stefaan Marysse, 75–94. Paris: L'Harmattan.

Vandeginste, Stef, and Luc Huyse. 2005. "Consociational Democracy for Rwanda?" In *Political Economy of the Great Lakes Region of Africa: The Pitfalls of Enforced Democracy and Globalization*, edited by Stefaan Marysse and Filip Reyntjens, 101–22. Basingstoke, UK: Palgrave Macmillan.

Van der Merwe, Hugo, Victoria Baxter, and Audrey R. Chapman, eds. 2009. *Assessing the Impact of Transitional Justice: Challenges for Empirical Research*. Washington, DC: U.S. Institute of Peace Press.

Van Gennep, Arthur. 1960 (1994). *The Rites of Passage*. London: Routledge.

Van Houtte, Jean, Filip Reyntjens, and Alberto Basomingera. 1981. "Litiges et besoins juridiques au Rwanda: Une enquête préliminaire." *Revue juridique du Rwanda* 188–203.

Van Leeuwen, Matthijs. 2001. "Rwanda's *Imidugudu* Programme and Earlier Experiences with Villagisation and Resettlement in East Africa." *Journal of Modern African Studies* 39 (4): 623–44.

Vansina, Jan. 2004. *Antecedents to Modern Rwanda: The Nyiginya Kingdom*. Madison: University of Wisconsin Press.

Varshney, Ashutosh. 2002. *Ethnic Conflict and Civic Life: Hindus and Muslims in India*. New Haven, CT: Yale University Press.

Venter, C. M. 2007. "Eliminating Fear through Recreating Community in Rwanda: The Role of the *Gacaca* Courts." *Texas Wesleyan Law Review* 13:577–97.

Viaene, Lieselotte. 2010a. "The Internal Logic of the Cosmos as 'Justice' and 'Reconciliation': Micro-Level Perceptions in Post-Conflict Guatemala." *Critique of Anthropology* 30 (3): 287–312.

———. 2010b. "Voices from the Shadows: The Role of Cultural Contexts in Transitional Justice Processes: Maya Q'eqchi' Perspectives from Post-Conflict Guatemala." PhD diss., University of Ghent.

Viaene, Lieselotte, and Brems, Eva. 2010. "Transitional Justice and Cultural Contexts: Learning from the Universality Debate." *Netherlands Quarterly of Human Rights* 28 (2): 199–224.

Vidal, Claudine. 1998. "Questions sur le rôle des paysans durant le génocide des Rwandais Tutsi." *Cahiers d'études africaines* 38 (150): 331–45.

———. 2001. "Les commémorations du génocide au Rwanda." *Les temps modernes* 613:1–46.

Vigh, Henrig. 2009. "Motion Squared: A Second Look at the Concept of Social Navigation." *Anthropological Theory* 9 (4): 419–38.

Villarreal, Magdalena. 1994. "Wielding and Yielding: Power, Subordination, and Gender Identity in the Context of a Mexican Development Project." PhD diss., Wageningen University.

Waldorf, Lars. 2006. "Mass Justice for Mass Atrocity: Rethinking Local Justice as Transitional Justice." *Temple Law Review* 79 (1): 1–88.

———. 2009. "Revisiting Hotel Rwanda: Genocide Ideology, Reconciliation, and Rescuers." *Journal of Genocide Research* 11 (1): 101–25.

———. 2010. "'Like Jews Waiting for Jesus': Posthumous Justice in Post-Genocide Rwanda." In *Localizing Transitional Justice: Interventions and Priorities after Mass Violence*, edited by Rosalind Shaw and Lars Waldorf, 183–202. Stanford, CA: Stanford University Press.

Warner, Michael. 2009. "Sources and Methods for the Study of Intelligence." In *Handbook of Intelligence Studies*, edited by Loch K. Johnson, 17–27. New York: Routledge.

Webster, Don. 2011. "The Uneasy Relationship between the ICTR and Gacaca." In *Remaking Rwanda: State Building and Human Rights after Mass Violence*, edited by Scott Straus and Lars Waldorf, 184–93. Madison: University of Wisconsin Press.

Wells, Sara A. 2005. "Gender, Sexual Violence, and Prospects for Justice at the *Gacaca* Courts in Rwanda." *Review of Law and Women's Studies* 14 (2): 167–96.

Westberg, Megan M. 2010. "Rwanda's Use of Transitional Justice after Genocide: The Gacaca Courts and the ICTR." *Kansas Law Review* 59 (1): 331–67.

Wierzynska, Aneta. 2004. "Consolidating Democracy through Transitional Justice: Rwanda's *Gacaca* Courts." *New York University Law Review* 79:1934–69.

Wilson, Richard A. 2001. *The Politics of Truth and Reconciliation in South Africa: Legitimizing the Post-Apartheid State.* Cambridge: Cambridge University Press.

Zorbas, Eugenia. 2004. "Reconciliation in Post-Genocide Rwanda." *African Journal of Legal Studies* 1 (1): 29–51.

Websites

Avocats Sans Frontières (ASF). http://www.asf.be/index.php?module=publicatiesandlang=enandid=177.

Institute of Research and Dialogue for Peace (IRDP). http://www.irdp.rw.

National Service of the Gacaca Courts (SNJG). http://www.inkiko-gacaca.gov.rw.

National Unity and Reconciliation Commission (NURC). http://www.nurc.gov.rw.

Penal Reform International (PRI). http://www.penalreform.org/transitional.html.

Index

Rukoma, 39, 55, 57, 64, 124, 134–39, 144–
45, 155, 157, 203n3
Runyoni, 38, 51–55, 60, 67, 69, 73, 122,
127–28, 130
Rusagara, Frank, 6–8
Rwanda: civil society in, 23–24; civil war
of, 5, 14–18, 38, 69, 76–82, 109–10,
113–14, 201n16; colonialism in, 15,
19–20; decentralization and, 3–4,
28–29, 65–68, 98–109, 119–20, 133,
160, 162, 165, 191n4; ethnicity in,
14–18, 44–45, 76–82; heart and, 13,
151–59; independence of, 15, 134;
language of, 31–32; legislation of, 6–7;
multiparty political system of, 14–17,
77, 139; NGOs in, 4, 8–9, 11–12, 20,
22, 24, 29, 70, 135, 190n13, 197n35;
ordinary courts in, 20–27, 68–71, 108,
120, 197n36; social imaginary of,
89–90, 118–22, 131–34, 141–42, 147–51,
163–67, 204n1; state power in, 12,
17–18, 20–22, 29, 32, 39, 87–88,
98–116, 133, 135, 157–58, 189n8, 193n21;
unity principle and, 5, 17–18, 24–27,
63, 80–81, 84–85, 90–93, 97, 111, 130,
189n8. *See also* courts; *gacaca* courts;
genocide; *and specific places*
Rwanda's Gamble (Harrell), 8

Schabas, William, 4
score-settling, 12, 120–25, 138, 167
Scott, James, 6, 203n1
Sebarenzi, Joseph, 200n14
sectors: cell-level appeals and, 42, 50, 55,
61, 67–68, 194n8, 198n53; decentralization and, 28–29, 99–104, 192n14;
descriptions of, 26–27; *gacaca* law
and, 25–26, 42; genocide crimes and,
78–85; social science research methods
and, 37–38; trial procedures of, 51–55.
See also hills
security (as right), 6–7, 82, 90–92, 130,
141, 152–54

self-censorship. *See* silence
sentencing, 68–75
settlements, 81–82
Shaw, Rosalind, 162, 164, 204n6, 205n12
Sierra Leone, 162, 205n12
silence, 12, 97, 111–16, 128–32, 138, 141–
42, 145, 165
SNJG (National Service of the Gacaca
Courts), 28, 42, 60–66, 114, 121, 143,
157–58, 189n3, 193n21, 196n11
snowball sampling, 47
social imaginary, 89–90, 118–22, 131–34,
141–42, 147–54, 163–67, 204n1
Sommers, Marc, 194n17
South Africa, 161–62, 165–66
South African Truth and Reconciliation
Commission, 161–62
Special Court for Sierra Leone, 164
Subotic, Jelena, 167
surveillance, 32, 101–4
surveys, 30, 35–36, 86, 92–97
survivors (of genocide), 79–86, 103, 118–
28, 135, 145, 149, 195n3

tacit knowledge, 31–32, 48, 118–19
Tanzania, 15, 131, 191n4
Taylor, Charles, 204n1
Taylor, Christopher C., 205n10
Teitel, Ruti, 166
temporality, 27–29
testimony, 12, 51–56, 61, 64–68, 80,
85–86, 95, 117–32, 141–42, 145. *See also*
accusations; information-collection
phase; property cases; truth
Theidon, Kimberly, 164, 204n6,
205n12
theoretical drive, 10, 190n17
Theunis, Guy, 193n23
Thomson, Susan, 189n7
Tinbergen, Jan, 161
transitional justice, 3–7, 10, 25, 30, 83,
160–67, 189n1, 191n4, 204n6
translation, 33–34, 40, 42, 47

Critical Human Rights